W9-AQL-679

MOTYA

A PHOENICIAN AND CARTHAGINIAN CITY
IN SICILY

MOTYA

A PHOENICIAN AND CARTHAGINIAN CITY IN SICILY

A report of the excavations undertaken during the years 1961-65 on behalf of the University of Leeds, The Institute of Archaeology of London University and Fairleigh Dickinson University, New Jersey.

BY

B. S. J. ISSERLIN AND JOAN DU PLAT TAYLOR

WITH CONTRIBUTIONS BY

N. COLDSTREAM, W. E. COLLINS, G. EVANS, E. MACNAMARA, C. P. NUTTALL, G. ORAM, E. PIKE, H. M. H. PIKE, G. F. TAGG, J. WAECHTER, C. WESTERN, C. WILKINSON

VOLUME I

FIELD WORK AND EXCAVATION

With 15 Plans, 24 Figures and 26 Plates

LEIDEN
E. J. BRILL
1974

ISBN 90 04 03839 6

PRINTED IN THE NETHERLANDS

CONTENTS

PREFACE

Of the three great Mediterranean peoples of classical antiquity—the Greeks, the Romans, and the Phoenicians with their Carthaginian colonists—it is the Phoenician and Punic world which is least known. In spite of the increased interest and activity in the field of Phoenician and Carthaginian studies which the past decade has witnessed, we are still far removed from possessing a full and coherent picture of ancient Phoenician-Punic city life of the kind which has been long available at Priene or Pompeii. There are, however, a number of sites which hold out a promise that excavation might provide just this kind of knowledge, and among these the site of the Phoenician colonial city, and later Carthaginian military base, of Motya near Marsala in Sicily has long ranked high. It was the late J. I. S. Whitaker whose extensive and painstaking researches between 1906 and 1919 provided the elements of an overall picture of this ancient town: his report *Motya, a Phoenician Colony in Sicily* (1921) is still a fundamental source of information. Later work has added to rather than modified his results, and anyone who comes to know Motya and its ruins cannot fail to be increasingly impressed by the clarity of his vision and the care with which his observations were made and recorded.

After the First World War, however, Whitaker found little opportunity to continue his researches, and except for a month's trial dig undertaken by Professor P. Marconi in 1930, activity slackened. It was nevertheless clear that the site was not yet exhausted; indeed in some ways investigation had hardly begun. Within the circuit wall, the ancient city and its plan were practically unknown; private houses and public buildings were little known; fortifications and harbour works deserved additional study, and the history of the city, as a whole, was as yet known only in outline. At the same time the absence of substantial layers due to building activity after the destruction of Motya in 397 B.C. seemed to offer the excavator interested in Phoenician and Punic antiquity unusually favourable conditions.

The idea that additional excavations at Motya might be feasible first occurred to the writer in 1951, and a year or two later it had become clear that such work would in fact find approval with the Whitaker family. The late excavator's wife, Mrs. Tina Whitaker, then still living in Rome with her daughters, received the idea of renewed digging at Motya kindly. It was in particular the younger daughter of the late excavator, Miss Delia Whitaker, later becoming, until her death in 1971, owner of Motya, who from the beginning showed the project every assistance. Thereafter her interest and support remained unfailing and vital at every stage. We hope that our thanks expresses in every way our debt to her. Nor must we forget our thanks to her for recommending us to the good offices of the local administrator of the estate, the late Col. G. Lipari who died in 1971; his steady support, unfailingly and generously put at our disposition, has been vital to our work, as has the help of his son, Signor E. Lipari, during the later years.

It was at first a matter of some difficulty to get support in England to renew excavations at Motya, but at Oxford, the late Mr. T. Dunbabin, and Mr. D. B. Harden, then at the Ashmolean Museum, lent the budding project their support. It was thanks to them that in 1955 a small trial expedition went out to Motya, directed by the writer and staffed by P. Parr and W. Culican, with the financial support of the Ashmolean Museum and the Craven Committee of Oxford University. It proved, however, rather more difficult to proceed from a trial dig to a full scale expedition, and a number of years passed before this stage could be reached. Ultimately it was found that on the basis of inter-University co-operation, an expedition could be sent out: the credit for helping to arrange this expedition must largely go to Miss O. Tufnell. The parties involved were the University of Leeds, Department of Semitic Languages and Literatures (now Department of Semitic Studies - to the Headship of which the writer had meanwhile acceded), and the Institute of Archaeology of the University of London. The participation of the latter meant not only that the Expedition benefited from the backing of considerable technical facilities, but also that Miss J. du Plat Taylor became the co-director and (in 1962-5) director of underwater research, and Mr. M. Cookson the expedition photographer. The benefit to the Motya expedition of Miss du Plat Taylor's experience and scholarship has been immense: her advice and criticism have borne on every aspect of both field work and the ensuing publication, even where this is not specially indicated. I want here to thank her, however inadequately, for all the time and effort she has given the Motya project over the years. Our illustrations show how much the Expedition owed to Mr. Cookson's work, until his untimely death.

The young expedition was fortunate in being able to establish a working partnership with a French excavation at Motya led by Professor P. Cintas, one of the outstanding authorities in the field of Punic and Phoenician studies. This partnership, happily maintained during the years 1961-2, involved the sharing of certain basic expenses while each party pursued separate excavations in different parts of the island. It is a pleasant duty in this connection to thank Professor Cintas for allowing us at the same time to draw freely on the vast store of his experience and erudition. Miss Tufnell during those years also participated in the field, laying the foundations of the *corpus* of Motya pottery; Mr. N. Coldstream joined the expedition as classicist and specialist for Greek pottery (later joined by Dr. A. Snodgrass who specialised on metal objects and weapons). At this time support came again from the Craven Committee of Oxford University, the Cambridge University Faculty of Classical Studies (Craven Fund), the University of Leeds, the City of Leeds Museum (whose assistant curator, Miss E. Pirie succeeded Miss Tufnell as registrator of pottery), and also from the Russell Trust and private donors. Over successive years, the funds now available permitted the prosecution of limited excavations in zones adjoining the North and South Gates, as well as underwater investigations undertaken with the help of a team of divers from Imperial College, London.

The Imperial College team was led by Brian Matthews, and Dr. Ellen Macnamara was archaeologist in charge; Dr. John Waechter assisted with the work in 1964. We are indebted to Dr. Graham Evans for the subsequent study of the core samples collected; and to Messrs. Martini and Rossi, the Royal Geographical Society, Imperial College, the Gordon Childe Fund, and the Society of Antiquaries for their generous financial support for the exploration.

We also gratefully acknowledge permission given by Prof. Theodor Kraus, director of the Deutsches Archäologisches Institut in Rome, to study the photographs and notes made by the late Dr. H. Schläger concerning the stagnone off Märsala.

A third stage in the work of the expedition was reached in 1963 when Fairleigh Dickinson University, N.J., was added to the list of sponsoring bodies. For this we have to thank Prof. T. H. Gaster, who in 1962-3 came to the University to Leeds as Montague Burton Visiting Lecturer, and President (later Chancellor) P. Sammartino, Head of the academic body of Fairleigh Dickinson University, who gave our programme his far-sighted interest. The new tripartite partnership meant an increase in excavation activity; we were able to open new lines of research which, at comparatively small cost, promised to give a preliminary idea of the content of the largely unexcavated central area of the island of Motya. One aspect concerned resistivity measuring, followed by limited test trenching. Here in particular we have to thank Messrs. Evershed and Vignoles, London, who in 1964 made it possible for Dr. G. Tagg, a well known specialist in this field from their research Department to be seconded to Motya. Another line of enquiry, actively pursued over a number of years, concerned the acquisition and interpretation of air photographs of Motya, including some specially taken for the Expedition. These comprised Italian photographs (for which we have to thank Prof. D. Adamesteanu, then at the *Aerofototeca* in Rome, and Brigadier-General G. Schmiedt of the *Istituto Geografico Militare* in Florence).

Messrs. Hunting Surveys took air photographs specially for us in 1967; and in 1968 pictures of Motya taken on training flights were made available to us by the Royal Air Force under NATO auspices, and by special permission of the Italian authorities. In this connection, besides the Italian authorities, we wish to thank the Rt. Hon. D. Healey, then H. M. Secretary for Defence, the R.A.F. Central Reconnaissance Establishment at Brampton and its Commanding Officer, Group-Captain E. B. Sismore, D.S.O., D.F.C., A.F.C., and in particular Flight-Lieut. B. O. Sibree, who generously noted, and supplied, our needs. We wish, lastly, to thank the Deutsches Archäologisches Institut in Rome for their kind permission to reproduce an air photo of Motya and the lagoon by the late Dr. H. Schläger.

It is a pleasure to record during the years 1963-5, the active participation of a number of both junior and senior members and supporters of Fairley Dickinson University in the field work at Motya, including Mrs. V. Pollak, Mr. S. Van Zandt, and Mrs. L. Gaster. Financial support during this stage in the Expedition's work came from the sponsoring Universities, besides the Society of Antiquaries, the Russell Trust, the Simon Marks Charitable Trust, and the British Academy as well as previously mentioned contributors. Among contributions from private sources we were grateful to receive one from Mrs. V. Pollak.

The first phase of our work at Motya came to an end in 1965. A second phase began in 1968, when the Dept. of Semitic Studies in the University of Sydney, Australia, joined us. During the year the Head of that Department, Mr. E.C.B. MacLaurin, himself joined us in the field. While the work of this second stage is largely left for treatment in a subsequent volume, it is occasionally referred to in this present report and we wish to express our thanks to Sydney University, and in particular to Mr. MacLaurin and his Department.

During the years we have worked in Sicily, we have been show every consideration and kindness by the Department of Antiquities in Palermo, and by its Soprintendente- first by Signora I. Bovio Marconi, and more recently by her successor, Prof. V. Tusa. Their advice, based on their unique knowledge of the antiquities of Sicily, has been invaluable; in particular Prof. Tusa, an authority in the field of Punic studies, during many a walk over the island of Motya gave us the benefit of his counsel. We are also greatly indebted to his wife, Signora A. Tusa-Cutroni, for undertaking the study of our coins. In Rome, we wish to thank the British School, and in particular the Director, Prof. J. Ward-Perkins, who over the years has lent his official support, while in Palermo, the British Consulate has helped us year by year in dealing with official matters. May this acknowledgment express our gratitude for the burden they have carried for so long. In England we must thank the Director of the Institute of Archaeology, Prof. W. F. Grimes, and the late Prof. V. G. Childe, his predecessor, and the Vice-Chancellor, Bursar and administrative staff of the University of Leeds who shouldered much additional work on our behalf: likewise Prof. H. J. King, lately Professor of Mining in the University of Leeds, and Dr. W. G. Collins, until recently of the Dept. of Engineering, for much help over the years.

Our debt to a number of Libraries and learned institutions is also considerable: the British Museum and Public Record Office in London, the Vatican Library in Rome, and the Librarian and Map Curator of the R. Geographical Society all showed us kindness. In Palermo we owe a great debt of gratitude to the *Archivio di Stato* and its Director, Prof. A. Baviera, the *Biblioteca Communale* and its Director, Prof. E. Alaimo, Dr. B. Caronia of the *Ufficio Tecnico per le Trazzere di Sicilia*, and Dr. F. Montalto, the Director of the *Commissariato per la Liquidazione degli Usi Civici della Sicilia*—all of whom generously put documentary material at our disposition or allowed us to quote extracts in our text. In Florence we are most grateful to the Istituto Geografico Militare, and to Brig.-Gen.-G. Schmiedt, for generous permission to reproduce part of Schmettau's map of Sicily (1 : 75000) from an original drawing used to make blocks for this map. In Munich, we are indebted to the *Staatsbibliothek* and the *Bayerisches Hauptstaatsarchiv*, *Geheimes Hausarchiv* and its Head, Prof. Dr. H. Rall, as well as H. R. H.

Duke Albert of Bavaria, for permission to consult papers relating to Sicily in the early 19th century; similarly we have to thank Dr. Bellot, director of the *Staats- und Stadtbibliothek*, Augsburg, and Dr. H. Drexler of the *Augsburger Allgemeine Zeitung* there, for research into their files relating to H. Schliemann. We owe particular thanks to Prof. F. R. Walton of the Gennadius Library, Athens for making available to us photocopies of Schliemann's diary relating to his stay at Motya, and for the trouble he generously took in elucidating certain passages in the diary, where the writing was no longer fully legible. In Athens we are also greatly indebted to the American excavations in the Agora and in particular to Prof. P. E. Corbett, and to Dr. B. A. Sparkes for their expert advice on our Attic pottery. Further, Dr. Sparkes kindly supplied advance information about volume XII (The Black and Plain Pottery) of the Report by himself and the late Miss L. Talcott, and we wish to thank both of them.

We want to thank all the members of the staff of our Expedition, both senior and junior, listed overleaf, for their labours: and we cannot omit on this occasion to say how fortunate we were in having workmen to whose energy, skill, and unfailing courtesy and good humour we are greatly indebted.

We have listed overleaf all those who supported us financially. Among those we should given special thanks to the Russell Trust and its Head, Major D. Russell, for repeatedly helping us with additional, as well as regular grants, which repeatedly allowed us to continue vital investigations for which funds would otherwise not have been available. The debt of thanks which we owe them is thus a very special one, and if useful results could be achieved by our work at Motya and presented here, then a good deal of the credit must go to the steady support and encouragement we received from Major Russell and the Russell Trust. We are also most grateful to the Faculty of Classics in Cambridge for making available a grant of £ 500 towards the preparation and publication of this report. Its publication was finally assured by additional grants from the Russell Trust and Leeds University.

Since we began working at Motya, important excavations have been undertaken by a joint mission of the *Istituto al Oriente* of the University of Rome under Prof. S. Moscati, and the *Soprintendenza alle Antichità of Palermo*, under Prof. V. Tusa. Their work, which has led to discoveries of outstanding importance, has been published with exemplary speed: we have greatly profited from the study of their volumes while preparing our own report. We have also profited from discussion with Prof. E. Titone, of Marsala, and from the study of his recent volume on Motya.

The wearisome task of typing the manuscript of this volume was undertaken by Mrs. P. Monkman, and the ladies of the General Secretarial Office, Leeds University, under the direction of Mrs. W. M. Digby.

The original text of the manuscript was partly scrutinized by Dr. E. Oren. Later it was systematically checked by Miss J. Davis, and thereafter subjected to very detailed scrutiny by Mr. D. B. Harden. To them all, and especially to Mr. Harden, who generously gave a great deal of his time to the considerable benefit of the text, we want to express our sincere thanks.

This report is dedicated to the memory of Miss Delia Whitaker, the late owner of Motya, as well as to her father. His work laid the foundations for future research at Motya: her generosity has made its continuation possible. I would like to conclude with a personal expression of thanks to my wife, without whose unobtrusive but steady help, our Motya Expedition would not have become a reality in 1961, or continued thereafter.

LIST OF DONORS AND CONTRIBUTORS
(1961-6)

The University of Leeds
The Institute of Archaeology, University of London
Fairleigh Dickinson University
The University of Oxford (Craven Fund)
The Faculty of Classics, University of Cambridge (Craven Fund)
The Russell Trust
The Society of Antiquaries, London
The British Academy
The Simon Marks Charitable Trust
The Ashmolean Museum, Oxford (1955 Expedition)
Leeds City Museum

Mr. D. de Ghetto
Mr. T. Goeritz
Mrs. B. Isserlin
Mrs. G. Pike
Mrs. V. Pollak
Miss G. Talbot
Miss J. du Plat Taylor

LIST OF PARTICIPANTS

Mr. G. D. Addison, 1963
Dr. A. R. al Ansari, 1965
Miss M. E. Best, 1961
Miss K. Blanchard, 1964
Mr. A. G. Bloomer, 1964
Miss B. Bornstein, 1965
Mr. D. Browne, 1965
Miss M. Cardale, 1965
Miss V. Carnegie, 1964-5
Mr. N. Coldstream, 1961 ff.
Miss T. Collingwood, 1961
Dr. N. Cooke, 1965
Mr. M. B. Cookson, 1961-4
Miss A. Craven, 1961
Dr. W. Culican, 1955
Miss L. Davren, 1964
Miss E. Dowman, 1966
Miss R. Droller, 1962
Miss B. E. Fielding, 1955
Mr. P. Fordham, 1962
Mr. D. A. de Ghetto, 1963, 5
Mr. H. M. Goldthorpe, 1963
Miss J. Grad, 1955
Mr. D. C. Graham, 1963
Mr. M. Hassall, 1965
Mrs. B. Isserlin, 1961 ff.
Miss M. Lewin, 1966
Mr. H. G. Macalister, 1963
Miss A. Madeira, 1963-4
Miss R. Maizel, 1964
Mr. W. G. Oram, 1963
Mr. P. Parr. 1955
Dr. and Mrs. H. H. M. Pike, 1966
Miss E. Pirie, 1963-5
Mrs. V. Pollak, 1963-4
Miss H. Razavi, 1961-2
Mr. C. Robinson, 1962
Mr. R. Robertson-Mackay, 1961
Mr. A. Robertson-Pearce, 1965
Miss C. Rodriguez, 1966
Mr. and Mrs. R. H. Searle, 1966
Miss G. Sanguinetti, 1962
Dr. A. Snodgrass, 1962 ff.
Dr. G. Tagg, 1964
Miss G. Talbot, 1955, 1961, 62
Miss O. Tufnell, 1961, 63-4
Mr. S. Van Zandt, 1963-4
Mr. E. von der Lippe, 1963
Dr. J. Waechter, 1964
Miss C. Warhurst, 1964
Mr. T. Wood, 1964
Mr. W. Yonkers, 1964

LIST OF PLANS AND SECTIONS

LIST OF PLATES

All photographs are by the late Mr. M. Cookson, except for the following:

Pl. 1 : 2; 5 : 2, 3; 12 : 2, 3	by Miss J. du Plat Taylor
Pl. 9 : 2 26 : 2–4	by A. Robertson-Pierce
Pl. 2 : 1	H. Schläger (courtesy of Deutsches Archäologisches Institut, Rome)
Pl. 2 : 2, 3	Italian Air Force photograph supplied by Aerofototeca, Rome
Pl. 3	by Messrs. Hunting Surveys Ltd.
Pl. 4 : 2; Pl. 7	Royal Air Force
Pl. 4 : 1	B. S. J. Isserlin
Pl. 11 : 2, 3	Miss G. Talbot
Pl. 19 : 1	Miss C. Warhurst
Pl. 8 : 1	C. B. MacLaurin
Pl. 9 : 3; 18 : 1, 2	A. Pegg
Pl. 14 : 5	Messrs. Lipari, Marsala

The photographs of Mr. Joseph and Miss Delia Whitaker (Pl. 1 : 1) were kindly supplied by the latter.

LIST OF FIGURES IN TEXT

KEY TO LAYER NUMBERS USED IN SECTIONS ON PLANS IV-XI (SOUTH GATE)

00. Dark brown—grey top soil, flecked, clayey near shore
0. Hard grey brown flecked and plastery (robbed)
1. Plastery tip
2. Sandy brown earth
3. Dark grey soil
4. Grey clay and brown earth: above XVIII-plastery streaks over sand
5. Brown sandy streaks and plastery
6. Sticky grey-green clay
7. Grey flecked, brown and yellow
8. Black and yellow sand with plastery streaks and burnt matter
9. Dark brown and grey sticky
10. Brown-grey plastery, flecked, and dark debris; ashy E and W of XXXVIII
11. Black flecked
12. Grey- black hard dark mud
13. Black mud
14. Yellow sand with black muddy streaks
15. Light brown flecked; S. of XXVII over yellow clay
16. Brown flecked
17. Grey flecked soil, bricky locally
18. Hard brown flecked
19. Dark brown-black
20. Black soil
21. Brown plastery and debris
22. Sand and black mud, mixed with mud-brick debris
23. Brown and grey sandy, locally with debris
24. Dark grey and blackish mud and sand; in Room 29 with charcoal
25. Greyish brown
26. ,, ,,
27. Brown loamy and debris
28. Trodden grey sandy and clay over pebbles; clay W of XXI
29. Brown- grey clay (above clayey sand and grey sand)
30. Coarse grey clay
31. Brown sand and shells
32. Dark grey sand
33. Grey soil and sand
34. Grey packing and ashy
35. Grey gritty sand
36. Grey and muddy; stony in section I-I
37. Black mud with shells

Pit A (1) Mixed fill, clay and plastery streaks
A (2) Mixed fill and clay
Pit B (1) Grey- brown and sandy
B (2) Brown hard pebbly

Shore deposit (Section I-I): top soil; mixed sandy and gravelly

Lower shore deposit (ibid): hard brown sandy clay

KEY TO LAYER NUMBERS USED IN SECTIONS ON PLANS XII-XIV (NORTH GATE)

0. Hard brown topsoil
1. Hard brown with chips and stones
2. Grey or brown soil
3. Sandy with limestone dust
4. Brown-grey sandy
5. Sandy brown-grey clay
6. Grey clay and sand
7. Loose brown (foundation trench)
8. Black ooze
9. Black mould
10. Natural gray and orange sand
11. Brown earth
12. Brown earth and sand
13. Dark grey clay and sand
14. Dark grey clay and sand
15. Natural grey-black
16. Brown sandy
17. Grey clayey sand
18. Dark brown clay
19. Brownish brick-earth and sand
20. Yellow clayey sand
21. Grey loam and clay
22. Grey sticky clay
23. Brown sand
24. Grey clay
25. Grey sand
26. Grey soil
27. Orange brown clay and sand
28. Lighter coloured sand
29. Wet grey sand with charcoal on top
30. Sand with iron pan
31. Black sand
32. Grey brown clayey sand
33. Grey mud
34. Fallen mud brick
35. Clayey brown earth
36. Grey and orange sand
37. Orange sand
38. Dark grey clay
39. Fine grey sand
40. Dark grey clay

LIST OF ABBREVIATIONS

ALUOS *Annual of Leeds University Oriental Society.*

CIS *Corpus Inscriptionum Semiticarum* de Academia Inscriptionum et Literarum Humaniorum conditum atque digestum. Paris, Académie des Inscriptions et Belles Lettres, Pars Prima, Tome 1-2, 1881. Paris.

Malta *Missione archeologica italiana a Malta. Rapporto preliminare della campagna* 1963 (by M. Cagiano de Azevado and others). Università di Roma, Istituto di Studi del Vicino Oriente (Rome, 1964)—here quoted as Vol I; II id., *Rapporto* 1964 (Rome, 1965); III, 1965 (1966); IV, 1966 (1967); V, 1967 (1968); VI, 1968 (1969).

Monte Sirai *Rapporto preliminare della Missione archeologica dell' Università di Roma e della Soprintendenza alle Antichità di Cagliari* (by F. Barreca and others). Università di Roma, Centro di Studi Semitici. Vol. I, 1964; II, 1965; III, 1966; IV, 1967. Rome.

Mozia *Rapporto preliminare della Missione archeologica della Soprintendenza alle Antichità della Sicilia occidentale e dell' Università di Roma* (by A. Ciasca and others). Università di Roma, Centro di Studi Semitici, Istituto di Studi del Vicino Oriente. Vol. I, 1964; II, 1966; III, 1967; IV, 1968; V, 1969; VI, 1970; VII, 1971, Rome.

PBSR *Papers of the British School at Rome.*

INTRODUCTION

1. The Name "Motya"

Information about the phonetic structure of the name Motya has to be gathered from two directions. The legends in the Phoenician script found on the coins issued by the city give the consonant structure as מטוא, מוטוא, המטוא, or אמטו (Tusa-Cutroni, in *Mozia* III, 97 ff.): i.e. מ(ו)טוא preceded by the definite article ה/א. Vowels are supplied by the Greek transcriptions: the standard spelling in the historical sources written in Attic or *koine* Greek is Μοτύη, corresponding to Sicilian Greek Μοτύα (Ziegler, 1933, col. 387); recently a Greek inscription of the early sixth century B.C. from Selinus has offered the alternative form ΜοτύϜαι with *digamma* preserved (Rocco, 1970, 27-33). On the combined evidence of these sources the (or a) pronunciation of the name should thus be Moṭúwa, or something similar.

The name of Motya has long been the object of learned investigation, the first attempt at an explanation being that by Bochart in 1646 (*Geographia Sacra, Seu Phaleg et Canaan*, ed. 1712, col. 509); and the question cannot yet be regarded as closed. A derivation from a Semitic root is assumed by most of the scholars who have dealt with the matter, but in detail there have been widely different solutions. Bochart himself interpreted the name to mean "protensa" on the basis of an assumed Semitic spelling מתוחה which the evidence of the coins has since proved to be untenable. Gesenius (1837, 297), who was aware of this fact, accordingly derived it from the root טוה attested in Hebrew, the meaning being "spinners' town". He also recalled (without stressing it) the Arabic root طوى and the noun طِيَّةٌ derived from it, meaning "hospitium, quod quis petit, longinquum". Gesenius' main proposal was accepted by a number of scholars who interpreted the name as spinners' or weavers' town, including Movers (1850, 334), Schröder (1869, 279), and Meyer (1931, 106); and Neiman followed it as recently as 1965 (114, note 8). Coglitore (1884, 20-2) and Whitaker (1921, 54), however, did not exclude other suggestions, and De Luynes in particular in his essay "Recherches sur l'emplacement de l'ancienne ville de Motya" (1855, 93) has discounted Gesenius' explanation on the grounds that Malta rather than Motya was famous for its textiles. While not totally rejecting an explanation from the Arabic root he proposed instead a comparison with the Aramaic מטא "advenit, parvenit". He also suggested as an alternative a connection with the name of the deity Mot mentioned by Philo of Byblos from Sanchuniathon (Eusebius, *Praeparatio Evangelica*, I, x, 1), and which he in turn linked with the root טוא "lutosus fuit" assumed by Gesenius (1828, 547 s.v. טאטא). This latter suggestion was likewise not ruled out by Whitaker. Coglitore (1884, 126) has also noted the possible interpretation of the medieval Arabic name of Motya as "linked isle" (implying apparently that Gisira Malbugi/Malbudi equals جَزِيرَةٌ مَرْبُوطَةٌ), as proposed earlier by Massa (1709, II, 487) and others: and, taking up another possible connotation of the Arabic root طوى, he suggested for the Phoenician "Motye" a similar meaning, the more apt because of the island's linkage with the mainland by means of the causeway.

Yet another suggestion was made by Ziegler (1933, 387). Discounting the previous interpretation of the word Motya as an appellative place name, he thought it was rather the name of the city goddess shown on the coins and mentioned in the tradition. In 1951 Friedrich made a suggestion radically different from all those mentioned above, namely that the name Motya was non-Semitic (1951, 40 : 102). It would thus presumably go back to the local native population.

When we review the suggestions listed above, we should keep in mind three criteria which should be satisfied before an interpretation can be regarded as established. Firstly, a Phoenician name should by preference be referred to a root lexically attested in Phoenician, rather than in another Semitic language (Hebrew being the second choice as the most closely related sister language). Secondly, any interpretation suggested should conform to suitable grammatical patterns known. Lastly, any given interpretation should suit actual conditions at Motya in the Phoenician period.

When we apply these criteria to the interpretations listed above, it will appear that none is completely satisfactory. It seems difficult at present to find among Phoenician vocabulary, known from ancient texts, proofs for the existence of any of the roots referred to here. We can, however, definitely *exclude* any attempt to pattern the name of the deity Mot, since the latter is spelled with ת, not ט, and similarly neither is a female (city) deity with the name like מטוא known. Coming to attempts based on Hebrew, we may note that the root טוא "lutosus fuit", assumed by Gesenius, and drawn on by de Luynes, is discarded or regarded as doubtful by standard modern dictionaries such as Brown, Driver, and Briggs (1906, 370, s.v. טאטא). טוה "to spin" is indeed known in Hebrew (ibid., 376) but what stem formation suitable for a place name and derived from this root would correspond to the transcription Μοτύη is not quite clear. This derivation deserves consideration, however.

Progressing now to interpretations based on other Semitic languages, we may begin with de Luynes' attempt to interpret from the Aramaic מטא. Formally such a derivation would have something in its favour, since a faʿūl/fuʿūl form מטוא would correspond tolerably well to the Greek transcription. An attempt could even be made to postulate the existence of the root in Phoenician, on the strength of the occurrence of mṣ'/mẓ' in Ugaritic (Gordon, 1965, 436, No. 1524) and the transition of ẓ into ṭ in cases like ṣr/Tyrus: but this remains rather doubtful.

Reviewing now interpretations on the base of Arabic roots, a suitable meaning "enfolded isle" or similar could be derived from طوى, and would meet presumed geographical conditions at Motya in antiquity, when the island was probably located in a deep bay open only from the south. The meaning "linked isle" also taken from طوى, however, seems less recommendable, since the causeway, the existence of which it implies, appears to have been built only in the 6th century B.C., well after the foundation of the city.

The Arabic وَطِئَ could, in view of its possible connotation "plain, level, soft, or easy to be travelled or to walk, or ride or lie upon" (Lane, 1893, 2949) give a meaning very suitably descriptive of the characteristic lowness of Motya, which has impressed travellers: but it is doubtful if a mafʿūl form מוטוא can be assumed here, even though the spelling מוטוא occurs on a coin (Tusa Cutroni, *Mozia* III, 110 : 5).

In view of so much uncertainty there is probably something to be said for Friedrich's suggestion that the name should be treated as non-Semitic: particularly since, as the archaeological evidence tends to show, the Phoenicians mingled at first with the local population whose name for the island they could well have taken over. The name would in that case presumably be Sican or Elymean. Specialists in those fields should be able to determine whether a suitable derivation can be offered from these languages. Meanwhile, however, a cautious attitude in this direction seems perhaps to be indicated: for, as E. Meyer noted long ago (1931, 106), the fact that the name Motya is, on the coins, usually preceded by the definite article may mean that it was meaningful as a descriptive noun to the Phoenicians. The question must thus remain undecided.

2. Literary and Epigraphical Sources for the History of Motya

The amount of knowledge about ancient Motya which can be gleaned from literary sources remains remarkably small when we consider the importance the city possesed, over a period of several centuries, as a focus of Phoenician trade and later as a Carthaginian military base. Our information is, moreover, one-sided and contains important lacunae; all Phoenician and Carthaginian historical works have perished and what would have been a main source of information is thus totally lacking. Of the works of those Greek writers (like Menander of Ephesus) who showed an interest in things Phoenician, or more particularly in the history of the Phoenicians and Carthaginians in Sicily, only a few fragments have survived: our main source is thus what Diodorus Siculus gathered in his *Bibliotheca* (Books XIII, 54, 61, 63, 88, and XIV, 47-55—especially XIV, 48-53). In addition to this, and Polyaenus, *Strategemata V*, 2, 61, there is a short entry under *Motya* in Stephen of Byzantium, taken from Hekataios and Philistos: a brief statement, in Thucydides (VI, 2, 6) and a confused remark in Pausanias (V, 25, 5—cf. Whitaker 1921, 46) complete the list. Even when textual references which do not mention Motya, but record events which must have affected here, are taken into consideration, it is still true that our texts tell us far more about the final siege to which the city succumbed than about the centuries that preceded it. It follows that we must not expect from them a balanced account of the history and development of Motya, or even a record of the main events in her story, especially those which were not of direct international importance.

Turning to epigraphic sources, we find that inscriptional materials from the city or from its outlying necropolis on the mainland at Birgi are scarce and do little add to our information. In Greek there are still only some fragmentary texts from tombstones dating from the 6th and 5th centuries B.C. Originally reported by Whitaker (1921, 286 ff.) they have recently been referred to by Jeffery (1961, 272). The brief Greek inscription from Selinus referred to above (Rocco, 1971, 27-33) offers us the first important epigraphic reference to Motya originating from the Greek sphere in Sicily: it is on the tombstone of Aristogeitos the son of Arcadion, who fell near, or under the walls of, Motya. Attributable probably to the early 6th century B.C., it has been tentatively linked by Rocco with the expedition of Pentathlos (580 B.C.) rather than that of Dorieus (510 B.C.) but these datings remain hypothetical; and the text cannot be used as evidence for the existence of city fortifications at Motya at a given point within the 6th century B.C. As for Phoenician, there is the long known tombstone inscription (CIS I, 137; Whitaker, 1921, 116 ff); and a number of texts recently added by the Italian expedition (Garbini in *Mozia* II, 109 ff.; III, 71 ff; IV, 95 ff.; Guzzo Amadisi, *Mozia* VI, 95-116). These date from the 6th century B.C. onwards, and are mainly of religious, onomastic and linguistic-epigraphic interest. Of public inscriptions of a civic or historical character there is as yet, no trace.

The Motyan coins, last dealt with by Mrs. A. Tusa Cutroni (in *Mozia* III, 97 ff; V, 173 ff.) and by G. K. Jenkins (1971) conclude the list of inscribed material of historical value. Emitted from the early 5th century to the end of the existence of the town, they are useful because of the links with the Greek world (Acragas, Selinus) which they indicate, but no other major contribution can at present be drawn from them.

3. The History of Research

The history of learned research concerning ancient Motya goes back to the time of the great classical scholars of the 16th and 17th centuries. The first main topic which engaged their attention was that of the location of the city, and answers offered to this question varied widely for a time. We may here refer, for detail, to the discussion contained in I. Coglitore's study (1883, 265 ff.) of the various suggestions made. The decisive step forward was, however, the proposal to locate the ancient town on the island of San Pantaleo in the lagoon (Stagnone) between Marsala and Trapani, made by Ph.

Cluverius (1619). Cluverius' arguments did not indeed immediately command complete assent—other suggestions were still being offered in the 19th century—but the case made in his book was never forgotten.

One of the results of the continued interest in the location proposed by Cluverius was to render San Pantaleo the object of visits by both scholars and travellers with an intelligent concern for the antiquities of Sicily. A number of these, form the 17th century onwards, left descriptions of what they saw or heard—ranging from a few sentences to full-scale essays. By no means all the more important travellers who have left us descriptions of Sicily in the later 18th or early 19th century visited San Pantaleo, however: thus, Hager, Bartels, Borch and Goethe gave no indication that the site was of interest to them, and they did not go there, nor was Motya mentioned in the travellers' guide-books which in the 18th and early 19th centuries indicated other ancient sites of interest in Sicily. The existing descriptions nevertheless contain information of interest.

It seems regrettable that, with the important exception of J. P. L. L. Houel, none of the artists who visited Sicily in the 17th, 18th and early 19th centuries apparently thought that anything at San Pantaleo deserved sketching, painting or publishing, even though several of them came as near as Trapani or Marsala, and Denon actually visited the island in 1788.

The amount of information to be derived from early maps is likewise very limited. However, a number of facts of interest can be gleaned from local documents concerned with rights of property or tenancy on San Pantaleo. This applies in particular to a volume in the *Archivio di Stato* from the Collegio Massimo of the Jesuits in Palermo (No. 7), which contains materials covering the period from the 11th to the 18th century. ("Case ex-gesuitiche, Collegio Massimo e Chiesa di Palermo").

Taken together, the above-mentioned materials enable us to gain some information not only about the progress of learned study, but also about the state of ancient monuments on San Pantaleo from the 17th century onwards. We also learn something about the use made of the land, and the pattern of roads, fields and habitation from time to time a knowledge of which is of value, e.g. where the interpretation of air photographs is concerned, since it should help us to distinguish features of post-classical periods more clearly.

Let us consider first texts of archaeological and antiquarian interest. No learned description of Motya antedating the publication of Cluverius' *Sicilia Antiqua* (1619) seems to exist. His work contains the following passage (Book II, Ch. I, 253):

> "Est autem hodieque insula, solo humili atque depresso, VI circiter stadia ab continente *Siciliae*, II ab *Aegithallo* promontorio passuum milia, VII ab *Lilybaeo* dissita, vulgari nunc vocabulo *Isola di Santo Pantaleone* dicta: in quam unam quum omnes supra scriptae historiae congruant, nullam jam dubium esse potest, quin haec illa sit, quae olim *Motyam* Carthaginiesium urbem sustinuit."

This text gives evidence of having been founded on first-hand observations gathered during the author's travels in Sicily. Nothing is said, however, about ancient ruins. It is possible that more may have been contained in the detailed journal kept by Cluverius during his tour, and on which he based his text to some extent: it was still used a number of years after the author's death by his former travelling companion, Holstenius, but must now be presumed lost (cf. Partsch, 1891, 16; Almagia, 1944, 71). There is, however, in the volume of papers from the Collegio Massimo of the Jesuits in Palermo a document written on November 14th, 1605—and thus contemporary with Cluverius—in which for the first time there is an archaeological observation. The passage concerned runs:

> "E detta isola è discosta da questa citta circa cinque miglia e di compreso da circa salmi deci

> di terra culti e inculti tutta pietrosa senza acqua la bestime ci anda per uno molo antico fatto di pietra alba(?) et arena lungo da circa uno miglio e menzo e largo otto passi l'inverno la detta bestiame vi passa con periculo..." (p. 169 verso).*

This seems to be the earliest reference to the causeway, recognised as ancient and described with fair accuracy.

However, the first more detailed description of the island of San Pantaleo and of the surrounding waters is that given by G. A. Massa in his comprehensive work *La Sicilia in Prospettiva* (1709), a book combining a thorough command of the learned sources with a detailed knowledge of contemporary Sicily. Under the entry "San Pantaleo" he writes (II, 488):

> "Stà in un gran secco, che mostra apparenza di Porto, perche ha l'onde sempre in calma e non esposte alla furia de' venti... è però di si poco fondo, che nè pure le piccole barche possono valicarlo, senza incagliare tratto tratto nelle secche. Non vi è hoggi altro di notabile, se non certa Peschiera di struttura moresca, e la Salina: attorno l'Isola presso le sponde del mare restano vestigie di mura, motivo al P. Cascini di persuadersi che vi sia fiorita un tempo qualche città de' Mori, non già l'antica Motia. Il suo terreno è assai fertile, e vi si produce copia di Ghiri..."

After Massa's book nothing of special interest to us seems to have been published for some time. However, the last thirty years of the 18th century brought a noticeable quickening of interest in Sicily and her antiquities, which also made itself felt in the case of Motya. Similarly, the number of travellers who visited her and wrote about her increased significantly.

Among these perhaps the first important figure is von Riedesel. He writes (1771, 22-3) the following about Motya:

> "Zwischen Trapani und Marsala ist eine kleine Insel, welche man jezo St. Pantaleo nennt, und die das alte Motya sein soll, wo, wie Thukidides sagt, die Phönizier eine Stadt baueten und von da Lilybaum überfielen und beunruhigten. Cluverius beweiset seiner Gewohnheit nach mit tausend Citationen dass dieses das alte Motya sey: er führet aber nichts von den Überbleibseln desselben an. Ich habe noch Kennzeichen der Stadtmauern mit Merkmalen von sieben Türmen gefunden: es deucht mich aber nicht die Bauart der Phönizier zu sein, indem die Steine derselben regelmässig gehauen sind: sie sind acht Palmen breit und viere hoch. Da in der Insel Ghozzo *(Gaulus)*, bey Malta, Mauern sind, welche der alten Mauer bey Fondi gleichen, so vermuthe ich, dass diese regelmässige Bauart in Motya von der Römer Zeiten sey, zumalen, da man verschiedene Urnen und Vasa Lacrimatoria dorten gefunden hat, welche unstreitig römisch sind..."

A short time after the beginning of active archaeological exploration at Motya (discussed below), Ignazio Paterno Castello, Principe di Biscari, published his *Viaggo per tutte le antichità della Sicilia* (1781). He mentions Motya and refers to the finding of a Punic inscription there by Principe Torremuzza in his capacity as Royal Sovraintendente of Antiquities for the Val di Mazzara district, in 1779, but does not otherwise bring any new information (1781, 154).

The year 1782, however, is of considerable interest in the annals of learned investigation at Motya, for it saw the start of publication in Paris of J.P.L.L. Houel's *Voyage pittoresque des isles de Sicile, de Malte et de Lipari*. Based on the careful observations made by this acute artist and writer (1776), this work is of very special value since it contains what appears to be the only published 18th-century view of Motyan

* I have to thank Prof. Baviera for her kind help with difficult readings in the MS.

antiquities (the North Gate-vol. I, pl. IX.). The textual passage concerned with Motya is as follows (ibid, I, 16):

> "Je quittai la route de Marsalla, afin d'aller voir l'île de S. Pantaleo, où l'on prétend qu'Hercule bâtit la ville de Mottya, ville qui a depuis appartenu aux Cartaginois, and que les Sarrasins ont détruite.
>
> "Cette île, qui n'est eloignée que d'un demi-mille du rivage de la Sicile, est à huit milles de Marsalla, & a six ou sept de Trapani. Elle a deux milles de tour. On y voit encore des portions considérables des murs de l'ancienne ville de Mottya. Une partie de ces murs consistoit en des espèces de bastions qui defendoient le midi de cette île. J'en ai dessiné un qui avoit trente-cinq pieds de face à l'orient, vingt-quatre au midi, et douze au couchant; il paroît que ces murs interrompus aujourd'hui, étoient autrefois contigus et faisoient le tour de l'île.
>
> "Planche Neuvieme. Vue du reste des murs de Mottya. J'ai representé la partie la plus considérable qui reste encore de cette ville. Ce sont deux bastions dont la face a trente pieds, & dont les flancs ont dix-huit. Ils s'élèvent à l'occident de l'île: il y a entre eux une ouverture de vingt-quatre pieds, qui semble avoir été une des portes de la ville. A gauche de ces bastions, le rivage qui suit vers le nord conduit à un autre bastion éloigné de quatre-vingt-huit toises; il a vingt-quatre pieds de face; et son flanc qui regarde l'orient, en a trente-cinq. Ce lieu étoit l'extremité de la ville. La mer s'avance presque au pied de ces murs.
>
> "En face de cette ouverture, où étoit la porte de Mottya, est une petite langue de terre A; elle va joindre à cent toises de là une autre petite île. Il n'y reste rien aujourd'hui; mais elle a été cultivée & peuplée autrefois.
>
> "On trouve à l'orient de l'île de S. Pantaleo des fragmens de tuiles, des canaux, de vases, de toutes sortes d'ouvrages en terre cuite.
>
> "Après avoir parcouru les rives de ces deux îles, je repris la route de Marsalla: mais avant d'y arriver, je rencontrai l'une des plus grandes salines qui'il y ait en Sicile. Je m' y'arrêtai, & je la dessinai."

As against this, F. Münter in his travels in Sicily (1785-6) did not take any special interest in San Pantaleo, though it is briefly referred to in his book.

The years 1785 and 1788 are, so far as Motya is concerned, connected with another opportunity missed. The former year saw the appearance in Paris of volume IV of J. C. Richard de Saint-Non's important illustrated work *Voyage pittoresque ou description des royaumes de Naples et de Sicile.* The text of this volume was essentially written by Baron D. V. Denon, a diplomatist and artist, who in 1781 had travelled with the large mission (including two architects and a painter) charged by Saint-Non to visit and draw the antiquities of Sicily. Three years later, D. V. Denon, after dissensions with Saint-Non, published his own independent book *Voyage en Sicile* (Paris, 1788). Denon and the mission, in the course of their travels, visited San Pantaleo, but while making a number of interesting observations he did not (unlike Houel) think anything here merited an illustration in his book. His text is as follows (1788, 108):

> "Nous prîmes une barque et allâmes a l'isle, qui a un mille de long sur un demi-mille de large. Elle appartenoit aux jesuites, et appartient maintenant au roi. Il y a une seule ferme, qui rapporte à peu près cent pistoles: nous cherchâmes vainement quelques vestiges de la ville détruite. Nous ne trouvâmes que quelques pierres antiques, dont on avoit construit un bastion moderne, aussi détruit: nous vîmes cependant beaucoup de *mattoni* épars dans les champs, des fragments de vases grecs de la plus grande finesse, et sur une pierre brute de deux pieds de haut sur quinze pouces de large cette inscription punique...

"Les paysans qui travailloient nous dirent qu'on avoit trouvé grand nombre de monnoies d'argent et de cuivre: ils m'en donnerent deux: l'une carthaginoise, ayant d'un côté une tête de femme d'un fort beau caractere, et au revers un cheval; l'autre monnoie étoit de Syracuse, mais presque entièrement effacée. Ils me donnerent aussi de fers de javelots et de traits en bronze. Ceux des traits étoient triangulaires, en forme de cône alongé, avec une pointe en arrière de chaque angle; ce qui en rendoit l'extraction très difficile, et la blessure fort dangereuse. De là nous allâmes à Marsala, à six milles plus loin..."

This passage is, with only slight variations, the same as the text in J. C. Richard de Saint-Non's *Voyage pittoresque de Naples et de Sicile*. The passage there (IV, 178 ff.) ends with the following words, which curiously anticipate Schliemann's negative judgment about Motya a century later: "Ne trouvant donc rien d'intéressant à voir dans l'isle de *San Pantaleone*, nous nouse rembarquâmes pour gagner *Marsala...*"

In 1790 Sir Richard Colt Hoare visited our part of Sicily. His reference to San Pantaleo in his book *A classical tour through Italy and Sicily* contains only one sentence of real interest; he writes (1819, 344): "It now contains only a farm house and before it was cultivated, I was creditably informed that the ruins of the ancient walls were yet to be traced". A few years later, in 1794, F. L. Graf zu Stolberg travelled in this part of Sicily, but his book, "Reise in Deutschland, der Schweiz, Italien und Sizilien", while mentioning Motya and the unusually flat nature of its relief, makes no remarks of archaeological interest. Neither A. de Sayve, *Voyage en Sicile, fait en* 1820 *et* 1821, Paris 1822, nor the *Souvenirs de la Sicile* by L. N. P. A. de Forbin, Paris, 1823, add any genuine information though they contain some spurious learning, including a tradition derived from Polyaenus, shared by some early Dutch maps, and still found in Schliemann's notes that from a hill on or near Motya one could see Cape Bon in Africa on a very clear day (Sayve, 1822, 129; Forbin, 1823, 67.).

Real progress is, on the other hand, marked by the appearance of Captain (later Admiral) W. H. Smyth's book *Memoir and description of the resources, inhabitants and hydrography of Sicily and its islands* (London, 1824) which is based on close acquaintance with the neighbourhood. He writes as follows (1824, 235):

> ...Fragments of wall, with two flanked gateways, consisting of large square stones, still exist; and as they appear to follow the tortuosities of the coast, the whole island was probably surrounded with fortifications. Coins are frequently found by the husbandmen, when tilling, and the ground is everywhere strewed with pieces of terra-cotta vases, and ancient brick. Among other rarities found here by Prince Torremuzza, were some curious leaden pipes, that communicated with the main land, probably over the famous causeway, near which was found the following Punic inscription:—(Here follows a rather rough copy of the inscription given by Whitaker, 1921, 116)...
>
> "...Its (i.e. Motya's) fine situation, as it were on a lake will best be understood by examining the plan contained in the Atlas; which will also shew the judgment of the Saracens in establishing a fishery on it".

In 1827 E. Boid published anonymously the impressions gathered on a journey made three years earlier (*Travels in Sicily and the Lipari Islands in the month of December, 1824, by a naval officer*). He seems to have been well informed, drawing both on local lore (thus he is the only traveller who gives an explanation for the name of Spagnola on the mainland, opposite Motya) and also well acquainted with the main traveller's accounts, such as Riedesel, some of whose remarks follows very closely without mentioning him by name. Whether he himself set foot on Motya is not quite clear, but his account (1827, 72 ff.) seems, nevertheless, based on very good authority.

A very important stage in the history of Motyan studies is marked by the appearance of A. de Luynes' essay "Recherches sur l'emplacement de l'ancienne ville de Motya" (1855). This included a detailed report by a French geologist, M. Gory, who at de Luynes' request studied Motya and its environs. His report on what he saw on the island runs as follows (1855, 96 ff):

> "Le lendemain j'ai pris une barque à Marsala et je me suis rendu à l'île de S. Pantaleo. La distance que j'avais à parcourir, est de 6 à 7 milles anglais (10 ou 11 Kilom.). Partout des bas-fonds. L'île est située à un mille anglais (1 Kilom., 609 m, 3) environ de la côte voisine. Du côté de la mer, à un demi mille, les îles de *Cerdinisi* et de *Burrone*; du côté de Trapani, l'îlot de *Sa. Maria* et, vers Marsala, celui de la *Scuola* qui touche presque à S. Pantaleo. Ces petites îles sont à fleur d'eau. Les deux plus grandes sont couvertes de salines. Toute la partie du bassin entre la terre et ces îles, appelée Stagnone, n'a pas, dans les endroits les plus profonds, plus de deux mètres.
>
> "La superficie totale de S. Pantaleo est de onze *Salmes* et demie. On peut en faire le tour en une heure. L'île n'a aucun relief. Son sol regulier s'élève de deux à quatre mètres au dessus du niveau de la mer. On y cultive du bled, des fèves, des lupins, des oliviers, des amandiers et quelques orangers. La population se compose de cent habitants réunis en un petit village d'une vingtaine de maisons.
>
> "A vingt pas du rivage, du côté qui regarde la Scuola et Marsala, j'ai trouvé une grande piscine en pierre et, tout près de là, des restes de mur d'enceinte en grandes pierres sans mortier. En face de Cerdinisi, également sur le rivage, un tombeau en pierres sèches de 0 m 35 de large sur 0 m 25 de haut. Un peu plus loin, on m'a montré l'emplacement d'un tombeau semblable découvert il y a 20 ans; il contenait un squelette avec un petit vase grec d'un côté et, assurait-on, un pain de l'autre. Quelques pas au delà, je trouvais des ossements humains avec des fragments de vases grecs et de poteries. J'avais déjà remarqué un grand nombre de ces debris.
>
> "Du côté qui regarde la côte de Sicile et le lieu appelé *Spagnuola*, à sic ou sept mètres de la mer, on voit deux grands massifs carrés en grandes pierres sans ciment de 9 m, 90 de long, évidemment les restes d'une porte de ville, et, tout juste en face, une espèce de chaussée recouverte seulement par quelques centimetres d'eau et par laquelle, en temps calme, on communique avec la terre. Un homme à cheval y passait au moment ou je mesurais ces ruines.
>
> "Dans l'interieur de l'île à quelques pas de là, est une citerne avec de grandes assises de pierre; çà et là, éparses sur le sol, des pierres de 1 m, 10 de long, une autre de 0 m, 70 sur 0 m, 45 avec des moulures et recouverte de stuc blanc. Des enfants m'apporterent huit on neuf petites medailles en bronze et une en argent (je crus reconnaître sur quelques unes le type de Motya), et des pointes de flèche en bronze que l'on trouve journellement dans l'île. On me parla de grands conduits en étain découverts il y a quelques années et qui servaient, à ce que l'on croit, à faire venir l'eau douce de la terre ferme.
>
> "Je me suis approché des autres îles d'assez près pour en reconnaitre le sol et je n'y ai pas aperçu les moindres restes d'anciennes constructions.
>
> "En résumé, si Motya a existé dans ces parages, c'est certainement dans l'île de S. Pantaleo qu'il faut en chercher l'emplacement."

De Luynes adds:

> "A ce témoignage du voyageur français j'ajouterai celui que me fournit une lettre du savant Sicilien Mr. Agostino Gallo à Mr. Gargallo Grimaldi, si connu par ses doctes travaux archéologiques et qui avait bien voulu demander de ma part des renseignements au sujet de Motya.

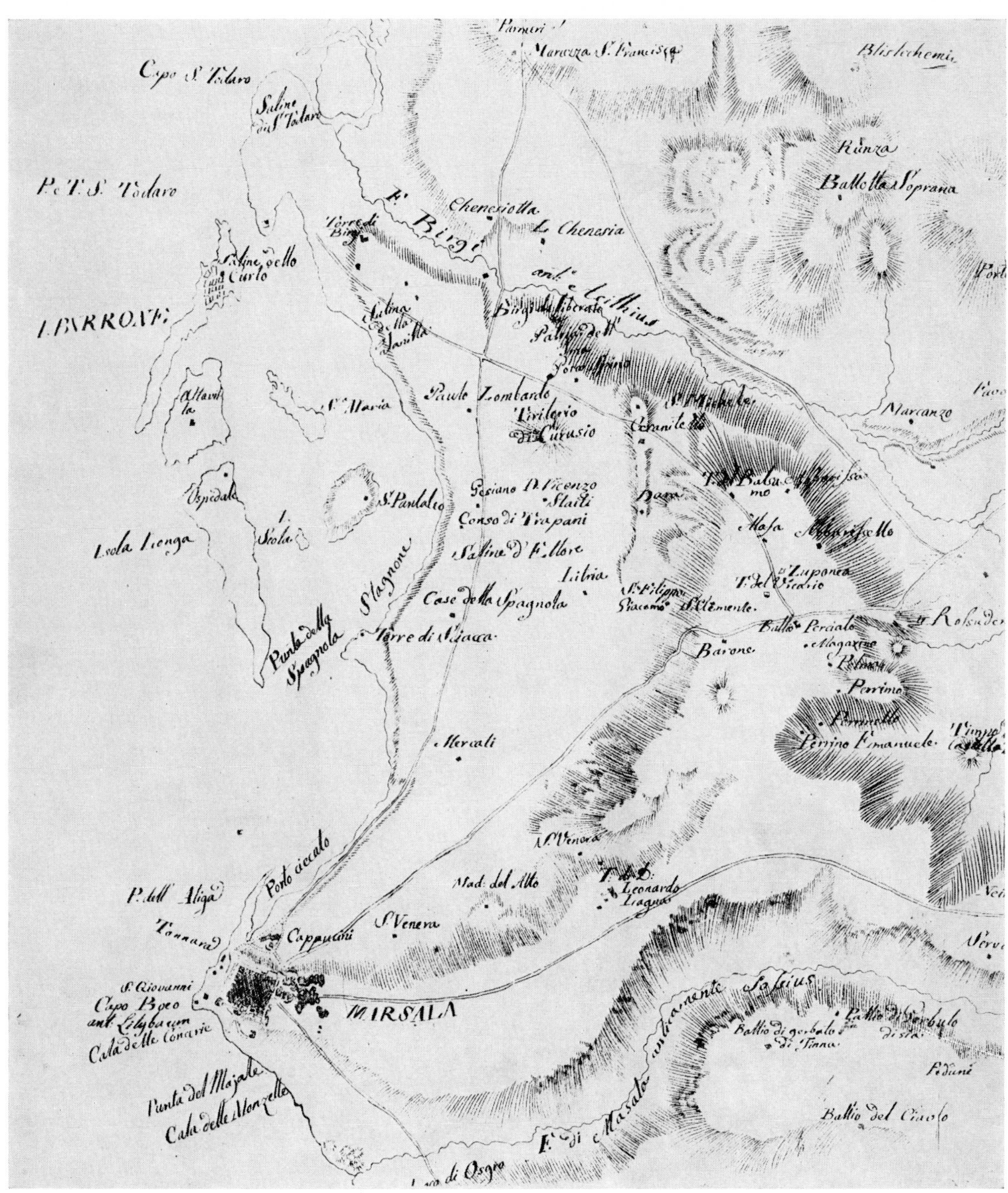

Fig. 1. Motya and environment on the map by S. von Schmettau (1719-21).

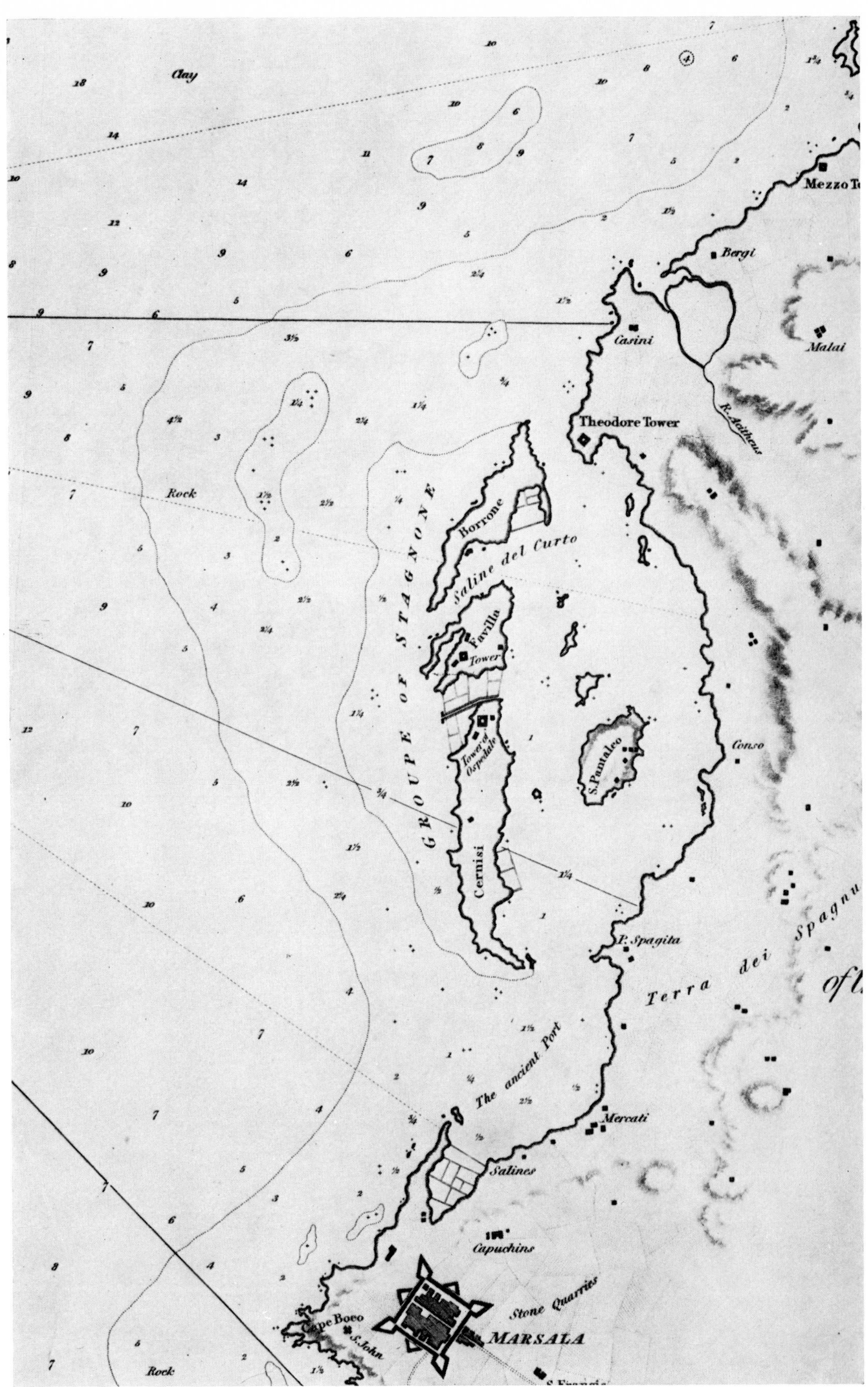

Fig. 2. The stagnone and Motya on W. H. Smyth's map (1824).

"...J'ai conféré avec le Prince de Trabio qui a visité et observé avec des yeux intelligents la petite île de S. Pantaleo ou S. Pantaleone. Il ne doute pas que ce ne soit le véritable emplacement de Motya selon l'opinion de Cluvier... À S. Pantaleo on voit encore l'isthme couvert de deux palmes d'eau tout au plus, qui réunissait cette ville à la rive la plus voisine, entre Marsala et Trapani, où devait s'étendre son territoire; il était planté de vignes dont le vin s'appelle encore *vino di Mozia*, comme me l'assure le Prince de Trabio, argument des plus irrésistibles pour placer Motya dans cette region..."

Eleven years after de Luynes, J. Schubring published in *Philologus*, XXIV, 1866, another study based on careful and detailed personal inspection of San Pantaleo, and which included a thorough review of what had been written about her. We reproduce below the section giving a description of the island (61 ff.):

"Was wir daher heute noch von spuren und resten von Motye sehen entstand alles vor Ol. 96. Das ist denn erstlich der alte molo, welcher die insel mit dem festland verbindet, zwar nicht über dem wasserspiegel erhaben, auch bemerkt man keine steine oder blöcke, die etwa an einzelnen stellen noch sichtbar wären (der isthmus von Syrakus war aus λίθοι λογάδες), sondern es ist eine unterseeische landbrücke, aber doch so prononcirt, so überall gleich breit und ununterbrochen, dass noch heute die bewohner von S. Pantaleo, sommer und winter, mit ihren maulthierkarren auf diesem damme zum festlande gelangen. Ferner sind noch im ganzen rund die fundamente der festungsmauern zu sehen, welche die etwa 20′ hohe insel an ihrem rande umgaben; auf der nordostseite sind noch einzelne thürme zu erkennen. Zwei thore hatte das alte Motya, ein landthor im norden, welches gegen den molo, die nekropolis und den continent sich öffnete, und ein hafenthor im süden. Das erstere ist sehr wohl erhalten und noch heut der schmuck von S. Pantaleo; zwei mächtige viereckige thorgebäude, von denen das eine 10,50 m. ausdehnung in der front, 9,70 m. in der tiefe, das andere 9,70 m. fronterstreckung hat, beschützten eine strasse von 8,50 m. breite. Sie sind aus sehr langen, aber nicht hohen quadern gefügt, zwischen denen oft kleinere als ausfüllung sitzen. Zwischen diesem thor und dem anfang des dammes sehen wir am wasser noch ein stück künstlichen fussbodens. Das südliche thor ist weniger gut erhalten; doch unterscheiden wir deutlich, wie sich an die starke eckbastion der südwestseite der westliche flügel des thores anschliesst; dann folgt die strasse, jetzt 14-16 meter breit, da sie als canal für eine kleine dort befindliche saline dienend erweitert ist, und endlich das östliche thorhaus, von dem die einfache mauer weiter geht.—In dem südwestlichen theile der stadt stand nicht ein grosser, wohl aber heiliger, bau; es haben sich daselbst in der ecke eine grosse anzahl trefflich gearbeiteter quadern mit stuck gefunden, welche von den bauern allmählich aus der erde herausgegraben und dort aufgeschichtet sind. Sie haben einschnitte für die eisenklammern.—Motye entnahm sein trinkwasser von dem quellreichen höhenzuge der Regalia, an welchem die strasse von Marsala vorbeiführt, demselben, der auch später Lilybaeum versorgte. Die wasserströme wurden von osten her unter dem meere in zinnernen aquäduktrohren geleitet, deren sich noch einige vorgefunden haben. Gut erhalten ist ein aus quadern gebauter wasserbehälter an der östlichen küste, in welchen die känale mündeten. Im innern der stadt gegen norden zu ist ein zweites wasserwerk, eine gebaute cisterne mit stuck inwendig, mit weitem bauch und engem hals, welche durch einen canal mit einer andern zerstörten bauanlage in verbindung gesetzt ist. Ob dieses zu einem leitungssystem gehörte, oder eine regenwassergrube war, will ich nicht entscheiden. Jetzt versorgt man sich nur mit himmlischem wasser.—Die zahlreichen gräber unserer merkwürdigen inselstadt befinden sich gegen norden auf dem continent; dort sind viele steinerne sarkophage in der erde gefunden, die in grosser anzahl noch unberührt waren. Der deckel lag noch oben und drinnen die vasen und gebeine. Die bauern behaupten, die anzahl der vasen sei immer eine gleiche zwei, vier oder sechs; sie werden an ort und stelle aufbewahrt und sind sämmtlich von nicht feinem thon, in antiker form, ohne bild oder verzierung. Münzen waren nicht in den gräbern, doch sammelt man deren auf dem stadtboden. Von den schön gearbeiteten sarkophagen war einer 2,20 m. lang, 0,70 m. breit, 0,60 m. hoch; ein anderer 3,30 m. lang, 1 m. breit, 1,20 m. hoch.—Zum schluss erwähne ich noch der sage, die in Marsala und S. Pantaleo mit seltener einmüthigkeit erzahlt wird nämlich dass professor Cicero auf der kleinen insel Scuola eine akademie gehalten habe; daher stamme auch der name Scuola."

The final stage of learned description of Motya in conjunction with the discussions of the ancient texts may be said to be reached with I. Coglitore's exhaustive study (1883-84).

Where archaeological matters are concerned he largely summarizes the work of his predecessors, though he adds to them from a first-hand knowledge of the island, but also in particular by giving a catalogue of finds made in the excavations undertaken there in his own day (1884, 8-17).

With Coglitore, the series of descriptions of Motya which are not largely excavation reports comes to an end, though it may be worth recalling that among later studies the article by K. Lehmann-Hartleben (1926, col. 182 ff, cf. v. Duhn, 1921, col. 201 ff.) brings some fresh facts based on the author's ocular inspection during a visit. The article "Motya" by Ziegler (1923, cols. 387-407) is largely a summary of the position at the time, though the author had visited the site.

The overall impression gained from the evidence of these earlier writers is that the aspect of the remains at Motya has changed but little over a number of centuries. There is, indeed, in the documents from the Collegio Massimo of the Jesuits in Palermo, repeated reference to removal of stone (which the authorities in Marsala prohibited). We notice also that the improvements in farming and the extension of the area under cultivation at Motya, which the documents allow us to follow from the 17th century onwards, very probably led to the removal of such traces of walling as were visible in the top soil in areas then newly taken under the plough (the description of Motya as "tutta pietrosa" in the above quoted document of 1605 is not repeated later on). Yet, while no doubt much damage was done to the ruins in these ways, there is no indication that any major ancient monuments existed here within the span of time which the written record covers, and have since disappeared. The causeway, the town wall with its towers and gates, the necropolis in the northern region with its ancient vases (later investigated more systematically by Whitaker) are the main elements referred to, with occasional remarks about such things as the Cappiddazzu region, or the occurrence of mud brick in the fields in other parts of the island, or finds of ancient arrowheads and coins. All this seems to hint that most of the visible ancient ruins inside the fortified perimeter must have been removed a very long time ago, and that for centuries fields and vineyards covered much of what remained of the ancient city. It is also of interest to note that the Arab occupation of the site was regarded as archaeologically significant, and that the "salinella" was considered by some authorities to be of Moorish construction.

4. Early Maps, and the Post-Classical Settlements on Motya

We next come to deal with the evidence of early maps. Those of the 16th century dealing with Sicily, including the one by Cluverius, are of no help to us. Some recognizable detail appears on the Dutch (and German, and later English) maps in the 18th century. Thus the map by G. van Keulen (Nieuwe Aftekening van het Eyland en Koninkryk Sicilia, Amsterdam, 1720) carries on the island of San Pantaleo the symbol for a small village (though it is not clear in which part of it this would have to be placed). On the other hand, the map of Sicily by Samuel Baron von Schmettau, prepared for the Emperor Charles VI to the scale of 1 : 75,000 in 1719-21 gives a reasonably accurate, though very small, picture of San Pantaleo, and seems to place an inhabited locality pretty well where the hamlet is now (Fig. 1). It deserves notice that a number of the early maps (including van Keulen's but not Schmettau's) indicate on or near Motya a hill from where Cape Bon may be seen—thus continuing a spurious learned tradition derived from Polyaenus.

The publication of Smyth's *Sicily and its Islands* in 1824 is of interest because of its map of the Stagnone, including San Pantaleo (Fig. 2). It is, however, not a very accurate map of the island. Smyth's map also is closely related to the admiralty chart of western Sicily published under his authorship, which was later brought up to date by G. R. Wilkinson (Mediterranean, Sicily, West coast, Trapani). While likewise not very exact, Wilkinson's map, brought out in 1864, indicates that all the houses on San Pantaleo were grouped as at present. The map of Motya and the lagoon, accompanying Schubring's essay (our Fig. 3), 1866, while very small, yet indicates for the first time some matters of archaeological interest.

A really satisfactory and detailed survey of San Pantaleo and the lagoon around it became available, however, in 1863 when the Italian Istituto Topografico Militare prepared a map to the scale of 1 : 50,000 (sheet f 256 (I), 257 (IV) (Fig. 4); a reduced reproduction accompanies Coglitore's essay). This is, in fact, the earliest map at present available which gives any detail about paths and fields divisions on San Pantaleo since search for earlier estate maps of the kind made by progressive landlords in the 18th century, and which the Jesuits may very likely have prepared when San Pantaleo belonged to them, has up to now proved fruitless. The hamlet is here given in its present shape and the field paths are essentially shown as they now exist, except that the path from the hamlet to the Cothon (which had not then been cleared to the present extent) continued straight on to meet the main north-south road near the point where it ends at the southern coast of the island, instead of curving round to the Cothon channel.

If we now combine the evidence offered by the early maps with indications from textual or archaeological evidence, certain facts suggest themselves.

In the history of Motya after the fall of the ancient city, it appears we can distinguish two periods: one, when a settlement of sorts still existed around the Cappiddazzu, and one when this had been given up. The recent Italian explorations, which have amplified the evidence in existence since the days of Whitaker, now hint at an occupation of the Cappiddazzu region, which stretched from the Roman and Byzantine to the Arab period. The church was built there apparently during the Byzantine age (V. Tusa, *Mozia* I, 23 and fig. 4; II, 24). One may wonder whether it still survived in the 12th century, when Motya became the property of the Basilian monks.

A second period is denoted by the existence of the present hamlet only near the Villa Whitaker. This appears to have existed in the 18th century, but we cannot yet say how much earlier. Whitaker was inclined to assume it existed in the Norman period (1921, 97). We may tentatively link it with the time from the 16th century onwards, when Motya belonged to the Jesuits.

The existence of the two centres of habitation may possibly be connected also with two different systems of fields and paths in the island. The present system most probably goes back to the Jesuits, since it involved overall planning in the island as a whole. Maps show it to have been in existence by the 19th century—at a time when property at Motya was split up into many small holdings. Such circumstances were unlikely to give rise to a coherent scheme, which should thus be regarded as a survival from a previous time of overall control. An earlier, different, system of field boundaries and paths appears to be hinted at in air photographs. This, which likewise looks like the outcome of large scale overall planning, may be tentatively linked with the time when Motya was a property of the Basilian monks. As such, it should be of interest to medieval historians concerned with agricultural administration in Sicily, and it should be studied and its genuineness investigated.

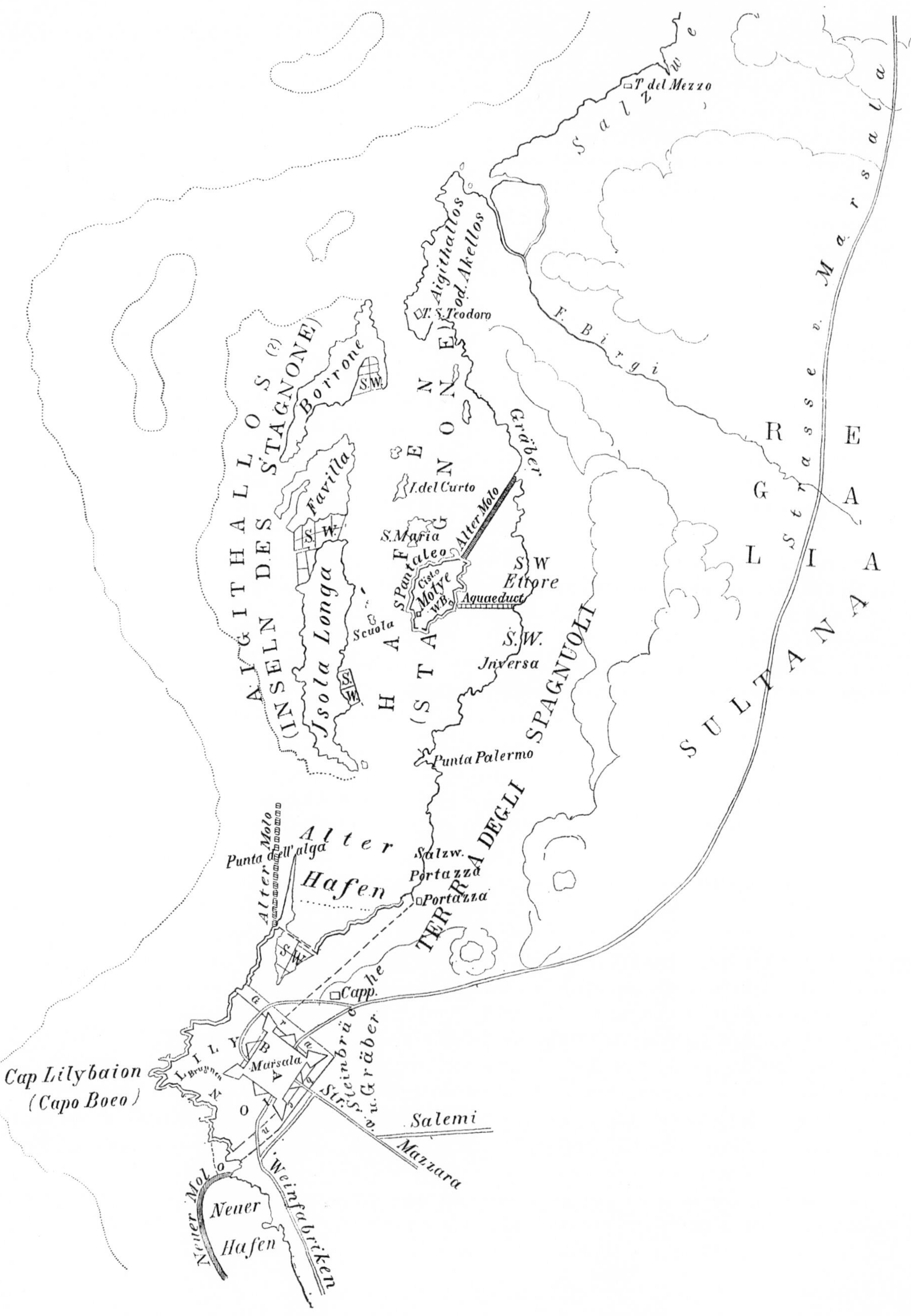

Fig. 3. Motya and the stagnone on J. Schubring's map (1866).

Fig. 4. The stagnone and Motya on the Italian military map, 1 : 50,000 (1863).

5. Archaeological Exploration

The history of archaeological excavation at Motya is lengthy, but not as well known as would be desirable. This applies in particular to the earliest diggings, the extent and results of which are almost totally undocumented.

As B. Pace relates in his *Arte e Civiltà della Sicilia Antica* (I, 30 ff.) the year 1779 saw the establishment of what may be described as an Antiquities Service for Sicily, the post of Custodian of Antiquities for the Val di Mazzara region was instituted and Prince Torremuzza was appointed as its first incumbent. San Pantaleo was included in this division, and as a passage referred to above (p. 5) in Prince Biscari's book shows, Torremuzza seems at once to have taken an active interest in Motya. It seems possible that it was then that the first excavations took place, as Whitaker suggests (1921, 113-4), and that Houel in 1782 saw the North Gate uncovered as the result of these activities. However, no written information about any such work has been traced. We know, nevertheless, that digging took place roughly a decade later, when Barone Rosario Alagna, Superintendent of Antiquities for the province of Trapani, worked here by order of Monsignore Alfonso Airoldi, then the Custodian of Antiquities in the Province of Val di Mazzara. Reports by Barone Alagna, to which Whitaker refers (1921, 117, note 2), still exist in the Biblioteca Communale in Palermo. They are contained in pages 14-24 of a volume of A. Airoldi's manuscripts entitled *Raccolta di scritture e documenti che riguardano le antichità e belle arti in Sicilia*, (which are marked 4 Qq.D. 42). Dated in 1793, certain letters relate to the discovery of such pieces as the great sculpture of a bull attacked by two dogs or lions (Whitaker, 1921, 116 and 115, fig. 1) but insufficient details are given about the provenance of these pieces, and indeed neither the location nor the extent and character of the digging can be traced from the documents. Since the assumption has been widely made that the region near the North Gate (where we also excavated) was concerned in this activity, this lack of information is particularly regrettable for us; we do not know in what condition our early predecessors may have found, or left, that area.

There appears after this to have been a considerable intermission in archaeological activity at San Pantaleo: excavations are next mentioned in 1865, 1869 and 1872, undertaken apparently on behalf of the Commissione delle antichità di Sicilia. These are referred to by Whitaker (1921, 122) and Coglitore (1884, 8), but again no satisfactory documentation is at present available.

In October 1875 Schliemann worked for a few days at Motya, his attention having been drawn to the site by R. Bonghi. In spite of the intention expressed in his letters (E. Meyer, *Briefwechsel Schliemann*, 1953, 298, 302) to publish accounts of his results in *Revue Archéologique* and the *Allgemeine Zeitung*, neither of these periodicals carries the promised articles. However, his diaries, giving entries for the days concerned in English and a summary of his results in Greek, still survive in the Gennadius Library in Athens. (For certain aspects of Schliemann's excavations at Motya see further Soprintendente Tusa in *Mozia*, I, 13-14, note 3; and the writer in *Antiquity*, XLII, 1968, 144 ff.).

Schliemann's account is of real interest, and the text of his reports (the Greek in English translation) will be found in Appendix 5 at the end of this book. However, there are no figures or plans to illustrate the text, and the interpretation of his statements, embodying (as we now know) in some respects erroneous conclusions, remains thus somewhat obscure. The use which can be made of his report in the study of the archaeological situation at Motya is, therefore, very limited. It is possible that a disturbance inside the North Gate (trench Zq) is attributable to a sounding mentioned by him.

There followed another pause in archaeological activity in Motya, until 1906, when Whitaker began his excavations, which he carried on, with intermissions during the first World War, until 1919. (As Whitaker himself states (1921, 124) the digging was under the supervision of Professor A. Salinas, then the Director of the Palermo Museum; the local direction being entrusted to Cavaliere G. Lipari-Cascio of Marsala). Whitaker's work marks an epoch in the story of archaeological research at San

Pantaleo, not only in scope and method, but also through his presentation of a comprehensive report *Motya, a Phoenician colony in Sicily* (London, Bell, 1921).

This book opens the series of printed reports on archaeological researches at Motya which, taken together, form the frame of reference for our own work. We must enumerate them briefly.

After Whitaker, digging was next carried out at Motya in 1930, when Professor P. Marconi arranged for additional excavation to be undertaken in the Cappiddazzu ruins by I. Messina, then his assistant at the Palermo Museum: the documentation concerning this has recently been published by Soprintendente Tusa (in *Mozia* I, p. 23-30).

Again there was an intermission, until the trial excavations by the small Oxford Mission, headed by the writer in 1955 (published in the *Papers of the British School at Rome*, XXVI (N.S. vol. XIII), 1958, 4 ff.) and their resumption on a larger scale in 1961. (Some of the results available in 1963 were presented in the *Annual of Leeds Oriental Society*, IV, 1962-3, 84-131, by the writer and others: a brief account by Miss J. du Plat Taylor appears in *Archaeology*, 17, 1964, 91-100.) The work of the Italian Mission, working at Motya on behalf of the Soprintendenza alle Antichità of Palermo, and of the Centro di Studi Semitici of the University of Rome directed by Professor S. Moscati, began in 1964. The results so far have been published with exemplary speed, in the seven preliminary report volumes *Mozia*, I-VII (Rome 1964-72).

In addition, E. Titone published in 1964 his independent study *Civiltà di Motya* which contains observations of value.

6. The Expedition: Aims and Methods

One of our chief aims in initiating work at Motya was to learn about Phoenician architecture, both public and private, including defence and harbour works. Faced with what was then a vast expanse of unexplored ground, we had obviously to be selective. We decided to investigate first those parts of the city which were near the North and South Gates, and the sea adjoining them, for it was clear that in those regions constructions of the types in which we were interested were available for study. Our main efforts were concentrated near the South Gate, where the ground was tested in 1955 (*PBSR*, 26, 1958, 4 ff.). Here a zone, ca. 40 m. by 15 m. situated inside the Gate was laid out on a grid of 4 by 4 m., separated by 1 m. baulks. The eastern half of the grid was at first aligned on the Cothon, but later the western part was re-aligned to conform with the line of the town wall. In this grid the upper layers were almost completely excavated: lower layers were dug down to natural in selected localities, to provide a number of long sections. A number of isolated exploratory trenches were also dug to supplement the gridded area. A limited amount of ground between the city wall and the sea was likewise investigated.

Work in this zone was under the joint direction of the writer and Miss du Plat Taylor, and supervised by Mr. Robertson Mackay in 1961, and later by Miss E. Pirie and Dr. A. Snodgrass. Chapter 7a is based on their field notes and interpretations. In the interpretation of the data here, as elsewhere, the part played by Miss du Plat Taylor was vital, and I wish gratefully to acknowledge it, while accepting responsibility for chapters over my signature.

In the region near the North Gate, an area ca. 16 by 7 m. outside the western gate bastion laid out in 4 m. squares between 50 cm. baulks, was excavated by Mr. N. Coldstream in 1961-2. In later years the road from the causeway to the city and ground adjoining it were investigated by surface stripping and trial trenches. This work was supervised by Dr. A Snodgrass and Miss C. Warhurst under the direction of Miss Taylor and the writer, and their notes form the basis for the description and interpretation in Chapter 8.

In addition, a number of exploratory trenches were dug in the centre of the island with the aim of obtaining some preliminary information about buildings and their alignment. These trenches were supervised by the writer; only surface levels were cleared systematically, lower strata being tested by a few soundings. The results are offered in chapter 9.

As the total information about ancient Motya available from excavation was bound to be limited, we were anxious to obtain some additional suggestions concerning the architecture and planning of the city by other means. The following methods were employed:

1. A study was made of reports by early travellers, early documents, maps, pictures, excavation reports, etc.
2. The scenery and topography of Motya and their possible archaeological relevance were investigated and a new contour map of the island was prepared by Mr. C. Robinson. This was later collated with detailed air photographs.
3. Air photographs (in black and white, colour, and infra-red) were collected and systematically studied. In the interpretation of the photographs we are greatly indebted to Dr. W. Collins, then of the Department of Civil Engineering of Leeds University, who also generously made the technical facilities of his Department available.
4. Electrical resistivity surveying was used to test unexcavated ground for possible buried archaeological features. "Megger"-Null balance testers were employed, since a proton-magnetometer was not available. The surveying was begun in 1963 by a group of students from the Department of Mining at Leeds University under Mr. G. D. Addison, mainly near the South Gate and Cothon; in 1964 it was continued by Dr. A. Tagg of Messrs. Evershed and Vignoles, assisted by Mr. A. Bloomer, another Leeds graduate, in a number of localities; in 1966 additional surveys, mainly near the Villa and the Cothon, were undertaken by Dr. H. M. M. Pike of the United Kingdom Atomic Energy Commission at Harwell, and Mrs. G. Pike, assisted by Mr. and Mrs. R. H. Searle of the same institution. The interpretation of the results obtained owes much to suggestions by Dr. Collins of the Department of Civil Engineering of Leeds University.
5. Geological investigations were undertaken by Miss du Plat Taylor, Dr. J. Waechter and Mr. W. G. Oram.
6. Underwater exploration was carried out under the direction of Miss du Plat Taylor, with the collaboration of Dr. J. Waechter and Miss E. Macnamara, by a team of divers from Imperial College, London, led by Mr. Brian Matthews, in 1962. (A more detailed investigation and excavation of the Cothon complex was begun by the writer in 1968. These researches are still proceeding and will be dealt with in a later report).
7. Since the firm date of 397 B.C. for the destruction of Motya is of more than local importance in pottery dating, the compilation of a corpus of stratified pottery was obviously a prime *desideratum*. This was begun by Miss O. Tufnell, and later continued by Miss E. Pirie and Miss du Plat Taylor, who also studied the coarse pottery, Greek vases being dealt with by Mr. N. Coldstream, while metal objects were studied by Dr. A. Snodgrass.

THE WORK OF THE EXPEDITION: EXPLORATION AND EXCAVATIONS

PART ONE

THE ISLAND AND ITS ENVIRONMENT

CHAPTER ONE

MOTYA AND THE LAGOON (STAGNONE): TOPOGRAPHY AND GEOLOGY

In 1962, a preliminary exploration of the stagnone or lagoon in which the island of Motya is situated was undertaken with the assistance of a team of divers from Imperial College, University of London; in 1964 further geological and topographic work was undertaken.

The map (Fig. 5, based on the 1 : 25000 map of Italy, 1941, sheets 256, 257) shows the lagoon enclosed by the Isola Grande. Motya lies in the centre, the Isola S. Maria, a long narrow strip, to the north, and the very small Isola la Scuola in the west.

To the north the entrance lies between the Torre S. Teodoro and Punta Tramontana on the Isola Grande. The main entrance is on the south near Marsala, between the Punta d'Alga and the World War II blockhouse marking the end of the reef.

North of the island, the ancient delta of the Chinosia or Birgi river shows the wide extent of the alluvial deposits. The latest mouth is still further north, but a canal now carries the flood water directly into the sea. North and south currents have no doubt spread this alluvium still further; and on the Admiralty chart 189 (1961) shoal water is shown outside the Isola Grande for at least two miles. The channel between Pta. Scario and Pta. Marsala on Favignana, a hazardous passage, is marked by lights.

The first chart prepared by Captain Smyth in 1815 (Fig. 2: somewhat distorted in comparison with modern surveys) shows three islands, Borrone, Favilla and Cernisi, the two latter being joined by salt-pans. Today all three are joined by salt-works, while other pans have been established within the lagoon at S. Teodoro, Infersa and Ettore. These mask the outline of the islands to a considerable extent, and have probably affected conditions within the lagoon. Di Girolamo (1898, 51) notes that the feudal concessions for the salt-pans date from the time of Philip II of Spain, who granted those between Cernisi, also called Isola Lunga, and Favilla to Bernardino Grignani in 1556, in succession to G. A. Bonnano, who had held it since 1522. Schmettau's map of 1719-21 shows salt-pans on Burrone.

On Wilkinson's edition of chart 189 (1864), the bar across the north entrance is shown. This is clearly visible in the air photographs (Pl. 2 : 2) and, in fact, it is possible to walk across the entrance. It appears that there can never have been a useful boat entrance on this side of the lagoon.

At the extreme south of the Isola Grande the reef can be seen on the air photograph (Pl. 2 : 1) continuing as a sharp line underwater. On this photograph the two sides of a wall are quite clear. A gap of some 100 m. separates the end from the Punta d'Alga whence it continues to the mainland north of Marsala.

The geological map of Italy (Foglio 257, 1959) indicates that the islands formed part of the original land-mass, composed of calcareous tufa containing *Strombus bubonius* and associated with the Tyrrhenian formation. The islands within the lagoon are shown as outcrops of this formation. It may be postulated that a promontory formerly existed ending in Punta Scario; but, that at some time the sea (or perhaps

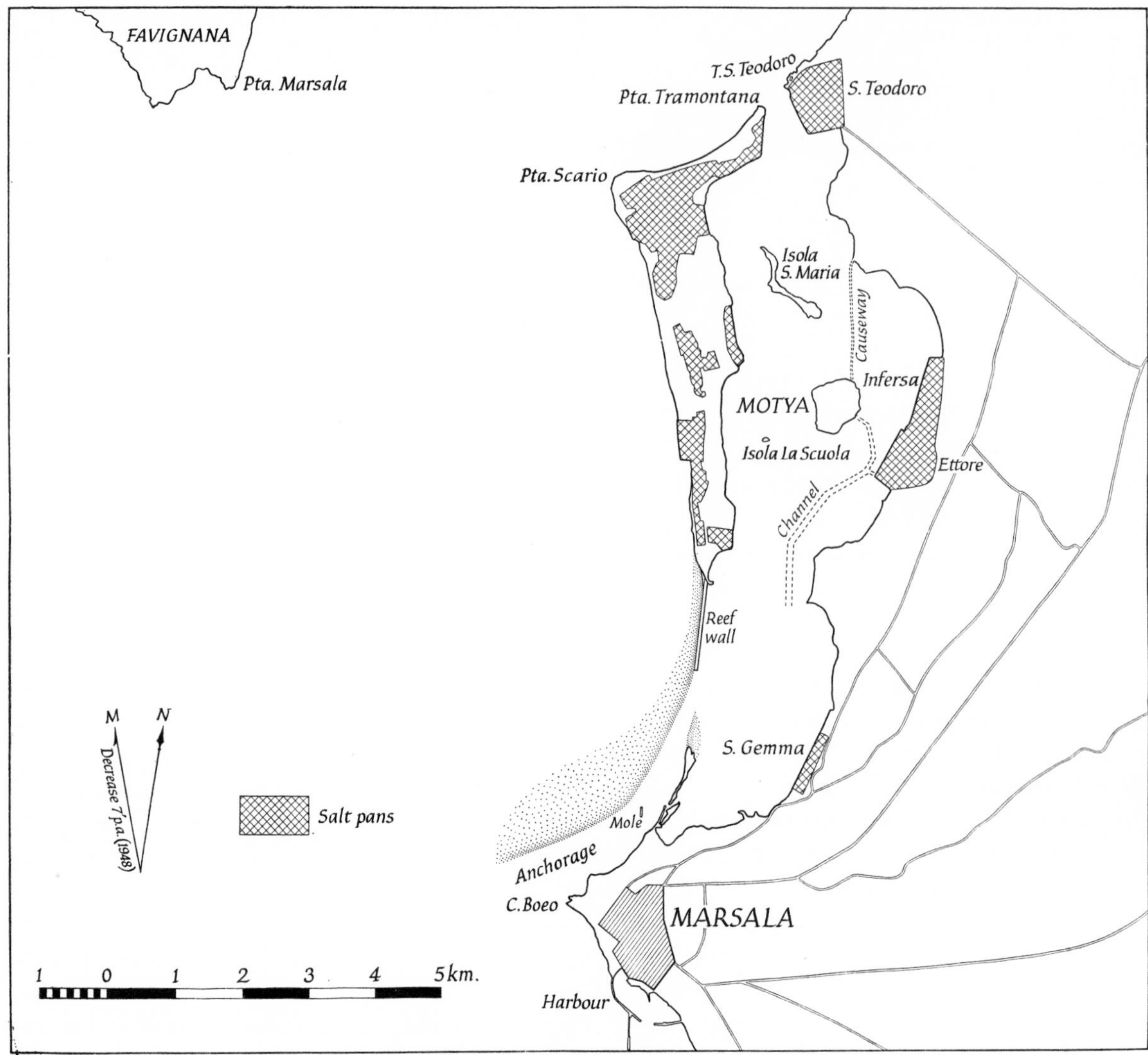

Fig. 5. Map of the stagnone showing features of archaeological interest.

an early mouth of the Chinosia), broke through the crust round the edge eroding the soft tufa and flooding the lagoon, leaving the islands with their cliff shores as isolated remains of the old land surface.

Within the lagoon today there is rarely more than a metre of water, except in the dredged channel from Marsala leading to Motya and the salt-pans opposite. Navigation elsewhere is difficult and there are many shoals on which quite small boats may ground, the whole bottom being covered with weed. As we hope to show, the filling up the lagoon is of recent origin. On Smyth's chart of 1815 there is a quarter fathom over the Isola Grande reef, one to one-and-a-quarter between Spagnola point and the island and one-and-a-half to two-and-a-half in the outer lagoon. Smyth (1824, 233) says: "the harbour could never have been a national object, having been only a kind of creek, whose utmost depth was 12 to 14 feet, and this I have proved by sounding through the mud to the live rock with a graduated iron rod". Later, in 1864, Wilkinson shows the depth as the same over the reef and half to a quarter fathom round Motya, as it is today; but there was only one-and-a-half to two fathoms in the outer lagoon. On the 1961 Admiralty chart, no more than a fathom is shown in the centre of the outer lagoon.

As seen in the air photographs (Pl. 2 : 1), the enclosing reef has a very clear line; but on examination from a boat and by wading the edge was more obscure. It is now covered with mud and weed and any trace of the wall, called by the fishermen "muro romano" was not visible in 1964. The inner shore of the Isola Grande was also masked by mud and weed; and on land, though scattered sherds were observed in several places, they were mostly of recent date. The smaller entrance shown by Schmiedt was not observed underwater, nor was the barrier "I" on his sketch map (1965, 261).

Some diving was done in the areas marked "anchorage" between Punta d'Alga and C. Boeo leading to the entrance of the lagoon. This channel is visible on the air photographs (Schmiedt, 1965, 260), covering the area P-O-N. It is bordered on the west by banks of sand and weed in a dune-like formation, at 3 m. or less, while the channel is 5-6 m. in depth. The banks shown by Schmiedt were not examined, but further south some rectangular areas of sand defined by banks of weed, having the appearance of structures, were noted. These areas contained sherds of amphorae (see "Coarse Pottery", Vol. II), but the banks, when probed with metal rods, contained no solid material.

The only structure found was the mole, not visible in the air photographs. This mole was built of individual, rectangular blocks dropped in a haphazard manner over a distance of some 200 m. The edges of the mole were fairly well defined, running practically straight, giving an average width of less than 5 m. The blocks measured 200 × 120 × 90, 210 × 145 × 60 and 200 × 120 × 68 cm. The top of the mole could not clearly be defined, for in one place blocks reached to within 50 cm. of the surface, and in another gap, they plunged to 2 m. The average depth of water was 2 m. The ends of the mole were relatively abrupt, ending on the seaward side against the banks of sand. As it lies directly athwart the channel, this mole is very likely the barrier of stones constructed by Carlo Aragona, High Admiral of Sicily in 1574-5, to keep pirates out of the lagoon (Columba, 1906, 46 (262).

The island of Motya, therefore, forms part of the geological formation of the mainland. Whitaker (1921, 49) describes the topography as he found it and notes that "the subsoil is composed of soft friable 'tufa' of a deep yellowish colour, but the outer crust in some parts is formed by a fairly hard rock of limestone". The geological sequence on the island is visible in one or two exposures around the shore. Dr. Waechter examined these exposures and writes:

> "The geological sequence of the island is not easy to determine owing to the lack of suitable exposures, the considerable disturbance of the surface in Phoenician times, and the fact that the shore sections are generally obscured by the town walling. There are, however, two sections, both on the shore, which show at least the upper part of the sequence. The West section (Pl. 5 : 2) about 50 m. south of the small Gateway (at G on Whitaker's end map, cf. our Fig. 9) shows the following sequence:
>
> 1. Light grey soil approximately 90 cm. in depth. This contains angular stones and sherds and clearly represents the disturbed upper soil contemporary with the main occupation of the site. The slight change of colour towards the base and the marked calcareous zone at the base, indicate that leaching has taken place.
> 2. Immediately below the concretions is a red soil ("terra fusca") about 35 cm. at its deepest. One impasto sherd was found in this soil and it probably represents the original pre-Phoenician soil of the island.
> 3. Calcareous "tufa": this is a little under a metre thick and is a crumbly, limy deposit whose origin is not yet clear.
> 4. Brown-grey clay. The depth of this not known as the base is obscured by the beach. Similar clays have been found at the North and South Gates and at the bottom of the lagoon, and it appears to be the base complex of the island.

"It is possible that the two upper layers represent two different soil complexes: the first, representing the major disturbance of the original red soil, has, in the course of time, developed a new profile, the base of which is the calcareous zone separating the red from the grey.

"On the east side of the island is a similar section between the eastern staircase and the small eastern gateway (B) (Pl. 5 : 3). This differs from the west section only in that the soil profiles are not so well developed, and by the presence of cobbles in the "tufa". This zone of cobbles dips sharply towards the south and decreases in depth. The widest part, towards the north, is about 70 cm. and southward it tails to nothing. In appearance these cobbles suggest the remnants of a storm beach, the shore of which runs roughly east and west, though it could also represent the remains of a shallow watercourse draining from the high ground on the mainland to the east. (This may be related to the "outcrop of current-bedded, water-worn pebbles on the shore S.E. of Birgi" observed by W. G. Oram).

"The remaining formations on the island, apart from the lagoon sands, are an outcrop of consolidated marine sands and the reefs on the west and south. The consolidated marine sands form the bulk of the knoll to the west of the South Gate; these sands contain large pieces of shell and are very pebbly towards the base, though the pebbles are only pea-size and do not compare with the larger cobbles from the east section. Traces of similar material occur at the base of the shallow shore section between the South Staircase (D) and the Jetty; but is not clear whether it is in place. These sands are part of a shoreline and do not represent dune sand; they probably extend right along the south side of the island. In the region of the South Gate and Cothon the sand was probably quarried away and used as building stone, since traces of similar material are found in the buildings over the greater part of the island. It is tempting to relate this shore deposit with the 'storm beach' of the east section but it was not possible to see the junction, nor was it possible to establish the relationship between this consolidated sand and the profile of the West section, since the latter dips southwards and is obscured by the modern shore deposits before it reaches the South Gate".

Similar sections of shore profiles are to be seen on the Isola di Santa Maria where the "tufa" is much thicker, 2 to 5 m.

W. G. Oram noted:

"The basal horizons consist of finely laminated bands of buff-yellow and white calcareous sands, the beds of which are contorted and show several types of flow folding".

At Spagnola, on the mainland south of Motya, the maximum thickness of "tufa" is 0.7 m. On the south side of the road from Marsala to Mazzara which crosses the same geological formation, a complete exposure can be seen in a clay quarry for the brickworks. Here the "tufa", 2-3 m. thick, overlies the same grey-green clay noted above.

Building Stone by W. G. Oram

"Four types are observed in the excavations:

Soft sandstone. This is a buff-coloured sandstone used for the main building features. It is a poorly cemented coarse sandstone composed of shell debris and coarse sub-angular sand grains; and is fossiliferous, containing several species of pecten. A similar rock containing the same fossils occurs in old pits near the railway station at Marsala.

Hard sandstone. A hard compact sandstone possibly with silica cement. It is found in small quantities in the building and may have been obtained from the South Gate (see above). The only observed outcrop was on the north end of the Isola Grande.

Conglomerate. This is similar to that occurring at Birgi, which is the obvious source for this material. Some of this rock could have occurred on the island and been available to the Phoenicians.

Hard limestone. This is not very common and is used mainly as 'fill'. It is known to occur near Trapani and on the Islands."

Whitaker (1921, 143) states that the blocks used in the bastions are

"of a limestone formation, not compact limestone, but what is known among Sicilian builders as tenacious limestone.

"An identical quality of stone is to be found on the adjacent mainland, not far from the Birgi district; and at a certain spot on the coast, called Nivaloro, a large number of blocks similar to those employed in the construction of Motya fortifications may be seen at the present day, lying on the shore, as if prepared for transport to the island.

"At Motya itself the outer crust of the rock lying immediately below the surface soil in some parts appears to be the same geological formation, and doubtless a good deal of this local material was employed in building the fortifications."

CHAPTER TWO

EXPLORATION OF THE LAGOON

The purpose of the underwater exploration was twofold: to discover the extent and depth of the ancient roadstead, and to make a geological-biological examination of the silt to endeavour to ascertain how it was formed; and to survey the causeway and such other underwater features as were discovered.

The general description of the lagoon has been set out above. The results of the random core-borings made by the Imperial College team, and the soundings made by Dr. Waechter must now be examined.

The bottom of the lagoon is covered by sand and mud on which grow *Posidonia oceanica (L) Del.* and *Cymodocea nodosia* (UCR/A) *Asch* weed; this also extends widely over to shallows on the seaward side of the Isola Grande. For transects of Mollusca, see Appendix 2.

Examining first the hand-excavated soundings made by Dr. Waechter near the Jetty, and east and west of the South Gate, the following typical bottom profiles were revealed:

15-20 cm. of fine mud, the present bottom of the lagoon.
A shallow shell-bed also in mud.
Below this a grey sand about 50 cm. thick resting on blue-grey clay, whose depth is unknown.

The base of the grey sand contains Phoenician pottery and cobbles from the east section, as well as shells. There is little doubt, in view of the pottery, that this represents the bottom of the lagoon in Phoenician times, a fact which would suggest that, at any rate on the east side of the island, the water was some 50 cm. deeper than at present. Traces of this sand and the underlying clay were found by core-boring in other parts of the lagoon, and there seems little doubt that the clay is the same as that at the base of the east and west sections. In the excavations outside the South Gate, the marine sands were also found to rest on it.

Dr. Graham Evans' analysis of samples from these sections are set out below:

Jetty Section

Top. Silty clay (mud and pelite) with shell and plant fragments and a few rock fragments.

-15 cm. Coarse shell, pottery and a few rock fragments mixed with typical lagoon sands and a little silt and clay. Contain Echinoid fragments possibly indicating lagoon more open during sedimentation. Greyish silty clay (rather like surface mud).

-75 cm. Coarse rock, poltens and shell fragments mixed with typical lagoon sand and a little silt and clay.

Bottom. Little comment other than that coarse layers may be due either to human interference or local change in dynamic conditions in a storm.

East Section

Top. Soil; iron-stained sand "terra rossa"; tufa-bound sand; cobble-bed bound tufa; "bare clay", really quartz sand bound by tufa.

Bottom. Little comment. Most sediment bound by precipitated calcium carbonate from ground waters, typical of arid climates. Section mainly sandy with cobble layers and old buried soil, "terra rossa".

West Section

Top. Grey soil; carbonate bearing sand/silt and clay; "terra rossa" iron stained sand; "kunka", tufa-bound quartz sand, (very hard); "bare clay", quartz sand bound by tufa (in ppte calcium carbonate) containing a few calcareous fragments.

Bottom. Similar to the last section. Sand dominates the section; being bound by "tufa" or "calicine"-like material deposited probably from ground waters. Again an old oxidized surface "terra rossa". The so-called "kunka" is merely a quartz sand with very strong calcium carbonate cementation.

The cores collected by the Imperial College group did not reach so deep; the maximum length was 55 cm., but they yielded a similar picture.

Motya sediments (By Dr. Graham Evans)

Sediments (surface and cores) consist of some gravel grade materials (i.e. greater than 2.0 mm.) with the dominant constituent being sand (less than 2.0 mm. and greater than 0.625 mm.), and "pelite" (less than 0.625 mm.). The latter term "pelite" means mud or silt plus clay. There is also considerable organic matter in the form of plant fibres, probably after *cymodocea* and *Podosinia*. Generally the majority of the samples are sand pelite mixtures. There is not a distinct pattern but generally the more pelitic (i.e. muddier) sediments tend to be found in the inner, more sheltered, parts of the lagoon.

The gravel grade is composed almost entirely of shell debris, mainly whole gastropod shells. There are also some pottery fragments and a few fragments of calcareous sandstone.

The sand grade consists of clean quartz grains, sometimes very well rounded, and calcium carbonate fragments in the form of shell debris; this debris is often the dominant constituent of the sand grade. Less important constituents are Foraminifera, either fresh or worn, Polyzoan fragments and less commonly Ostracods. Some of the muddier and more pelitic sediments contain small gypsum crystals (CaS_4O. $2H_2O$). This mineral has grown in the sediment (it is authigenic) by reaction between calcareous debris and included lagoon water. Less common constituents are some grey rock fragments, probably chert, small amounts of dark minerals and occasionally fragments of "brown oxidized earth", tufa and charcoal. The latter were common in the cothon infilling.

The sediment suggests that there is very little material entering the lagoon and that sedimentation is very slow. The remains of the Gastropods always make up a large and sometimes dominant part of the sand fraction, indicating that local production of material by organisms is equal to, or exceeds the amount of detrital material entering the area.

Echinoid debris is very rare and certainly points to a lack of sediment supply from the shallow marine areas outside the lagoon.

On the south and west sides of the island there are two series of reefs. The flatness of their surface and the regularity of their line suggested that they could have been artificial, but a closer inspection showed clearly that they were natural. Off the South Gate they were found to be resting on sand containing Phoenician pottery. These so-called "reefs" are made of a calcareous algae and *not* coral. It is probably close to the genus *Lithothamnion*; this generally behaves very much like coral, forming large reef-like structures with a very restricted depth range. The "reef" appears to be situated on a mass of calcareous sandstone which is also found as boulders in other parts of the lagoon.

The picture, then, seems to be a small sheltered lagoon into which move small amounts of sand, silt and clay from the marine areas to seaward and possibly locally off the land. There is a prolific growth of Gastropods and some other organisms together with weed (*Posidonia* and *Cymodocea*); this mixes with the material carried into the lagoon and may in many cases exceed it. The lack of sediment entering the lagoon is probably because of the lack of good sediment supply, in spite of the delta lying to the north-east. Sediment coming into the sea *via* the latter source probably moves away to the NE rather than to the SW; the protective islands off there would help to indicate this. The lagoon is the site of only slow deposition.

The cores show no marked and distinct trend and it must be assumed that conditions have remained fairly similar over the time represented by them.

It seems evident that the "marobia" (Whitaker, 1921, 52-3; Smyth, 1824, 224), a seasonal rise and fall of sea level of up to 50 cm. caused by certain winds, which stirs up the bottom and carries weed and detritus with it, does not, as was previously thought, cause silting within the lagoon, but only a local movement of bottom material.

CHAPTER THREE

THE SURVEY OF THE CAUSEWAY

It is of interest to make some observations of the methods used and the difficulties encountered even in extremely shallow water. Almost all of the bottom of the lagoon is covered with a fine mud which, when disturbed, immediately clouds the water and makes any observation difficult. Rocks lying below the sea-level are pitted and encrusted by marine growth and it is often very hard to decide the extent of a single stone and whether or not it had been dressed. Some attempt was made to dig down along the side of the causeway within the harbour, where the curb-stone was found (Plan I), but the hole filled with a fine silt and here, as elsewhere, it was necessary to resort to probing with a two-metre rod. Cores were taken to a depth of one metre.

The line of the causeway and the walls of the harbour show clearly on the air photographs, the former doubled by the even firmer line of the modern cart-track (Pl. 2 : 3), for the route is still used by the local high-wheeled carts and they may be seen leaving the island and apparently setting out to sea.

The causeway runs directly out of the North Gate and follows an almost straight course northwards to Birgi, the mainland promontory opposite, some 1700 m. distant (Plan I). About 550 m. from the Birgi foreshore the causeway becomes impossible to follow across the stony shallows and it remains a problem what form it took at this point. It disappears at a depth below sea-level of about one metre; so the modern rise of waterlevel and consequent change of shore line cannot be supposed to account for its disappearance.

(All the stated depths are taken below low water mark. There are no true tides but there are daily fluctuations).

The structure of the causeway is a tip of stones, water-worn and averaging 30 to 50 cm. in diameter; the base of the structure is irregular in width, but averages some 12.5 m. The base now lies in sandy silt; below this is the mud bed of the lagoon, which may be probed to a depth of 2 m. without finding a bottom. At the point where the causeway, directly outside the North Gate, crosses the tidal level, we found small stones *in situ* which formed a cobble pavement. This area was the foreshore in Punic times and the cobbles would have been set in an earth or sand foundation, just as they were in the roadway leading out of the gate. Further out, on the true causeway over the tip of stones, the paving was of flat, irregular slabs of some 40 to 60 cm. across (Plan I, plan at A-B). This type of paving seems to have been a speciality of the causeway; road surfacing on the land is either cobbles or made of large stones neither so flat nor so thin. Almost all the paving on the causeway has vanished, particularly along the track followed by the drivers of the carts, who prefer the sandy bottom which soon settles in a slight depression. Thus for long stretches where the modern cart-track runs along the centre of the causeway, the edges are now higher than the middle, as is shown in Profile A-B. However, in the places where the carts run alongside the causeway, the paving slabs may sometimes be seen still in position at the middle, and there is little doubt that originally the paving covered a surface down the centre of the causeway to a width of some 7 m., a comfortable two-track cart-way. The wheel-ruts of a double cart-track are visible passing through the North Gate and have been laid bare continuing northwards towards the causeway; no ruts were, however, found on the stones of the causeway itself.

At a point some 560 m. north of the Motya foreshore there is a more solidly built part of the causeway (Plan I, plan at C-D). Here, for about 14 m., there is no tip of stones and the sides, about 10 m. apart, are formed of large blocks. Directly outside these blocks it is possible to probe to 2 m. without finding a bottom. The modern cart-track runs across the centre, and here there is no paving left, but a hard bottom under 20 to 50 cm. of sand. The rest of the area retains some of its paving and the structure may have been a halting place with a jetty, or the foundations of a light building.

The length of the causeway is not all in the same state of preservation. From a point about 240 m. north of the Motya foreshore and continuing for 160 m. the foundation tip is tolerably complete and here and there are slabs of paving; the next section of 165 m., that is from the point where the modern cart-track abandons the causeway to the point C-D where it regains the centre, the causeway is very dilapidated. No paving is left, and the foundations often rise to only 75 cm. below water-level. In this section there are two narrow breaches, which have probably been made to allow the passage of small craft. Beyond the point C-D the causeway has suffered rather less until it reaches the point off the Birgi foreshore where it disappears. It is impossible to say which, if any, of these dilapidated sections represent the breach made by the Motyans before the siege of Dionysius (Diodorus, XIV, 48); indeed it remains open to speculation whether or not Dionysius repaired the damage.

At those points where the surface may still be observed, the level of the causeway is remarkably constant. Taking a datum of the surface of the central stone in the roadway as it passes through the North Gate, the causeway drops 85 cm. in the first 80 m. north of the gate; 100 m. further it rises a little to minus 77 cm. A further 150 m. north the level averages minus 86 cm. and the paving of the structure at C-D is within 5 cm. of this height. Such uniformity of level suggests that these parts of the causeway have not sunk appreciably and as one can hardly suppose the Motyans built an under-water roadway, it is further proof that the sea-level has risen since ancient times. Whitaker (1921, 51-2) believed the sea-level unchanged; but see Isserlin in *PBSR* (1958, 4) on the rise of the ground water-level.

The causeway paving now averages 5 to 15 cm. below low-water mark; the average rise and fall is 30 cm., but exceptionally, when the wind joins the "tide", the rise is up to 60 cm. (During February, March and April, there may be a phenomenal fall of sea-level of up to 50 cm.; when this occurs the causeway is in part or completely exposed. See note on Admiralty chart 189).

Thus, if the Motyans built the causeway as a dry road in all normal tides, one may postulate a rise in sea-level of at least 50 cm.

As has been mentioned above, the air-photographs showed submerged walls outside the North Gate (Pl. 2 : 3). These walls are sturdy constructions, now some 25 to 50 cm. below water-level and 1.5 to 2 m. in width. They are made of quite large stones, now so pitted and encrusted that it is impossible to observe if they were originally dressed. There is a tumble of stones fallen from the walls on either side and across the harbour mouth, but it is possible to probe in places alongside the walls to a depth of 2 m. It would be interesting to know the depth of the foundations of these walls; probing indicated they were not very deep.

These walls form a small harbour built up against the west side of the causeway, which was itself, no doubt, used as a quay. One large, partly cut, stone was found in position at the edge of the causeway; it lay on a lower stone and probing showed a hard foundation beneath. Immediately outside this stone it is possible to probe to 2 m. In the area where the north harbour wall joins the causeway, there is an indefinite platform, part of which is still covered by paving slabs. The edge of this platform bordering the harbour is impossible to follow with the probe; there are no large stones at the edge and it seems that the foundation may have slipped into the harbour area, as probing discloses many stones there. Nearer the foreshore, however, in the area bounded by the causeway to the east and the southern harbour wall to the west it is possible to probe to 2 m.

Parallel to the shore line and now some 20 cm., below sea-level, there is a flat-topped reef. This reef starts within the harbour, passes the southern wall, and continues westward outside. A close examination revealed nothing which may be said to be without doubt artificial; yet in view of the Phoenician practice of utlizing natural rock (H. Frost, 1963 *passim*) and its position in the harbour, one can but conclude that it formed a jetty. This small harbour at the land-locked end of the lagoon would have been suitable for the small craft plying in the stagnone.

No internal evidence has been discovered for dating the causeway or the harbour. The former is certainly aligned with the bastions of the North Gate but no evidence for relative dating has been forthcoming. In the circumstances it is best to follow Dunbabin (1948, 332), who suggests that the causeway was built about the time the cemetery was transferred from Motya to Birgi during the second or third quarter of the 6th century B.C. During the middle of that century the small temple was founded which flanks the roadway outside the North Gate and emphasizes the new importance of this approach to the city. This was the period after the death of Pentathlos, when the Motyans, backed by the growing imperial power of Carthage, played an active part in defending the Punic west of Sicily. The causeway could have facilitated both peaceful and military contacts with the mainland and it is worth noting that it is directed towards the territory of their Elymian allies.

A later generation of Motyans may well have regretted this joining of their island-city to the mainland, contrary to usual Phoenician practice. Diodorus Siculus describes how the Motyans, threatened by Dionysius, breached the causeway and how Dionysius replied by constructing moles over which he brought his siege-engines up under the walls. It is open to discussion whether or not Dionysius used the causeway. Whitaker (1921, 77) thought that he did. "Dionysius... ordered the reconstruction of the road". Diodorus must have thought of two structures and he is followed by some historians, e.g. Bury in his *History of Greece*, 649 where he says Dionysius set his men to build "a mole far greater than the causeway the Motyans had destroyed". The later version may well have gained ground from the analogy with Alexander's famous siege of Tyre, described by Diodorus himself (XVII 40, seq.) and Arrian (Anab., 18-22).

There is no sign of a second construction across the lagoon, and, moreover, there is a certain weight of evidence to suggest that an attack took place at the north end of the island; quantities of arrowheads have been found here and there are signs of burning on the stones of the walls. It is, therefore, possible to make the conjecture that the causeway was in fact used by Dionysius' assault forces.

It is possible, too, that the causeway contributed in another way to the decline of the city. The main anchorage lay to the south of the island; this was one good reason for building the causeway to the north which, though by no means the shortest way across the lagoon, nor conspicuously shallow, had the advantage of causing least hindrance to shipping. Though it is clear from Diodorus' description that the lagoon was for all practical purposes land-locked, except from the south, yet the construction of the causeway would have prevented any currents circulating round the island (no signs of any sluices remain) and would thus have hastened the silting.

The present submergence of the causeway raises the question of a small eustatic rise in sea-level for which, in spite of vacillating views on the subject, evidence is piling up.

On the island, Dr. Isserlin noted in 1955 that one of the tombs he had dug had been flooded (*PBSR* 1958, 19); the west temple at the North Gate, of which the foundations were left exposed for one season, was flooded right up to the footings, a depth which would have entirely covered the old shoreline of the first occupation. At the South Gate the footings of the early buildings on the shore are awash.

But if we assume a lowering of the water-level by just 50 cm. the picture would be very different. The buildings mentioned above would be clear of the water; and in addition to the causeway, the small harbour moles and the rock reef at the North Gate would be serviceable. There would still be enough water for a small boat to approach the east steps as suggested by Whitaker (1921, 52) though from the soundings, there could never have been more than two metres depth in the immediate neighbourhood of the island.

In respect of the lagoon, the encircling islands could have been more closely joined, as suggested on di Girolamo's map, though he gives no source for it. The natural bar across the S. Teodoro entrance at the north would be above water; as would the long reef to the south of Isola Grande thereby affording a better protection to the outer harbour on which the wall could have been built. Any barriers between the other islands are now obscured, but Miss Frost (1971, 5-12) during her exploration of the wrecks off Borrone, has reported the discovery of an ancient, stone-lined channel between Borrone and Favilla leading into the lagoon. Lastly, Freeman (1893-4) notes that a temple and mole are to be seen beneath the sea, off Cape Boeo; and one may note that the blocking mole off Marsala is also submerged by 50 cm. whereas to be an effective deterrent it should have been visible.

The lagoon must have been clear of weed in Phoenician times and the currents which still flow along the coast both in a northerly and southerly direction could have entered through the narrow channels and scoured the lagoon. There is still no natural silting off Marsala, which must imply some current in that area today.

That, in ancient times, there was a strong current running through the lagoon entrance is born out by Polybius (I, 42) who noted that Lilybaeum "is excellently defended... on the side facing the sea by shoaly water, the passage through which into the harbour requires great skill and practice"; and in describing the Romans' efforts to prevent blockade-runners getting in and out of the harbour, he writes (47) "in consequence the Romans, to whom this was a great annoyance, tried to fill up the mouth of the harbour. For the most part indeed, their attempt was useless both owing to the depth of the sea and because none of the stuff they threw in would remain in place or hold together in the least, but all they shot in used to be at once shifted by the force of the current. However in one place where there were more shoals a solid bank was formed at the cost of infinite pains, and on this a four-banked ship that was coming out at night grounded".

When the sea-level change took place, thereby perhaps reducing the strength of the currents, we have no evidence though it would appear that it was probably not until post-Roman times. The botanical and sedimentary evidence favour a recent formation of the filling in fairly static water; and one may wonder if the closing up of the islands by salt-pans or, indeed, the building the Phoenician causeway, may not have commenced the process. On the other hand, the submergence of the Aragonese mole may indicate a much later rise in sea level.

PART TWO

THE CITY

CHAPTER FOUR

THE ISLAND OF MOTYA: TOPOGRAPHY IN DETAIL

The main geological features of Motya and its environs have been described and discussed above (pp 19 ff.). The island consists essentially of a base of thick marine clays, overlaid locally by whitish-yellow tufa which is covered by a hard crust of concretions and is in turn overlaid by the natural, red or chocolate terra rossa. The tufa now appears over the clay as an archipelago of discontinuous reefs or islands. In the northern half of Motya, there is a substantial area where it can be seen at water-level near the westernmost point of the island, dipping below the water to the west but rising eastwards. Near the western gateway described by Whitaker (1921, 184) it has attained a height of ca. 2 m. above sea level. Mantled thereafter along the coast by scree and debris, it has been found in the Tophet at a similar height (Ciasca in *Mozia* II, 44) and to the east in the near-by trench 6 dug by ourselves in 1955; it reappears at much the same level in the area of the old necropolis dug by Whitaker and is still visible as a cliff some 100 m. south of the Eastern Staircase. Inland we found it at the base of our trial trench 1 (1955), north of the centre of the island.

The tufa, as we now know, also forms the base of the hill on which the Villa Whitaker is situated, for recently (1967) when a pit some 4 m. deep was dug to accommodate a new cistern just north of the extension to the Museum, the tufa, covered by the hard crust overlaid by red earth was, as the locals informed me, encountered at a depth of ca. 3.50 m; it thus exists in this area at much the same height as in the north. A third region where it is known to occur is near the Cothon canal and basin; while less than 1 m. above sea-level to the east of the channel, it rises to nearly 2 m. west of the Cothon basin. There are no doubt other occurrences; but elsewhere the marine clays form the base, as in the area adjoining the South Gate.

These base formations, which may be assumed to owe their shape to marine abrasion, on the whole do not make for a very striking or accentuated general relief, even though some fairly marked rises and falls of the rock surface, in the Tophet region in particular, have been noted by Ciasca (*Mozia* II, 44; III, 13); nor has the inconsiderable amount of soil and debris overtopping them modified the situation strongly.

Accordingly, the island of Motya appears flat in the main (already Cluverius called it "solo humili atque depresso"—cf. Pl. 4 : 1), though in some ways it would be more appropriate to compare it with a shallow saucer with slightly raised edges; for while the depth of soil in the interior tends not to be very considerable—a matter of 2-3 m.—a somewhat deeper mantle of debris and earth—up to ca. 6 m. —has tended to collect near the edges of the island where the ancient city's strong walls have given protection against erosion. However the flatness of the island is not absolute, and a study of the contour map (Plan II) in fact brings out the existence of several clearly defined topographical divisions, including in particular two main areas of somewhat greater altitude (cf. Fig. 6).

We may begin by noticing the existence of an irregular piece of higher ground in the northern

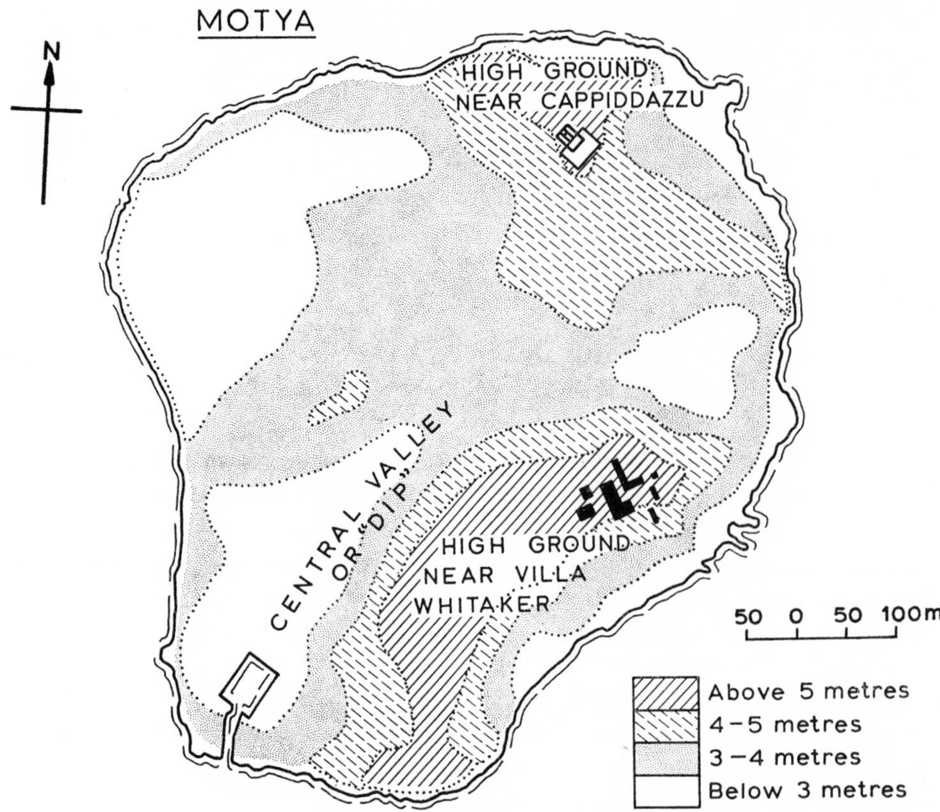

Fig. 6. Simplified relief map of Motya.

part of the island, near the Cappiddazzu. This area within or near the 5 m. contour, slopes gradually southwards towards the centre of the island, where there is a large, gently shelving plateau, the lower part of which may be said to be defined by the 3 m. contour which borders it, in its very irregular course, to the South and West. A limited rise of land within this general plateau (contained by the 4 m. contours) may be noticed southwest of the centre of the island, about halfway along the field path which branches off the road from the Villa to the Cothon, and leads to the Tophet and New Necropolis. However, a much more important feature is the hillock making up the south-eastern part of the island, which rises fairly steeply to a small platform in parts above the 7 m. line, in the region adjoining the Villa and modern hamlet. This hillock may in fact be said to be the dominating topographical feature of Motya. It is bordered, on the northern side, by a roughly circular depression descending to ca. 2 m.; while its south-western flank forms one side of a gentle, but topographically important, central "dip" or valley, the other side of which is constituted by the isolated high ground south-west of the centre of the island, noticed earlier. This valley drains in a generally southerly direction, and begins gently, but becomes increasingly accentuated, and must have been a noticeable feature of the ancient city. The Cothon is set in its lower reaches, not far from where one would have expected natural drainage to have issued seawards through low marshy ground. Other lowlying terrain occurs in a small bay near the House of Mosaics, and was noticed by Whitaker (1921, 188); while the large "bay" of ground below the 3 m. line, near the western corner of the island, is so shallow as to be of no obvious topographical significance.

We must now consider the possible bearing of this topographical situation, taken in conjunction with the known archaeological data, on the organization and lay-out of the ancient town. Several conclusions suggest themselves.

Dealing, firstly, with the high ground near the Cappiddazzu, Whitaker's excavations have shown that this was a district which contained very substantially constructed edifices, including some important public buildings (a temple, perhaps an agora) and a main artery of traffic, and that it was inhabited for a long time. In fact, until now it is only in this part of the island that excavations have brought to light considerable stretches of walling sufficiently powerful and solid to carry the burden of the multiple-storied houses implied by Diodorus Siculus (XIV, 51). The 5 m. contour here may thus give a hint of the approximate extent of what we may call the "civic centre" of Motya, even though some quite important buildings may well have been elsewhere.

While much less is at present known archaeologically about the other main region of high ground near the villa and hamlet, it seems likely that here, too, a high level and the presence of important buildings may have gone together. To begin with, this part of the island has the benefit of breezes little felt in the airless interior, and is therefore a more pleasant area to be in than the latter. Whitaker built his Villa here on dominating ground; the hamlet preceded him and no doubt the situation would have appealed also to the ancient Motyans (the "House of the Mosaics" is, in fact, situated just below the hill). The ground near the buildings in the hamlet is full of ancient potsherds, and the rustic houses and boundary walls contain substantial amounts of stone, including some good ashlar, cleared from the near-by fields and gardens. Recently (1966) more exact evidence of ancient habitation on the hill came to light when the foundation trenches for a northern extension to the Museum buildings were dug. They revealed parts of a building complex apparently dating from the 5th century B.C.; deeper digging near-by for a new cistern (1967) showed that archaeological layers hereabouts are some 3.50 m. thick, and sherds of pottery which came to light included some 7th and 6th century fragments. (Mr. Coldstream classified and dated sample sherds submitted to him as follows: East Greek, late 6th Century or more likely 7th; Corinthian kotyle, probably 6th century; Black glaze, not Attic, late 5th; Black glaze, not Attic, not before 5th century).

The extent of the archaeological zone in this area can again to some extent be delimited by a study of contours combined with other lines of evidence.

The high ground referred to is a slightly curved oblong, the back of which touches the seas for a short distance near where the stairs lead down from the high ground to the "Phoenician house" found by Whitaker (1921, 159-160). Visitors approaching the hillock along the paths leading up from the Cothon, the landing stage, and the centre of the island will in every case note a sudden and significantly marked rise which they must negotiate before gaining the plateau on which the modern buildings are situated. On the road approaching from the Cothon, and that from the centre of the island traces of unexcavated heavy rubble walls may be observed running obliquely across the path near the beginnings of the rise. On the road coming in from the centre, the boundary of this rise coincides roughly with the position of the 5 m. contour line. This contour approaches the road from the southwest, and after having continued beyond it on the same alignment for some 30 m., it swings round to a generally south-eastern direction. Having followed this for ca. 75 m., it abruptly turns southwest at an almost exact right angle (which is mirrored, in a vaguer way, by the 4 m. contour below).

The course of the contour lines does not look natural. Together with the traces of walling, and the sudden ascents to the upper plateau, they seem to suggest that we are in a region where man-made deposits in the nature of an inner "tell" were once held in position by terraces or retaining walls. Such could, of course, have been built at various times, but the period when the city flourished would seem to be the most likely one. In that case the hill would have represented a second urban zone, probably inhabited by the well-to-do, and possibly also including public buildings, as did the upper city or "Byrsa" at Carthage. Some ashlar stones of unusual size or quality can be observed among the cottages near the Villa. The hillock thus seems to deserve careful investigation, even though the lengthy record of occupation hereabouts will have entailed much disturbance, pit-cuttings, reuse of stone, etc.

Elsewhere on the island the aid which topographical study may give seems limited (though a hollow, at times filled by a stagnant pool largely choked by stones, in the north part of the island (P on map, Plan II) may deserve attention. There are, however, certain archaeological data, observable at present or observed in the past, in various regions of the island, which may offer hints as to the kinds of structures which once existed in certain parts of Motya. Among these are several stone column drums turned up by the plough in the field just north of the hut to the west of the central crossroads—a region surveyed by resistivity measurements (see p. 42) and now (1969) partly excavated by Soprintendente Tusa (*Mozia* V, 19 ff.). Again Schubring reports (1866, 61) the existence of quantities of fine ashlar with stucco covering in the neighbourhood of the south-west corner of the island which, he thought, might indicate the existence of a temple in this region. Other elements mentioned by him, such as a large receptacle for drinking water piped in from the mainland (1866, 62), seem difficult to locate now.

All told, such considerations, combined with the results of the very limited excavations so far undertaken, can only partially help to fill in what is still largely a blank area within the circuit of the Town Wall. In particular, they seem to leave wide open the important question whether an overall town plan existed at Motya. This has been raised by earlier authors, and received widely differing answers. Pace (1938, 365-7) noting the existence of the main north and south gates suggested that there must at least have been a *cardo* across the city linking them. Against this, Lehmann-Hartleben (1926, 183) maintained that the excavated ruins in the interior of the island, though few in number and widely scattered, showed absence of any overall system of orientation, and that accordingly there could not have been a comprehensive town plan.

Since there is now more evidence than when he wrote, it seems worth while to investigate afresh the orientation of all the known ancient constructions to see whether the city originally possessed in whole or in part, anything like a regular grid system of streets; and for this purpose we shall in each case cite the axis approximating most closely to a north-south direction.

Adopting this procedure it becomes apparent that the orientation of quite a number of features located in various parts of the island approximates to a greater or lesser extent (ca. $\pm$ 5°) to the direction of 40° E. of N. This applies to the main road leading in from the North Gate and the house just inside the walls behind the postern (Whitaker, 1921, 158-9 fig. 13). The Cappiddazzu near by is similarly orientated: so are the walls of houses encountered in our test trenches (A on map, Plan II) near the central crossroads. The same general direction is encountered in the buildings recently excavated by Soprintendente Tusa in 1968-9 near the field hut in the centre of the island, where resistivity measurements undertaken in 1963 had already predicted this (cf. *Mozia* V, 19 ff.). Progressing further southwards, a very similar orientation is displayed by walls unearthed in our long trial trench (B on map, Plan II) which parallels the field path from the Cothon road to the Tophet. Finally, at the southern end of the island, the Cothon again conforms to this scheme of alignment.

We have so far followed our system across the island from north to south. It can also be detected in the neighbourhood of the hillock on which the Villa Whitaker stands, as, for example, in the walls of the building discovered when the foundation trenches for the extension of the Museum were dug in 1966 and in the walling of an ancient construction, visible in a trench or pit, dug at an uncertain date inside the angle made by the bifurcation of the road from the hamlet to the Cothon, and the field path which branches off it and makes for the Tophet.

There are, thus, indications that over long distances in the interior of Motya a master scheme of planning was widely followed. We must not however be surprised if there were exceptions to it, or a lack of exactness in layout. Thus the orientation of a building situated some 100 m. west of the Villa by a turn in the field path, partly excavated by Whitaker, but recently cleared by Soprintendente Tusa, (*Mozia* V, 10) shows a definite deviation.

Also, measurements taken in the peripheral regions of the island give widely different readings. The little temple found outside the North Gate (see p. 69 ff.), the buildings in the Tophet, the houses excavated near the South Gate, the "House of the Mosaics", and the constructions behind the Eastern Staircase, all differ widely in their layout, and their alignment seems to be determined more by the lie

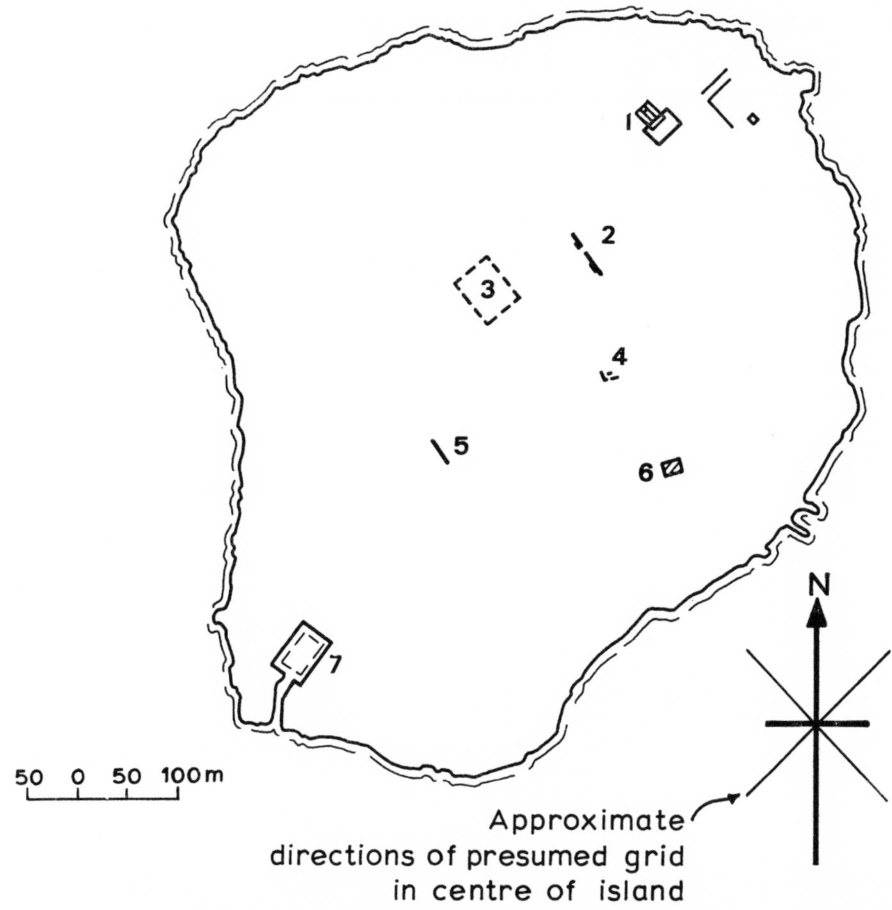

On this figure, 1 marks the Cappiddazzu temple, 2 Trench A on Plan II, 3 the area near the field hut in the centre of the island, 4 the building ca. 100 m. west of the Villa, 5 Trench B on Plan II, 6 the extension of the Museum, 7 the Cothon).

Fig. 7. Sketch map of Motya, showing localities where the existence of an urban grid plan seems indicated.

of the land than by overall planning. It thus seems likely that at Motya we must distinguish a peripheral zone, to which overall planning did not apply, from a central region, in which it did.

There is even a hint—though at present no more—that in the central, planned region of the city, a recurrent standard planning unit was employed. It seems to be represented by the N-S dimension of the Cappiddazzu—35.4 m. according to *Mozia* I, 35. As the air photograph (Pl. 3) will at once make evident, similar units of length occur nearby.

The walling flanking the east side of the main road entering Motya through the North Gate, up to the angle where the open space, regarded as an agora by Whitaker, (1921, 173) begins, is not much longer (ca. 37.4 m.). The width of the presumed agora itself, beginning from this angle and up to the prolongation of the north wall of the Cappiddazzu enclosure, is also much the same, allowing for the existence of roads flanking it on the north and south sides (ca. 43 m.). The width of the Cothon, again, is of a very similar size (35.5 m.) (du Plat Taylor, 1964, 92). It is interesting to note that this distance differs little from an *actus* of 120 Attic feet.

Can we say when such overall planning introduced to Motya?

The Cappiddazzu temple complex was founded in the 6th century B.C. (Tusa, *Mozia*, III, 10); so perhaps this century marked the beginnings of the scheme; though its main development may well have taken place later, in the 5th century B.C., and in places it was apparently still adhered to in the 4th. Fig. 7 shows in a simplified form those parts of the island where there is evidence for the existence of a grid.

CHAPTER FIVE

AIR PHOTOGRAPHY

For the purpose of our investigations we had at our disposition the following material:

1. A set of war-time black-and-white air photographs of the island and surrounding waters, taken by the RAF during a flight in 1943, was made available to us by the British War Office, by agreement with the Italian authorities. Later on another RAF war-time photograph, taken in that year, was made available for study by Keele University.
2. Photographs taken by the Italian Air Force, during and after the last war, were sent to us by the Aerofototeca in Rome, then under the direction of Professor D. Adamesteanu, in 1962, and others by Brigadiere G. Schmiedt of the Istituto Geografico Militare in Florence.
3. A set of black-and-white photographs was taken specially for us, to our specifications, by Messrs. Hunting Surveys Limited in November, 1967.

All these pictures were taken vertically.

4. In addition, we obtained by permission of the British Ministry of Defence copies of certain air photographs which had been taken in May and June, 1968, by RAF reconnaissance planes on training flights under NATO auspices, with special permission of the Italian authorities. These pictures included sets of infra-red photographs in black and white, both vertical and oblique, taken in May, 1968; and also infra-red ("false colour") and natural colour pictures, vertical and oblique, taken one month later. Of these the colour and "false colour" have proved of special interest, and our report below will rely on them particularly.

Of all the pictures in our possession, those taken in recent years are far the best in definition and steroscopic effect, and they were furthermore taken from a more suitable, lower altitude than the earlier ones.

In spite of this, the most recent pictures are not in all respects the most revealing and they must be studied throughout in conjunction with the earlier photographs. The reason is that even in the comparatively short period between 1942 and 1967 methods of cultivation on Motya (and, in particular, modern ploughing by tractor) have removed or blurred a number of old features. Accordingly, it seems best to proceed by giving the reader the net results of the joint analysis of all the material available for study.

In the working up and interpretation of our photographs we were greatly helped by Dr. W. Collins then of the Department of Civil Engineering of Leeds University, and the analysis given below is largely based on his specialist advice.

In order to arrive at a correct understanding of the data, we must obviously disregard all features which are likely to be comparatively modern. This applies to the present system of field-boundary walls and paths, arranged so as to define a system of rectangular plots, and which is noticeable in particular in the northern part of the island. Somewhat more doubtful is the correct assignation of a system of light-coloured streaks defining darker rectangular plots in the same region. Since they run parallel with the present field-boundary system, but take no account of the rather different direction of the ancient main road entering the city through the North Gate, it seems likely that these lines should likewise be regarded as dating from a time after the fall of the city, and perhaps indicating a fairly modern forerunner of the present field system at a slight lateral displacement. With somewhat less assurance, we may also feel inclined to assign to this same period, between the fall of the ancient city and the present day, certain light streaks in the same region, not very different in direction from the above. All the features which we feel should be disregarded, where the topography of ancient Motya is concerned, are shown on Fig. 8.

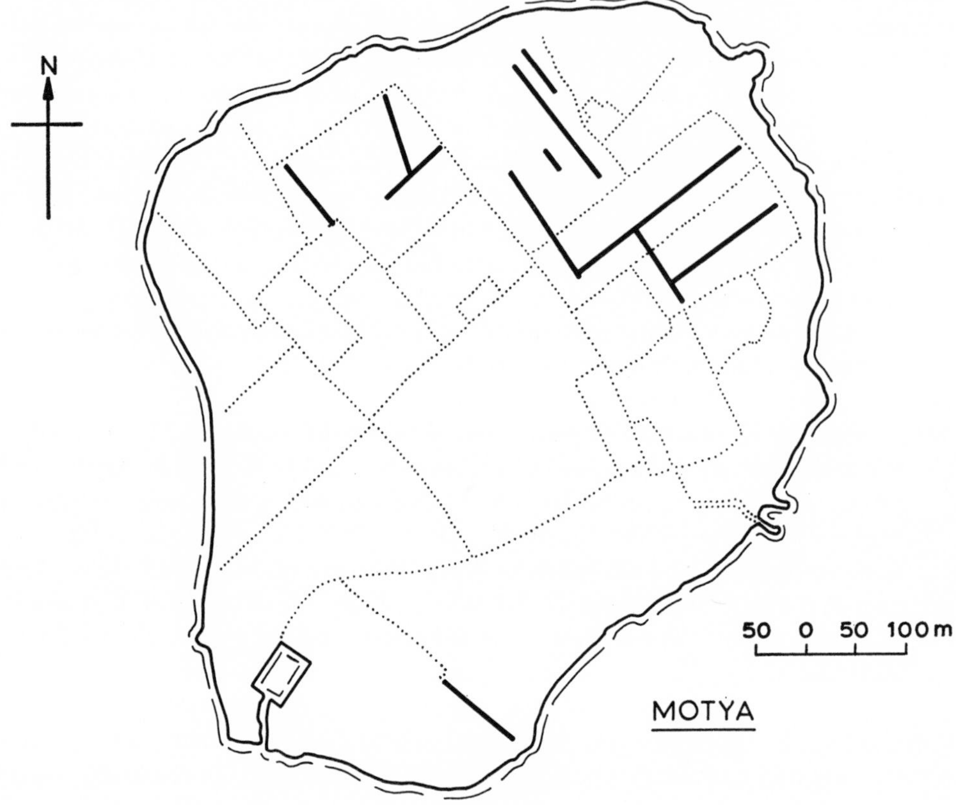

Fig. 8. Sketch map showing features on air photographs probably not significant for the topography of ancient Motya.

We must now look at those features on the air photographs which remain when the ones referred to above are eliminated, and which might thus be significantly related to the ruins of the ancient city (for reference in what follows, cf. Pl. 3 and Pl. 7).

We may begin by referring to the light lines shown in the water north, and west of, the North Gate. Part of them, substantiated by underwater investigation as ancient harbour works, have been referred to in detail in chapter 3. We note, in particular, the nearly straight line of reefs which runs almost exactly parallel to the city walls over a length of some 100 m. at ca. 35 m. distance, west of the N. Gate. Its regularity points to the adaptation of an originally natural bank of rock to urban needs, perhaps as a quay wall, and a number of ashlar blocks probably displaced shorewards by winter storm can be discerned in the shallow water just behind it. A slight fall in the water-level would convert these shallows into dry land—as they possibly were in antiquity. G. Schmiedt (1965) seems to have come to similar conclusions.

Continuing inwards from the North Gate, the early Italian photographs and perhaps the RAF photographs show, to the south of the Cappiddazzu, an indistinct line which roughly prolongs the direction of the main road leading into the city from the North Gate; this line divides areas of different soil colour within the same vineyard. It seems to meet the modern E-W road running from the Villa to the Tophet roughly where the present path leading northwards to the causeway branches off (i.e. near the centre of the island). Being aligned as it is, this is obviously a feature of potential urbanistic interest, though very indistinct. If genuine it may indicate a lane or road. Its course can be followed, with greater clarity, on the same alignment, further to the south, until it emerges as a definite light-coloured streak to the west and north-west of the Cothon basin. It is paralleled in this part of its course by another very definite streak on the north-eastern side of the Cothon. An additional feature in the region near the Cothon is a curved white line which originates in a light coloured patch adjoining the western side of the basin, and which swings round to the NE until it fades out just beyond the path from the Villa to the Cothon. In addition, in the fields in the northern and central parts of Motya a number of light and dark coloured areas, some of them with fairly straight edges, can be discerned. If these areas are outlined, faint straight lines adjoining them sometimes become noticeable which prolong the run of boundaries between the light and dark areas, and a fairly regular, if obviously incomplete pattern, seems to emerge. For details cf. Pl. 7.

When attempting to interpret the evidence summarised above, we may assume that light coloured areas on the pictures probably indicate soil with a comparatively high content of fragments of stone or plaster, originating from ruined buildings; dark areas, on the other hand, should be due to the presence of a depth of comparatively pure humus where no buildings stood. The tracing of these edges of such light or dark coloured areas might thus give some hints as to planning.

Looking at our photographs with this in mind, the regular pattern referred to above recalls town plans on a grid pattern such as the Greek "Hippodamian" type. In addition, the line which appears to prolong the course of the main road leading from the North Gate towards the Cappiddazzu might reflect, though vaguely, the course of a "cardo". As for the semi-circular curved line to the north-west of the Cothon, it partly corresponds (as we shall see) to a feature indicated by resistivity measurement and also to a slight rise in the ground; it may well reflect traces of a curving wall and can, in fact, be seen to form part of a large circle, of which the curving revetment wall inside the South Gate opening, discovered by Whitaker (1921, 183) could form another segment. The whole circle of walling could, when complete, have served as a circumvallation for the Cothon. Whether it was ever completed we have, however, no means of telling.

CHAPTER SIX

ELECTRICAL RESISTIVITY SURVEYS AND THEIR RESULTS

In addition to the methods described above, it was thought that resistivity measuring might be usefully employed at Motya to obtain some preliminary idea as to the location and character of structures in some large areas which are still archaeologically unexplored. The underlying principles of this method are well known, and have been briefly described by Dr. G. F. Tagg with special reference to Motya in the *Evershed News*, 8, 2, 1965, 1-7.

At Motya there were reasons to hope that resistivity surveying might provide useful results: one was the fact, referred to above, that the base rock appeared to be fairly homogeneous over considerable distances; the other that the soil of Motya, again often of a fairly constant depth, consists largely of sandy and loamy ingredients which differ sharply from the limestone used for foundation courses of mud-brick walls and in ashlar masonry.

Resistivity measurement of selected areas was therefore taken in hand and pursued over a number of years (1963, 1964, 1966) in order to build up a resistivity map comprising significant sections of the island. The areas so tested are indicated on the map (Fig. 9).

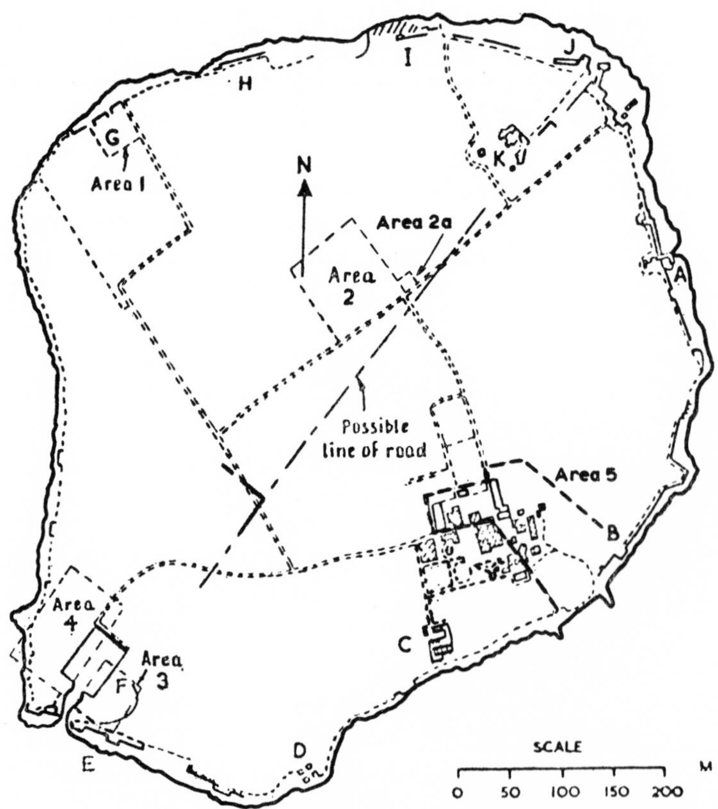

Fig. 9. Sketch map of Motya showing areas where resistivity measuring was carried out.

Two procedures of surveying were vailable. The first of these consisted of resistivity traverses, single or widely spaced, in which readings of high resistivity were likely to correspond to the approximate location of walls or possibly ditches. The other involves systematic surveying of selected areas by means of grids of electrode locations, which would permit the drawing of resistivity "contour maps" of lines linking points with similar readings. Electrode spacings in both procedures were usually, 1, 1.5, or 2 m. (in 1964, 10 ft. (or 3 m.) spacings were employed widely) but wider spacing permitting testing for more deeply buried structures, depth of soil, etc. was also sometimes used.

Tests with different probe spacings over the same traverse showed that the subsoil had a fairly uniform resistivity of 2500 ohm cm. at all depths between 1 and 4 m. This low resistivity was presumably due to the content of brackish water: at depths less than 1 m the average resistivity of the very dry soil was of the order of 5000 ohm cm. Contact resistance was so high that the Martin Clark meter could only be used if the probes were watered. This procedure lowered the apparent resistivity by a few per cent; it was not required when using the Evershed meter.

The maximum resistivity measured was of the order of 20,000 ohm cm. with 1 m. probe spacing, 10,000 ohm cm. with 2 m. probe spacing. The difference between these two resistivities suggest that there was a good conducting path at depths below about 2 m., probably through subsoil beneath the buried structure or possibly through very wet limestone.

Some tests of the local validity of the method were available in 1963 and additional checks have come to hand in subsequent years as excavations were undertaken in areas previously surveyed by resistivity measurement. The relative reliability of the resistivity grid will be illustrated best by comparing predictions based on resistivity contour readings with the actual results of digging in two selected areas. One of these is the western part of area 3 inside the South Gate, shown in Fig. 16. Here the prediction has been confirmed to a fair extent by excavation; some of the high readings not correspond-

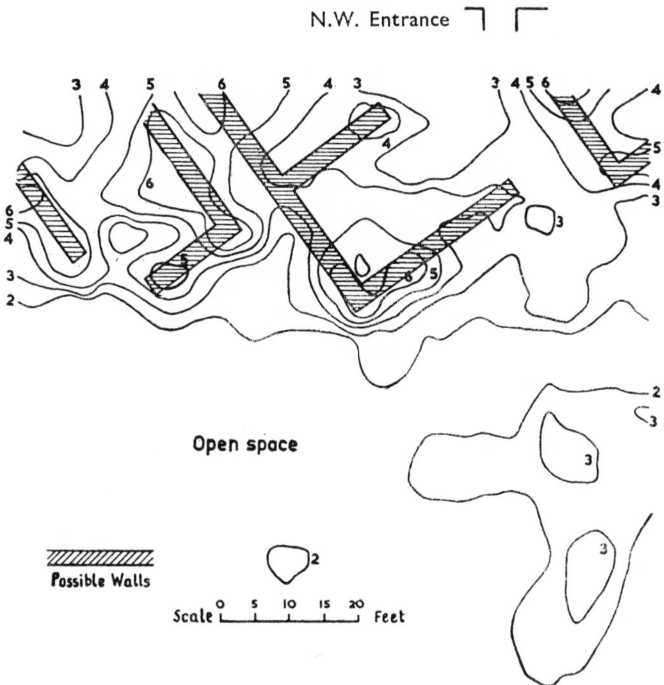

Fig. 10. Area (1) of resistivity survey: findings and interpretation (after G. Tagg, *The Evershed News*, 8, 2, 1965, p. 8, fig. 10).

ing to walls were due to spills of rubble from destroyed buildings. The second was the southern part of area 2 near the centre of the island, surveyed by us in 1964, and which has since (in 1968-9) been excavated by Soprintendente Tusa. Here the resistivity contour map correctly foreshadowed the essential alignment of the structures later uncovered, though detail remained in some doubt (Fig. 13). Similarly, near our long test trenches B, simple traverses helped to predict fairly correctly the existence of significant features, though the nature of these might sometimes be misunderstood.

Altogether, it may be said, on the basis of information available, that major architectural features at Motya are unlikely to be missed by resistivity surveying, and that a zone of high readings is very likely to contain a building. In addition, peaks, or pronounced kinks on upward readings, are likely to correspond to the location of walls crossing the traverse line at or near the points in question.

In reviewing the main results of our surveys, we begin near the small western gateway referred to by Whitaker (1921, 184). Here an area ca. 30 m. square (1 on the plan, Fig. 9) was surveyed by Dr. Tagg in 1964. Traverse lines were 10 ft. apart, with readings along the traverses spaced at distances of 5 ft. The zone near the city wall gave evidence of having been built up, while the area further inland appeared to have been an open space. Dr. Tagg's interpretation of the findings is indicated in Fig. 10. He though there was evidence that an underground channel, hidden beneath the present plough land, was making from the near-by marshy hollow (P on map, Plan II) for the coast to the WNW, but this needs further investigation.

Near the centre of the island Mr. Bloomer, in consultation with Dr. Tagg, investigated the area marked 2 on the plan, Fig. 9. Part of this area was surveyed in detail by means of a network of parallel traverses set 5 ft. (1.5 m.) apart, 10 ft. (3 m.) being the distance between reading along the traverses, whereas other sectors were given less detailed treatment; the results are shown in Figs. 11 and 12 respectively.

Interpretation in detail was not easy, but it seemed possible, in general terms, to discern an area bordered by roads or ambulatories to the N and S, by buildings on the E, and with some isolated structures in a wide open area. Where tested by excavation, this prediction has proved essentially accurate. For a comparison of the archaeological findings with previous resistivity readings in this area which has now been excavated by Soprintendente Tusa see Fig. 13.

An additional small area (2a) ca. 12 by 12 m. was set out in the angle between the path to the North Gate and the lane to the Tophet in 1966, and tested by Dr. and Mrs. Pike with traverses set 2 or 1 m. apart, electrode spacings being 1 m. The resulting map is shown in Fig. 14. This shows an area some 10 m. across where the mean resistivity in the top 1 m. had values only varying between 15,000 and 10,000 ohm cm., suggesting either continuous masonry or bedrock near to the surface.

The regions to the N, S and E of areas 2 and 2a were probed by Dr. Tagg by means of widely spaced traverses. The general impression gained by him was that a road or lane may have traversed the island here, continuing perhaps southwards; a side-road branching off it has also been tentatively suggested (cf. Fig. 9).

Southwards from the neighbourhood of area 2, widely spaced traverses extended across the central "dip" to the vicinity of the Cothon. These seemed to show that built-up ground extends on both sides of the valley and continues down the slope. However, the area directly north of the Cothon would, for ca. 35 m., seem to have been essentially free of buildings; the soil hereabouts was apparently very deep. On the other hand, both the eastern and western sides of this empty area to the north of the Cothon seem to some extent to have been flanked by buildings, as the ground west of the basin apparently was. To the east of the Cothon we have at present little indication that there were many buildings, and indeed this zone needs further investigation.

The neighbourhood where most detailed work was done was to the west of the Cothon (area 4 on map 1, cf. Fig. 15). Here, in 1963, Mr. Addison's team, on the basis of systematic plottings of maximum

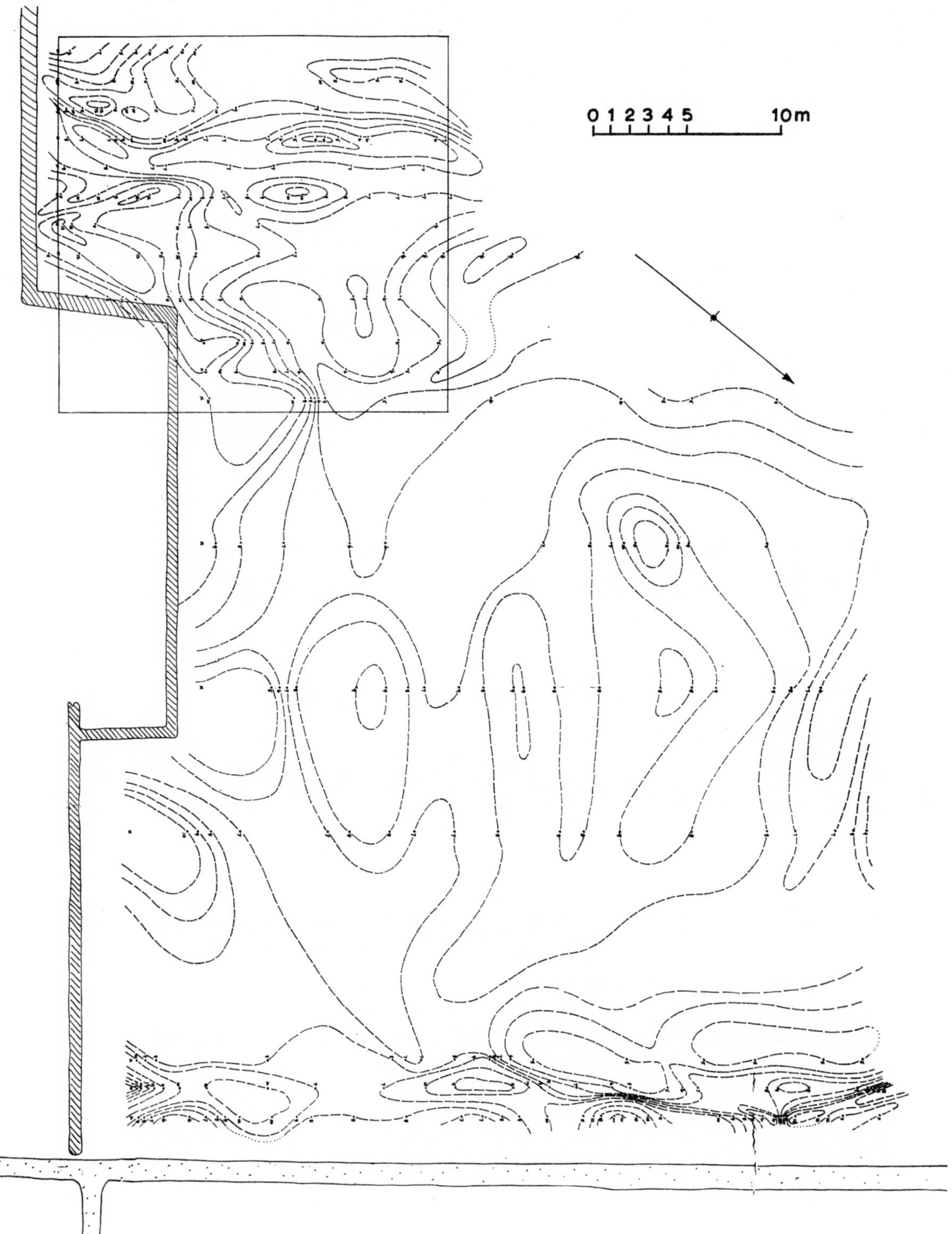

Fig. 11. Resistivity map of area (2) in centre of island.

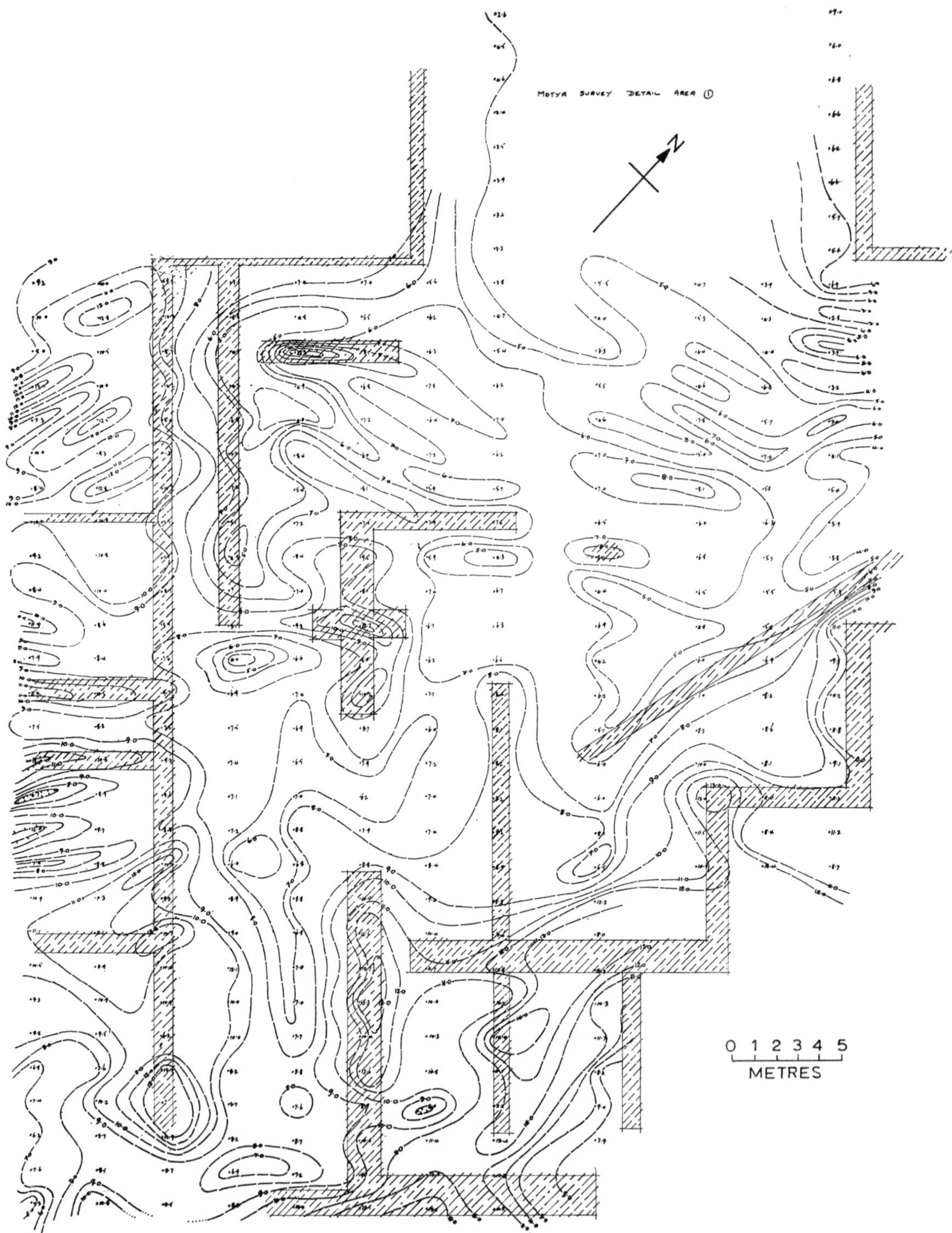

Fig. 12. Map of part of area (2) surveyed in greater detail. Suggested wall plottings are show in hatching.

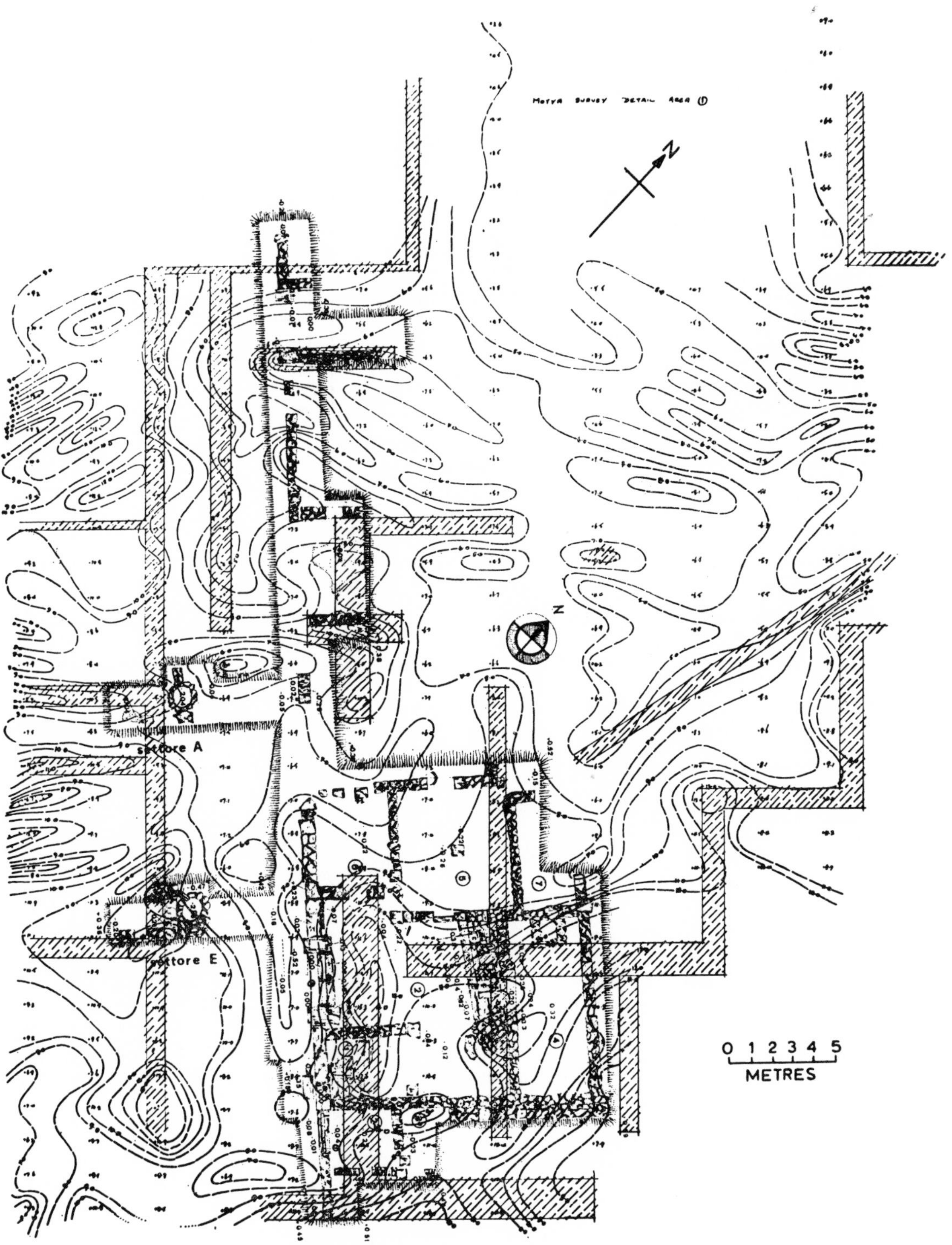

Fig. 13. Sketch map showing buildings excavated in the area given in fig. 11. Walling found is superimposed on the resistivity contours, and on walls predicted on the strength of these.

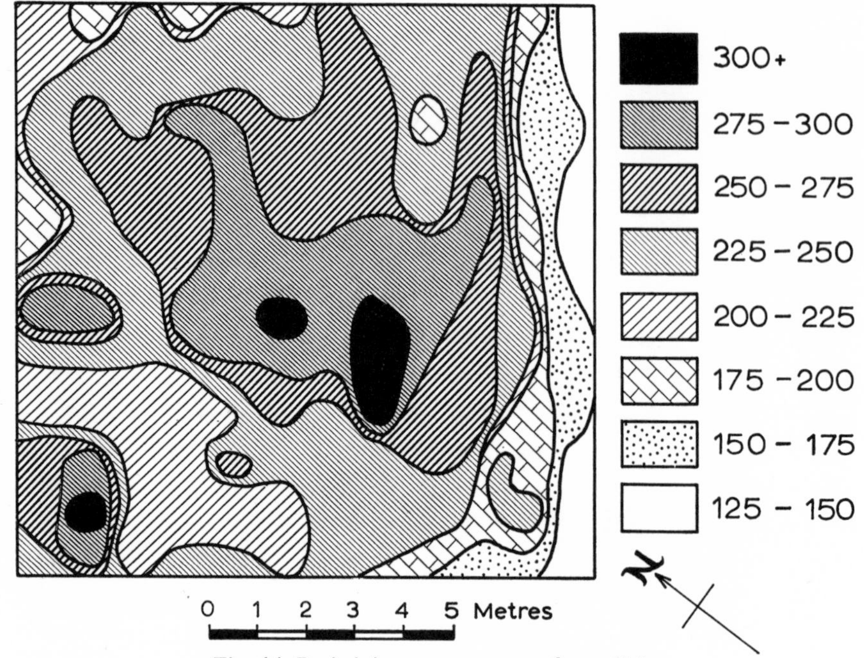

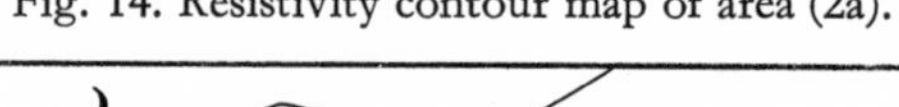

Fig. 14. Resistivity contour map of area (2a).

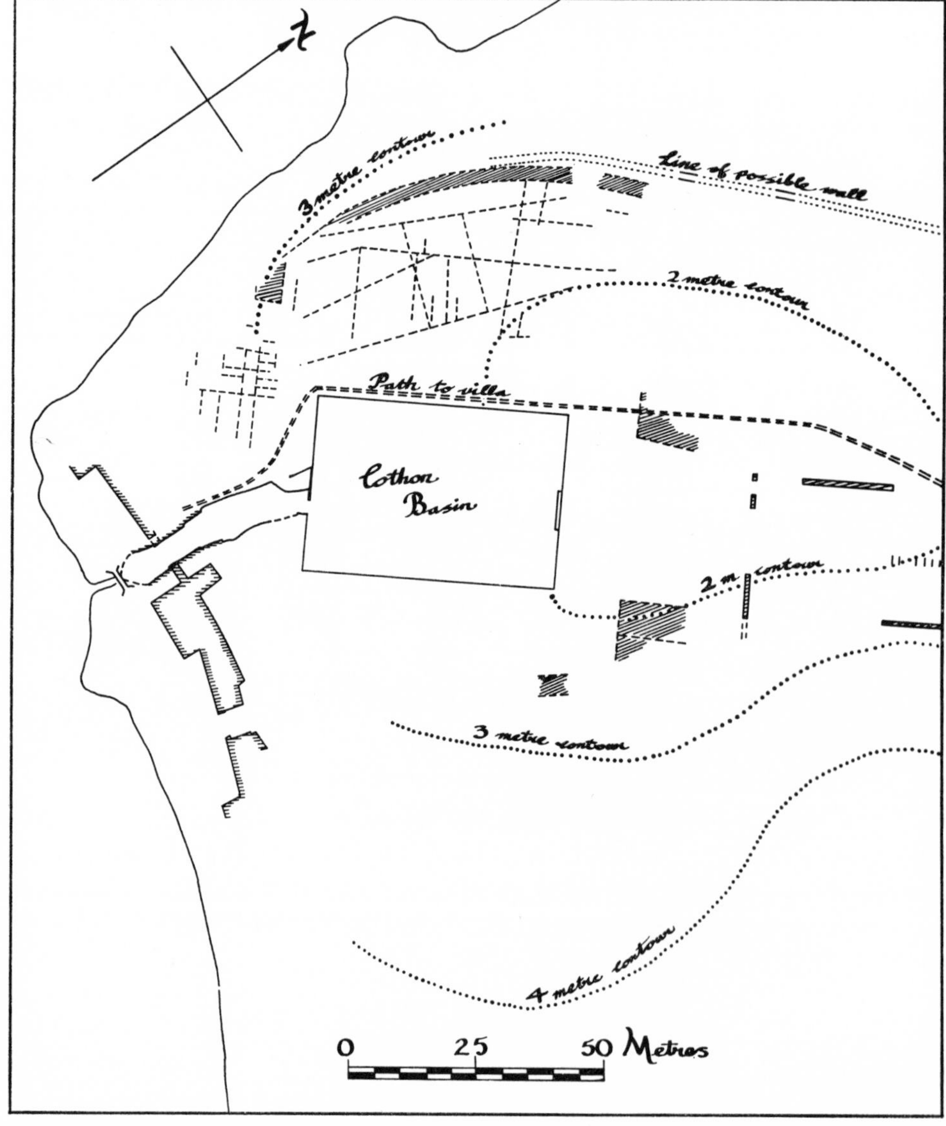

Fig. 15. Map showing results of resistivity measuring in the neighbourhood of the cothon.

readings, noted signs of a possible large building, and similar indications were encountered in 1966 by Mr. and Mrs. Searle. To the NW of this, a belt of high resistivity runs along the 3 m. contour. It tends to show maxima near its outer edges, and accordingly it has been tentatively interpreted as reflecting a two-faced wall with a less solid infilling between the outer faces; a rectangular area of high resistivity adjoining its southern end might be a building, such as a tower. This, or a related curving feature, was traced further northwards by Mr. and Mrs. Searle. They found it swung NE, perhaps crossing the path from the Villa near where the 2 m. contour traverses it. They also noticed that there is visual evidence of a slight plateau extending roughly from the suggested line of curving walling to the town wall; the feature was traced up to the point where it crosses the road at a bend, but was not pursued any further owing to lack of time.

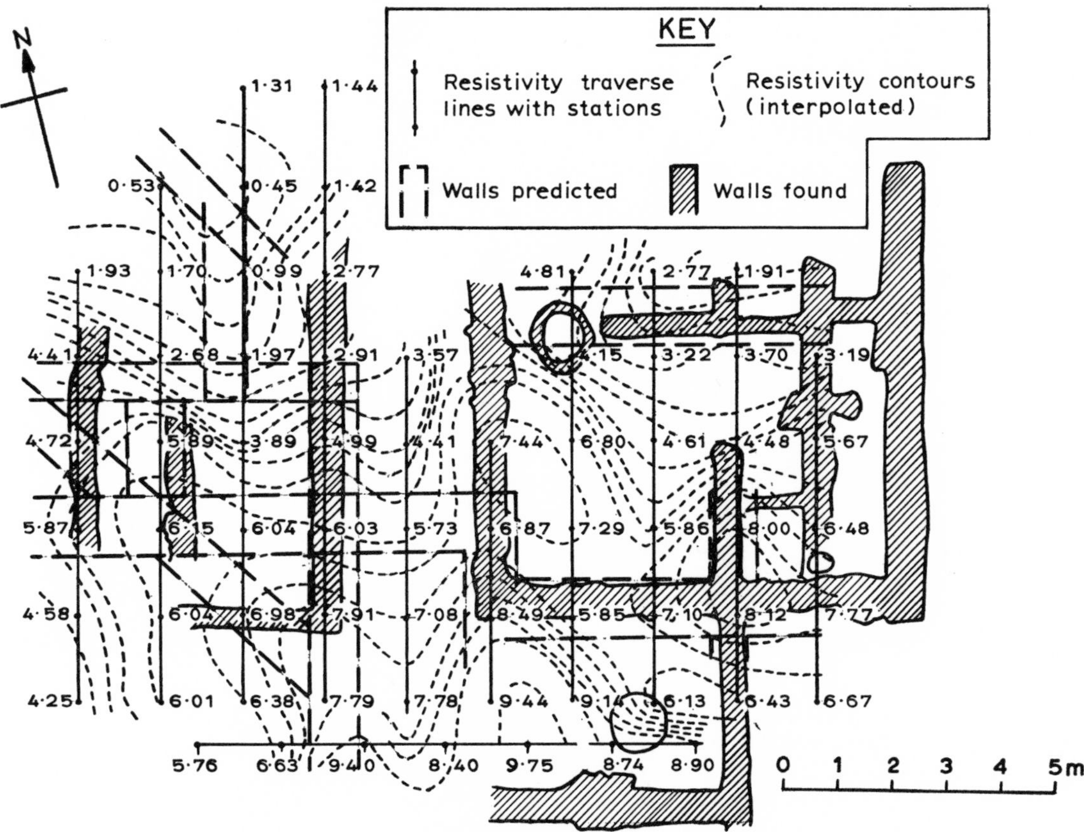

Fig. 16. Resistivity map of the central part of area (3) inside the South Gate, showing resistivity contours, walls predicted, and walls found.

Lastly we come to the region of the hamlet (Fig. 17) (area 5, cf. the map, Fig. 9). Here, as will be remembered (above, p. 33) the recent discovery of ancient walls north of the original Museum provides evidence about some building alignments. Resistivity measurement in the plot under the pine trees some 20 m. to the west (Fig. 17A) appear to point to the existence of constructions with rather similar alignments. Readings immediately north of the Museum area (Fig. 17B) are less easily interpreted (though a little further northwards there appears to be heavy stone walling, running diagonally across the road to the Tophet just inside the 5 m. contour which seems to be similarly orientated). Readings inside the adjoining orchard and on the ground east of it (Fig. 17C) hint at the presence of substantial constructions, but more traversing would be needed to determine their alignment. However, an isolat-

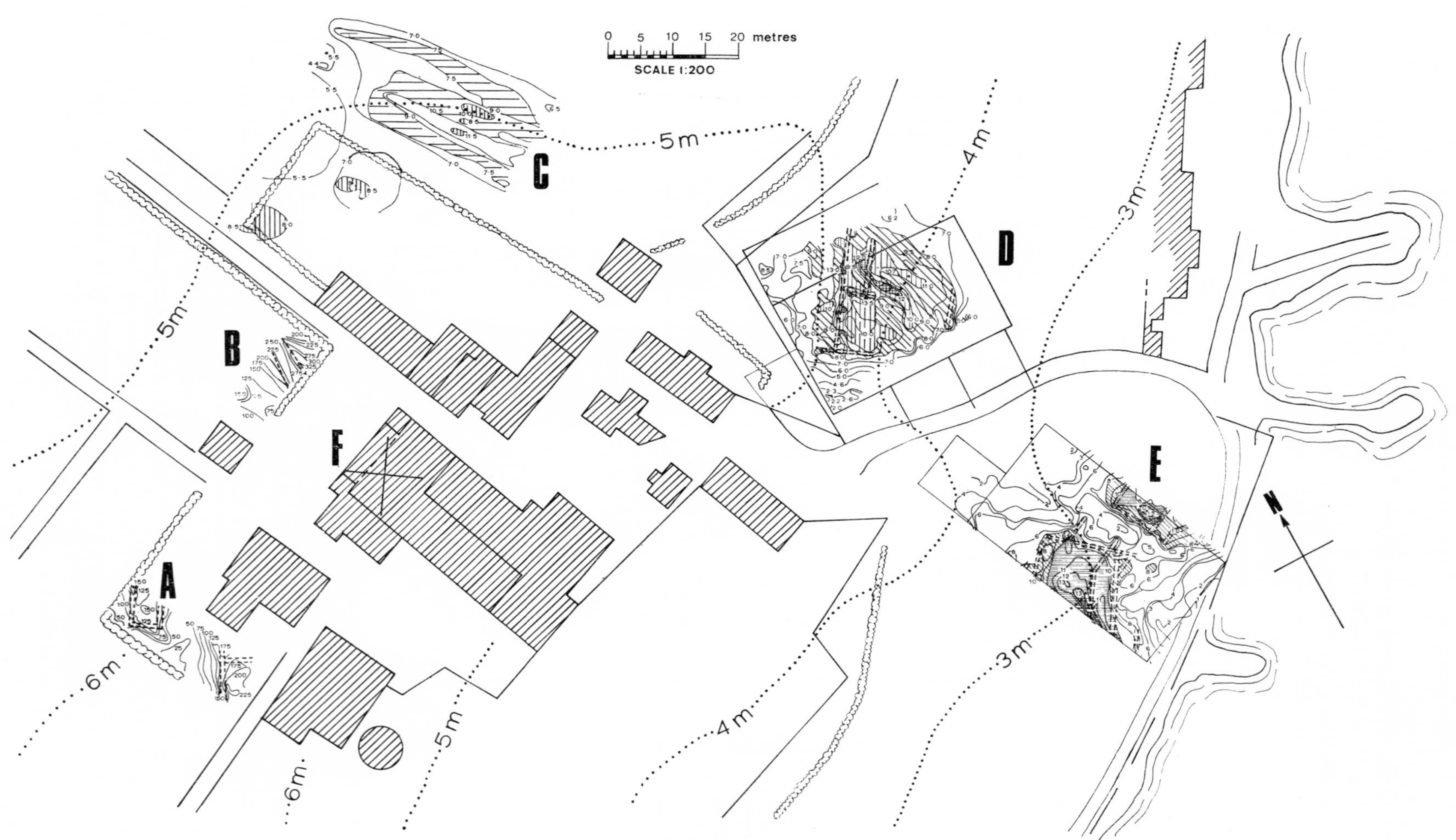

Fig. 17. Map showing the areas near the Villa (5) surveyed by resistivity measuring.

ed block of buildings a little distance southwards (Fig. 17D) seems well defined; a belt of low readings between it and the path probably corresponds to open ground; more sporadic traverses to the west and east seem to point to the existence of more buildings lower down the slopes of the hill on which the hamlet is situated. In its alignment the isolated building just referred to seems to conform to the orientation, attested or assumed, of structures in the hamlet region.

South-east of the road to the mole, another area (Fig. 17E) was surveyed, and again gave readings hinting at the existence of buildings. The resistivity contours here seem, on balance, to be on the same alignment as that of the "House of the Mosaics" some 100 m. further south-westwards, though part of the surveyed zone could be aligned in the same way as the structures higher up. Incidentally, the area of low resistivity within Fig. 17E may represent a lane between two buildings, or possibly a court or even gateway, allowing access to the upper reaches of the hill.

There was insufficient time to carry out repeated surveys of any one area with different probe spacings, which might have elucidated more detail of the structures, especially if the traverses had been re-aligned parallel to suspected walls. For example, Fig. 18 shows the resistivity measurements from two traverses, with 1 m. and 2 m. spacings, along the western boundary of area 17D. Both sets of readings show the double peak characteristic of a traverse across a solid piece of masonry, between 10 and 16 m. from the S.W. corner. However, there is very little correlation between the two sets between 16 and 25 m. from the corner, so that this is probably an area of tumble.

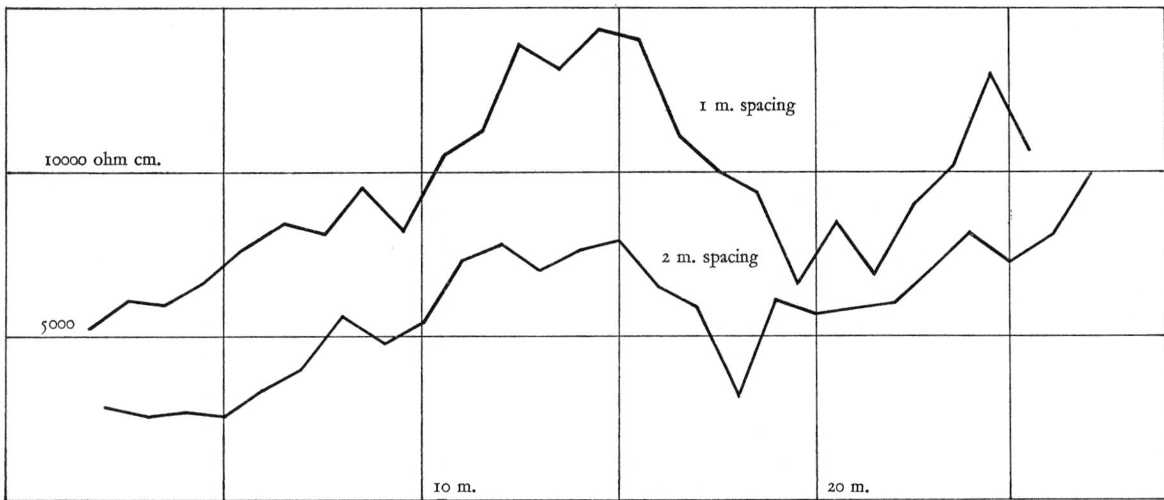

Fig. 18. Graphs representing resistivity measurements from two traverses (with 1m and 2m spacings) along the western boundary of area (5D).

CHAPTER SEVEN

THE SOUTH GATE EXCAVATIONS

General Topography

The traveller who comes to Motya by boat from Marsala will notice, near the south-western corner of the island, the remains of three big bastions which jut seawards from the city wall; even in their present diminished state they give a clear indication of their former strength and importance (cf. Pl. 8 : 1). Of these the one at the extreme south-west corner of Motya, and its more easterly neighbour (i.e. the central one of the three bastions) help to defend the entrance to the Cothon and basin (cf. plan, Pl. I). The central and easternmost of the three bastions, on the other hand, flank the South Gate and together with the adjoining wall they form part of the zone investigated (cf. Pl. 8 : 2).

Whitaker (1921, 177 ff.) wrote in some detail about the South Gate, the adjoining city wall and its bastions. He mentioned briefly the buildings inside the walls, of which very little was revealed in his time, but he nevertheless assessed correctly its character as a sailors' quarter (1921, 182). He noted the absence of a paved roadway leading in from the Gate, and from his plan (1921, 186) the absence of a radial road following the city wall on the inside is also obvious. On the other hand he observed, traced and described a roughly constructed wall just inside the Gate and which, running across the line of entry, completely blocked the access from the gateway to the city. This structure (Pl. 8:3—now shown to be a revetment wall) begins from a projection of the city wall on the north-west side of the Gate, and follows a semi-circular course for some 90 m. (wall XIX, cf. Plan III). Whitaker assigned its construction to the time of the final assault on the city (1921, 183-4). In addition, he observed that the opening of the Gate had been filled up by a barricade, probably at the time of the final siege: this he afterwards removed (1921, 182 and 179, fig. 19).

The picture of the South Gate region as Whitaker left it can thus be summed up as comprising the city wall, gate, and bastions, with no known features *extra muros*: inside the defences, the Cothon with the channel and quays, a very incompletely known civilian (mariners') quarter, and a blocking wall. Our first task was, therefore, to make a more intensive and detailed investigation of the region inside and outside the walls and of the little known civilian quarter, as well as of the town's defences; and also, as far as possible, to trace the historical development which this region has undergone.

Since our investigations show that the state of things revealed by Whitaker was preceded by stages when conditions were rather different, it seems best to describe these successive stages, discussing architectural and other features in their historical context as they are reached.

Natural Conditions

As has been stated in Part I the natural strata of Motya underlying recent soil consist essentially of heavy, greenish-yellow marine clays, locally capped by whitish tufa which tends to form a hard crust on its upper surface: the original red earth (terra rossa) is found immediately above this where the sequence has not been disturbed. Near the South Gate, the tufa above the clay survives only within a zone defined roughly by the City wall complex on the south, the Cothon on the north, the Cothon Channel on the west and Wall II on the east. Even here, no trace has been found of the hard top crust,

B. Emmison

Fig. 19. Theoretical reconstruction of the Town Wall (in section).

or the red earth above; they may have been removed for building stone and to make mud brick. Elsewhere the underlying clay is the surviving basic layer.

As a result, while the natural formation in this part of the island appears to be on the whole remarkably level, there is a slight rise where the tufa still covers the clay. A glance at Sections AA, (East to West—Plan IV) and BB, (North to South—Plan V) will convey the overall situation.

Above the basic tufa or clay, layers of generally shelly or gravelly sand occur in the regions near the sea, becoming deeper and more numerous as one approaches the water. This is well illustrated in Trench 6, which runs seawards from the outside of the South Gate (cf. Section I-I, Plan VIII). Here layer (37), the lowest reached above the natural clay, consists of a mixture of black sand and small gravel and seashell fragments; according to the detailed analysis undertaken by Mr. C. P. Nuttall of the British Museum (Natural History), given in appendix 1 below, this deposit may have been laid down in shallow water near a beach, or perhaps just above water on the adjoining shore. It seems that at the time when Phoenician occupation began there was an inlet extending towards the present position of the South Gate, and most of the area was liable to the deposition of sand by storm, floods, spray and wind.

In much of the area excavated to the north of the town wall, a blackish or dark sticky layer averaging some 20 cm in thickness was encountered, though this was not found in the eastern sector. It lay immediately above the natural clay or tufa, or above the sand spread over the natural subsoil. It appeared to consist mainly of the remnants of old swamp soil intermixed with clayey material and is apparently not native to the location where it is now found. In some places the earliest walls are associated with it, while in others the black layer shades upwards into streaks of black, interspersed with streaks of yellow sand. These latter betoken, or are associated with, the earliest walking levels.

This deposit is represented by layer (9) in the eastern half of the excavated zone (cf. Sections A-A, D-D, E-E, F-F on Plans IV, VI and VII; Pl. 12 : 3); further west, layer (13), visible in the western parts of Sections A-A and D-D, and in B-B (Plans IV, V, VI; cf. also Pl. 14 : 3 and 16 : 2) is similar in character.

The Settlement*

Phase IA

The earliest walls stand on the natural subsoil or the sand covering it, usually without any recognizabel foundation trenches through the black mud. They consist of limestone or conglomerate boulders and rubble, poorly coursed and bonded with clay mortar. In some place bigger blocks or slabs are also used. These walls, averaging 40-60 cm in width and 50 cm in height, represent the stone footings intended to carry upper walls of mud brick, which have now disappeared.

At the eastern limit of the excavation there are no certain traces of this phase near the present Town Wall. However, inside the curved revetment Wall XIX (in rooms 1-6) we find a system of walls arranged on a rectangular plan (cf. for this Plan III, and Pl. 13 : 1). The best preserved is Wall IIIA (a spine wall) which in places still exists to floor level, or a little above. From it, Walls XVIIA and XVIIIA branch off northwards, Walls XVIA and XXA southwards. Wall IIA, running likewise N-S, crosses IIIA, with which it is not bonded (there being a straight joint N and S of IIIA).

To the south IIA abuts on a big conglomerate boulder at the angle with Wall I (Pl. 12 : 3), roughly in line with a large ashlar block at the southern end of wall XXA; no trace of a connecting Wall between XXA and IIA is now visible. XXA may have continued further southwards: XVIA pretty certainly did, as a robber trench found on the alignment of its prolongation outside wall XIX shows. Walls I and VA (the latter partly hidden by later walls) are constructed mostly of bigger stones, and appear not to be bonded with Wall II (cf. Section A-A, Plan IV). Two other early walls (XIV-XV), encountered below Wall V in Room 8 may also belong to this phase, forming a continuation of VA, but they certainly existed in the next constructional Phase (IIA). Wall IVA, which enclosed Room 6 on the north, may have joined walling continuing the line of XIV.

The floor of the earliest building appears to have consisted of trodden clay, traces of which have survived in a few places. In Room 3 (Section F-F, Plan VII) there are some indications of a yellow floor (8) above black and yellow (9) with occupational material (7) above. In the adjoining Room 1 (*PBSR*, 1958, 8, fig. 4) the yellow and black layer (27) also exists directly over sand (28) above the yellowish-greeny clay, though a recognizable floor was not visible. In Room 4 these levels were not excavated; but Section A-A (Plan IV) in Room 5 shows a division between a dark brown to black bottom stratum

* In the light of fuller information now available the attribution of some of the walls to building phases in the preliminary report in *ALUOS* IV, 1964, p. 114 ff, has been modified. Walls which continued in use on the same alignment (with modifications) through phases I, II and III will be distinguished by the addition of A (for phase I), B (for phase II) and C (for phase III). Thus IIIB would be the stage of Wall III in use during phase II. As before, the designations Phase IA, IIA, and IIIA will be used to indicate the stage of ***construction***: while IB, IIB, IIIB refer to the periods of ***use and destruction.***

(9) and streaks of burnt debris and plaster above (8): the latter, a destruction deposit, evidently rests on a trodden floor. Room 6 shows a similar division. The adjoining Rooms 7-8 seem to be outside the western limits of our building, and probably belong to a later phase. Further to the east, in the sector penetrated by Pit A, only fragmentary evidence survives. Of the floors in Rooms 1, 1a, and 1b nothing remains. South of the big boulder at the angle of Walls I and II there are no structures and Room 1a may have been a large courtyard or a space open to the shore. However, in Room 2b north of Wall III (behind Section G-G, Plan VII) a patch of grey clay flooring remains above a yellow speckled layer similar to layer (9) which in turn overlies the natural subsoil.

No thresholds or door pivot stones survive, though it seems possible that the larger ashlar blocks at the south end of Wall XX may have served as a threshold. However, from what has been said we can discern the outlines of a large building, comprising rooms arranged symmetrically to the east and west of a courtyard (or possibly large room), with other rooms to the north of it. A passage or lane may have passed to the east of Wall XX. It seems possible that Wall III acted as a dividing wall, to the north and south of which there were different constructions. No trace of the original roofing, in particular roof tiles, was found among the debris of this building: we may assume it was covered by branches carrying a flat clay roof.

West of this building we find somewhat scattered and scrappy remains of other earlier structures. In Room 17a, Wall XXXII (Section D-D, Plan VI) should have been begun in this phase, though it continued without visible modifications in Phase IIA; and so too, perhaps should the lowest rough part of Wall XXXI (Section B-B, Plan V, and cf. Pl. 14 : 3) underlying the paved surface which forms a base for the later Town Wall. The same remarks apply to what are essentially the same constructive elements further westward in Room 17b (cf. Pl. 15 : 4). The scattered large boulders at the bottom of the trench there and in Room 21b may perhaps be remains of an early structure; the stone is not from the island. In Room 21c (cf. Section D-D, Plan VI and Pl. 16 : 1) the upper and lower paving, irregularly constructed from flagstones and boulders, is based on the natural tufa and butts against black mud (13), as Section D-D shows. It is an early element, the construction of which might belong to this phase. The total picture made up by all these features is presented in the plan, Plan X.

Date

Stratified evidence concerning the dating of Phase IA is available only from a limited number of *loci*, since in most of the excavated zone either the deepest layers were not reached, or later disturbances (such as Pits A and B) had affected the sequence down to natural subsoil. However, where the black sticky layer (9) survived above the natural subsoil (i.e. mainly in Rooms 5 and 6) a number of datable Greek sherds were found. Among these, nos. 6, 7, 9 and 10 (see catalogue, Volume II, Chapter 1)—all from Room 6 (9) (cf. Section F′-F′, Plan VI)—are from Corinthian kotylai ascribed to ca. 700 B.C.-675 B.C. This should mean that settlement in this part of the island could have started ca. 700 B.C., but that the actual buildings with which we are here concerned were only put up some 25 (or more) years later. The coarse wares from this stratum (nos. 354-367), (see Volume II, chapter 2) would fit such a date. These, on the other hand, present no evidence which would require a date lower than ca. 675-670 for the construction of the buildings discussed.

Phase IB. Occupation and Destruction of IA

The structures assigned to the first phase were found in a fairly ruinous condition. Walls were mostly reduced to stumps, the mud brick being absent above the stone footings which themselves had been pulled about and scattered, especially on the eastern side of Pit A. Where the floor survived, it was covered by débris likewise attesting destruction.

The ruined walls disintegrated into a loose, but substantial scatter of stones and boulders, especially to the east of Wall XX and just by the north-west corner of Room 28. Here a paved effect was produced as the stones had been walked on (cf. Pl. 10 : 1). A looser scatter was observed in the gateway (cf. Pl. 9 : 3). To the west of Wall XVI and its continuation southwards, the scatter of stones was not found. Another small pavement-like scatter of stones in Room 3a (south of Wall I—omitted in plan) may be similarly explained.

Débris layers assignable to this phase were discernible in various parts of the big building of Phase I especially in Rooms 1a and 1b, 5 and 6 (cf. Sections A-A, D-D, F-F, F′-F′, layers 7 and 8, and Pl. 12 : 3).

Date

The finds attributable to the occupation and destruction of buildings of Phase I come from the same neighbourhood as before. Greek sherd no. 63 (from Room 2(4)—section A-A, Plan IV) comes from a Corinthian skyphos of the middle of the 7th century B.C. while sherd No. 52 (from the débris layer (2) in Room 1b—(Section G-G, Plan VII) is a Siceliot copy of Greek types attributable to the first half of the 6th century (though contamination cannot be ruled out in the latter case). The occupation of the buildings should thus have continued through the 7th century and perhaps into the 6th.

Phase IIA

The fallen mud brick and other débris of Phase IB were shortly to be levelled in preparation for the erection of another set of rooms, laid out to a large extent on the lines of their predecessors. The make-up material associated with this reconstruction is not clearly divided from the débris levels below, though there may be a change in pottery. This applies to the levelling layers associated with the floors, particularly in Rooms 3, 5, 6 and part of 1 (cf. Sections A-A, D-D, F-F, F′-F′ (7), Plans IV, VI, VII, XI). Phase IIA also brought far more extensive occupation in the South Gate region, with new buildings occupying a considerable amount of previously vacant ground; and there seem to have been several sub-phases, even though it is difficult to separate them in detail.

In a number of places, we can discern the débris of structures of Phase IB which were levelled when the foundations of the succeeding Phase IIA were put down. Such levelling layers can be discerned in the Section A-A (Plan IV) in Room 5, and in the next-door Room 6 (Plan XI, Section F′-F′). In Rooms 3 and 1 such layers may also exist.

In the region of Pit A almost nothing firmly assignable to this phase appears to have survived, though the upper part of the rubbish covering remains of Phase I may be attributed to it (cf. Sections G-G, G′-G′ (2)—Plan VII, XI), except where it is contaminated by Pit A (especially near wall XIX).

In the area north of Wall III the western half of Wall XVIII in Room 2 was perhaps heightened: it retains a whitish filling (floor?) (cf. Section A-A (5)—Plan IV) including some pebbles which may, however, originally have continued further east. This was in turn overlaid by débris and filling, above which, with a very irregular, step-like broken edge, rises the area of pebble paving laid at the same levels as the pebble paving in room 5 to the west. The levels below this paving should also be attributed to phase IIA (cf. Sections A-A, G-G, G′-G′ (4)—Plans IV, VII, XI).

Elsewhere in the eastern part of the excavated zone it is difficult to identify layers attributable to this phase, since nearly everything was destroyed by Pit A.

In the region of the central building of Phase I the walls of the second phase are largely superimposed on those of the preceding stage; in places they are set slightly back or askew (as in Room 6). The stones employed to make the fairly crude, two-faced rubble walls are of medium size. Similar rubble also caps, somewhat discordantly, the lower work of Wall IIA, running across Wall III (in Room 3, Wall XII is founded at a higher level than Wall I and it probably belongs to the next Phase IIIA).

In Rooms 3-6 we can attribute Walls IIB, IIIB, IVB, VB (heightened) VIIIB (lower part), XIII and XIV to Phase IIA. Just east of Wall IIB above a step, north of Wall IIIB, what may be the foundations of a very rough wall of boulders shallowly founded in plaster, are visible (Wall XVIIIa). They include two fragments of a flat stone with a large central perforation, perhaps a broken stone anchor. Further south, Wall XIXa belongs to this stage; see below, p. 66.

The floors of this period, consisting of plaster (probably within rooms) and of pebbles irregularly set in plaster (perhaps in courtyards) have survived in a number of places.

In Room 3 (Sections D-D, F-F, Plan VI, VII) the plaster floor above (7) which originally went up to Wall XIII, is now broken by the insertion of Wall XII in Phase III. In Room 4 the grey plaster floor above (7) belongs to this phase and the same plaster, renewed several times, is also seen in Room 2, where it is cut by Pit A (cf. Tr. 3 (1955), Isserlin in *PBSR* 1958, 8 fig. 4 for the N.W. corner of Room 1; Layers 21-3 there equal (4) in Sections A-A, G-G.) In Room 5 there is a cobble paving set in the clay (cf. Pl. 13 : 2 and section G′-G′, Plan XI). Further east Pit A has removed all traces of this stage.

Essentially what is left of this complex can be described as a building with a long room or courtyard (Rooms 5 and 6) flanked by rooms on the south (where the structure may have continued under the town wall); extensions to the east are destroyed and any to the north are unexcavated. Structural elements are again lacking, though a gap, originally ca. 2 m wide (but later filled up) in Wall II, and extending northwards from a point 2.20 m. to the north of the intersection of Wall II with Wall III, may have been an entrance to room or courtyard 5-6, from the east. This latter was in use for domestic purposes since a hearth (shown in Section G′-G′, Pl. XI), and a fragment of a quern were found on the floor and another piece of quern in the floor make-up. Essentially the plan of the building probably continued that existing in Phase I.

So far as can be judged from the finds in our limited trenches, there is no evidence for other rooms immediately adjoining Wall V further west. However, some distance to the S.W., in Room 17a a floor above the hard brown (18) in Room 17 (cf. Sections B-B, D-D, Plans V, VI and Pl. 14 : 3) is pretty well at the same absolute level as the floors of Phase IIa further east. We may equate this floor and also the pavement-like top of Wall XXXI in section B-B, with the structures assigned to Phase IIA. Nearby, the N-S wall XXXII between Rooms 16 and 17a, founded in Phase I, was still in use. The pavement-like top of the wall underneath the Town Wall was also encountered in a limited sondage in Room 21d, and in 22a (cf. Pl. 15 : 4) after having run below the opening of the casemate in Room 17b (cf. section K-K, Plan IX). Wall XXIXB running E-W in Rooms 17a/17b parallel to the town wall and ca. 3 m. north of it (cf. section B-B on Plan IV) should also be assigned to this phase. We shall come back to it. Progressing westwards, we should attribute to this phase Wall XLI superimposed on the paved area in Room 21b, (see above). The pavement in Room 21c bears some slight cuttings which look as if the paving might have been slotted to receive the foundation courses of other lines of walling now removed: but it is difficult to be certain about this. It seems possible that Blocks A and B (cf. Pl. 16 : 1) now resting on the pavement may represent remnants of an ashlar building belonging to a stage within Phase II. In spite of their unusual size, however, they may, from the beginning, have formed part of the present tower structure, at the bottom of which they now stand. It should be noted that they are set, at different heights, one on the upper part of the pavement and the other on the lower (Section D-D, Plan VI). Perhaps this means that the pavement area was in a partly ruined state when these blocks were set on it.

All these walls are located in a narrow zone just north of the town wall. The area further northwards is occupied by what appears to be a large dump, about the character and history of which we are informed by Sections A-A (Plan IV) and B-B (Plan V). As the latter indicates, Wall XXIX lies on the southern end of this large mass of soil; Section AA shows that it extends between the Cothon channel in the west and Wall XIV in the east, and its northern end can be seen in Trench 20 (Section M-M).

The stratigraphic sequence in the area within these limits consists essentially of three layers: at the bottom there is blackish muddy soil (13); above it is dark mud (12) and on the top, black speckled soil (11). The black soil, as we saw, probably represents the same swamp earth which we found associated with Phase IA elsewhere; the blackish muddy soil and the black speckled soil can be most easily explained as representing spoil from the excavation of the Cothon channel and basin. This excavation would have penetrated first through swamp earth, and then into the underlying clay and tufa, and the character of the dumped material would have changed accordingly. As Section B-B also shows, the foundations of Wall XXIX are laid above the black soil (13), but into the dark mud (12) and the wall retains the black speckled soil (11): deposition of material may thus have continued for some time. Retaining walls corresponding to Wall XXIX seem to have fringed the dump elsewhere. To the west, wall XL, shown in Section A-A, founded on black muddy earth like XXIX, retains the filling. It is poorly built, with only one proper outer face on the west: originally it may have continued southwards as far as the tower, but Pit B has obliterated it. Further north, continuing the line, Wall XLb in Trench 18 is perhaps similar in date. Other sections of a retaining wall may have existed in Trenches 17, 19, and 20 but they have been robbed: cuttings visible in the natural subsoil indicate their presumed positions. A retaining wall delimiting the dump in a wide sweep seems a likely feature of Phase IIA. To the east, the foundation trenches cut for Wall VB-XIV appear to mark the end of the dump.

From the beginning the intention seems to have been to use the area which is covered by the dump, for domestic purposes. An indication is afforded by the well (W1) found in Room 12, which must have existed in Phase IIA or earlier: when the filling was subsequently deposited around it, the well-shaft was heightened and supported by a conical pile of rubble covered at the base by yellow clay (cf. Section B′-B′, Plan V. and, Pl. 14 : 4). Its continued use must have been regarded as desirable.

While the present line of the town wall delimits the constructions belonging to Phase IIA on the southern side, there are indications that they originally extended beneath it. Thus, to the south of Room 10, Trench 22, cut in an opening in the face of the Town Wall made by rainwash revealed, below a later filling of decayed mud-brick with occasional boulders, a plaster floor attributable to this phase. At a distance of 2.90 m from the outer face of the City Wall this floor abutted on a wall, still standing to a height of 1.30 m above the floor; it was covered with white plaster. This could have been the original rear wall of the building north of the city wall. Further to the east, in the South Gateway, robber trenches dug into the rubble of Phase II after its destruction seem also to indicate the existence of walls which have now disappeared, belonging perhaps to this period (Cf. Pl. 9 : 3, and Plan III). A definite, and important series of constructions belonging to Phase IIA was also discovered outside the Gateway (see below).

The Building Outside the South Gate

This large but very ruined building adjoins the western gate bastion (Cf. Plan III). The date of its foundation is uncertain; it could have belonged to Phase I, but was certainly in existence in Phase II. Neither its eastern nor its western limits have been determined and its southern extremity was in parts much destroyed by marine erosion. Near the Gateway, no traces of it appeared in Trench 8; and it is doubtful whether what appear to be remnants of a badly collapsed rubble wall (XLVIII) in Trench 6 (Section I-I, Plan VIII) belong to this complex.

In most places only the lowest foundation courses, or rather the bedding on which the foundations proper were to be placed, survive. Nowhere is any wall above foundation level still *in situ*, though some washed-out clay or mud deposits may have been remains of mud brick. It looks, in fact, as if at the time of the construction of the Town Wall, the building was truncated out of existence (cf. Section J-J, Plan VIII), but spot heights indicate that originally the top of its foundation could have reached a level roughly corresponding to the top of the wall foundations of Phase IIA, north of the City Wall (see

Section K-K, Plan IX). The discernible remainder, left after thorough robbing, consists of small rounded boulders with an outer facing of larger stones set into the natural clay: in one or two places these are still topped by irregular blocks of stone. Pl. 9 : 2 presents a typical stretch of this walling. The considerable width of the foundations, varying from ca. 1.20 to 1.55 m, their method of construction, and the size of the stones, all differ from the ordinary house foundations (which consist mostly of two-faced rubble walls some 50 cm in thickness).

The part of the building so far uncovered comprises a central room or courtyard (Room 25), ca. 6 m from N to S by 3.30 m from E to W, which contains, slightly off centre, a well cut into the natural clay. This courtyard is flanked by long narrow compartments, ca. 1.30-1.60 m in width; Room 26 to the east is fragmentary but more completely preserved Rooms 23 and 24 have been uncovered further to the west. To the north the building is truncated by the city wall and bastion. What appears to be a foundation trench for the latter cuts into it near the south-east corner.

Little can be said about the function of the building. The thickness of its walls seems to hint at a public rather than a private character, and the narrow rooms could be stores. Such an arrangement also recalls a casemate wall, known to have been employed by the Phoenicians for defence, though the width of the rooms exceeds those in normal casemates. This building could, in that case, have preceded the Town Wall as a work intended for defence, as well as for other purposes.

To regard it as a quay made up from compartments seems less likely in view of the presence of the well W3 in Room 25.

Like the other constructions attributable to Phase IIA the building outside the South Gate seems to have been in existence by the middle of the 6th century B.C. Among associated finds, a piece of wood, apparently a ship's timber, deserves notice (See Vol. II, chapter 6).

We noted above that there seem to be reasons to connect the construction of the Cothon channel and basin with Phase IIA. These features (shown in Pl. 17 : 1 and 2) are still under investigation, and it is intended to deal with them in a later volume: but something can already be said about the eastern quay flanking the channel and the ground immediately adjoining, subject to revision in the light of future exploration.

The quay along the Cothon Channel

This installation was first excavated and described by Whitaker (1921, 191 ff.). It is, as he stated, constructed of very good sandstone ashlar, though perhaps not all the ashlar blocks, which include stones deviating considerably from the average in size, were originally intended for this work. As our test trenches (Tr. 14, Tr. 15a, b, cf. Pl. 17:1, 2 and section L-L, Plan IX) revealed, the space between the southern end of the quay wall and the western end of the casemate construction was occupied by a very rough cobbled layer (pavement? (33), upper half) above grey sand, which appears to date from the time when the casemate or store building was in use, and associated finds assigned it to the second half of the 6th century B.C. The quay wall appears to have been laid into a cut in in the cobble layer. So also was a wall foundation (XLII cf. Pl. 18:1) running E-W just south of the wing wall, the function and date of which are not yet clear.

The Tower, Room 21

It would further appear that the construction of the Tower, the ruins of which flank the eastern side of the Cothon channel north of the city wall goes back to this late stage of Phase IIA: for the quay paving appears to be integrated with it, ending against the line of the original west wall (cf. for this Plan IV). The original shape of the Tower is no longer entirely clear: in particular the south wall appears to have extended under the north face of the Town Wall and wing wall. Only the east wall of the tower (which was constructed on top of the slab pavements in Room 21c) was found standing above foundation level. As Pl. 16 : 2 shows, it consists of ashlar blocks of good quality but unequal size. The coursing is somewhat irregular, and the inequalities are evened out by stone chips (cf. Whitaker's type E walling, 1921, 147, fig. 10). What remains of the building measures ca. 4 m from east to west, and 6 m from north to south in its original state. The tower seems to have included some internal partitions (a few stones marking the beginning of an angle are still in position next to Block A). The rubble walling to the south of the big ashlar block B (cf. Plan III and Pl. 16 : 1) may indicate the position of an original doorway later blocked up. From what has been said, it will be obvious that Phase IIA continued for some not inconsiderable time. It must also have involved a number of sub-phases: these include the rebuilding of the area occupied earlier by the domestic structures of Phase IA; the erection of the building outside the South Gate and bastion; the construction of the Cothon channel and its masonry quays, and the deposition of the dump linked with these events. However, it is not possible at present to be specific in detail about the dating, relative or absolute, of these sub-phases, beyond what has been stated.

Date

Dating evidence for Phase IIA as a whole, even in general terms, is still not plentiful, and much of what there is comes from the same localities as before.

Sherds of 7th century date are contained in IIA floor make-ups, as in Room 6. However, the Greek sherds, catalogue nos. 15 and 23 (Corinthian kotylae, Room 29), no. 78 (same location-Corinthian kylix), no. 33 (Corinthian kotyle from Room 17b (17), cf. Section D-D, Pl. VI), nos. 44, 48 (Corinthian kotyle and Siceliot imitation—both from Room 29) take us from the late 7th century into the early 6th. Some of the sherds in Room 22 may belong to Phase IIB rather than IIA, but in view of what was said earlier about the dating of Phase IB, a construction date for the buildings of Phase IIA inside the South Gate over structures of Phase I within the early decennia of the 6th century, and perhaps as late as ca. 550 B.C. should not be far wrong.

As for the mysterious building outside the South Gate, the fact that the layers concerned are mostly unsealed makes it difficult to feel certain about the time when it was constructed. Room 25, layer (30) (section J-J, Plan VIII) has furnished a sherd from a Corinthian kotyle (no. 27) of the early part of the 6th century: no. 40, also from Room 25 (30) is of the same period. However, there are later (5th century Attic) sherds from this same level (nos. 271, 272, 273, 279) which probably owe their presence to intrusion.

Sherds found in the "dump" are predominantly of the 7th century (nos. 3 from Room 14 (11); no. 19 from Room 18 (11); no. 109 from Room 12 (14), cf. section B-B, Plan V); but sherd no. 280 from layer (13) above the well casing in Room 12 (section B′-B′, Plan V) comes from an Attic lekythos datable after the mid-5th century. Deposition here may have continued up to fairly late times, in fact until the area was built over in Phase IIIA.

Evidence concerning the date when the Cothon channel was dug and the quays built is not yet complete, and present deductions may have to be modified as investigations proceed. Since pottery of the late 6th century was found in layers stratigraphically earlier than the quay, the latter could have been constructed towards the end of that century: or alternatively in the early part of the 5th century, if some 5th century sherds found in unsealed locations prove in the light of additional information not to be intrusive. There is at present no indication that the quays belong to more than one period.

We cannot at present give any more detailed indication of the time within Phase IIA when the original Tower was erected.

Phase IIB. Destruction

In certain parts of the region there are indications of a substantial destruction at the end of Phase

IIA. Outside the South Gate, the big casemate building was reduced to a shallow stump; as the sections (J-J, K-K, Plans VIII, IX) show, this was covered by a layer of clay (30) in places interlaced with shelly sands derived from the shore. Similar clays (30) are encountered also in the Gate region, in Trench 5, Section I-I, Plan VIII. In addition, test Trenches 5 a-e (also given on Section I-I) have shown that the whole of the present Gateway is situated over debris (covered by a later clay deposit) which should belong to the demolition of the wall of Phase IIA originally present in this region (cf. Pl. 9 : 3). Similar demolition debris are also present in rooms 28 and 29 inside the Gate (cf. Section H'-H', (28) Plan, VIII). Destruction layers are recognizable also further west along the inside of the town wall. Similarly, in the southern part of Room 16 an earthy layer, just below the foundations of the town wall covers floors of Phase IIA.

Date

Deposits of Phase IIB comprise the occupation materials of Phase IIA, as well as the later debris covering these. Though there are still some 7th century sherds on floors, yet together the finds seem to point to occupation extending from the early or mid-6th into the 5th century. Sherds no. 46 from Room 28 (27) (cf. Section H'-H', Plan VIII), no. 85 from Room 6 (10) (cf. Section F'-F', Plan XI) cover the earlier, 6th century part of this range. Sherd no. 335, from an Attic olpe of the 5th century found in Room 5(10), cf. Plan XI, Section G'-G', belongs to the later part. The closing date for the destruction of Phase IIA is somewhat indefinite, but it may have been near the middle of the 5th century B.C. or perhaps a little later.

Phase IIIA

Later in the 5th century B.C. the destruction described in the preceding section was followed by a major rebuilding. In particular the city defences, the ruins of which now dominate the scene near the South Gate, were begun. They were built on a new alignment set back from the frontage of the earlier casemate construction, and impinged in turn on what had been the residential region during Phase IIA. The housing complex was rebuilt on this restricted area, but it was now extended into the zone over the dump-complex. Both the town wall and the inhabited area to the north underwent some modification in this final phase before the catastrophic events of 397 B.C.

The Town Wall: Plan and methods of construction

The layout and the essential features of construction of the South Gate and adjoining walls and bastions were described in some detail by Whitaker (1921, 177 ff.), whose small map of the region (1921, 186, Plan E) usefully supplements the text by bringing out the very irregular plan of the whole complex. In what follows we shall amplify his views in the light of our own results.

The fortifications appear to consist of a stone socle and an upper work. The foundations, where tested in a deep sounding almost to water level below the floor of the casemate (Room 22, Section K-K, Plan IX), consisted of a solid packing of rough slabs and boulders, probably the continuation of the pavement—like Wall XXXI ascribed to Phase IIA. The floor thus belongs apparently to Phase II, and was adapted to its new function within the defences. Older work of this stage seems to have been generally incorporated and adapted for its secondary role as part of the foundation for the superimposed town wall.

Above these foundations the wall rises. It is provided with a stone facing on both the inner and outer sides, preserved to an average height of ca. 2-3 m; the foundations of these facings, where visible on the north and south sides of the wall, incorporate a number of large blocks irregularly placed and evidently taken from some earlier structure. Where cut by Trench 22, the inner facing was ca. 1 m. thick. As Whitaker noted, the masonry of the facing was mainly built of small quarry-split slabs laid in irregular courses and bound together by mud mortar (see Pls. 8 : 2; 9 : 1; Pl. 15, 1, 2, 4—Whitaker's type C, (1921, 145 fig. 8)) except for some ashlar with marginal drafting in the S. Gateway (Pl. 8 : 3, 9 : 3). On the inside of the wall small limestone fragments predominate. On the outer side however, large slabs or blocks of tenacious schistose stone of the kind elsewhere used for towers and bastion foundations (Whitaker, 1921, 142-4) predominate on the south and west sides of the bastion (Pl. 9 : 1). Such slabs also form much of the top of the bastion (similar stones are also noticeable on top of the tower (Room 21, cf. Pl. 16 : 1 top left) and in the wing wall running across the quay (cf. Pl. 18 : 1). Locally, the facing does not rise vertically for all its height, but the upper part is set back by one or two "steps".

While the bastion was apparently pretty solidly made of stone, Tr. 22 showed that the core of the Town Wall comprised, at least in places, a mud-brick fill. This appears to have been capped by a levelling layer of stone running above the core filling and bringing the total height of the stages mentioned to ca. 3 m: it would have provided a flat surface on which to place the next constructional section. This consisted of mud-brick, which was best preserved east of Room 22 (Pl. 15 : 1). The flattish bricks were probably made from the local natural red and grey earth and included many pebbles and grains of limestone grit; they are well laid in a regular bond, the courses being cemented together by mud mortar. The commonest brick sizes were 42-50 × 10-11 × 25-20 cm; others (32 × 8 cm—third dimension uncertain) were observed in the filling of the casemate (room 22). Mud mortar between courses might range up to 10 cm in thickness. The original height of this mud-brick stage above the lower work is not known, but on the basis of our findings Whitaker's original assumption of a total height for the town-wall of ca. 8-9 m. in all (1921, 152) seems reasonable. No signs of tie-beams were found in the brick-work. Neither do we know what the outer facing of the brick wall was like. Hower, since it is known that the walls carried heavy stone battlements (1921, 180), it seems preferable to assume that the stone facing was carried right up to a rampart walk at least on the outer side of the wall: from the recovery of a number of flat stone slabs (in Tr. 4a (1955)) which appeared to have slipped from the upper part of the wall, it seems likely that the wall top was provided with a paving of flat stone slabs serving as a "chemin de ronde" behind the parapet and battlements. The discovery nearby of stone gutters (cf. Whitaker, 1921, 182) makes it clear how the rain water was drained off. It is not entirely obvious just where the stone cornice, parts of which were noted by Whitaker (ibid.) would have been placed: perhaps they were more a feature of the Gate than of the wall in general, though Krischen accepted a coping in his reconstruction of the city wall of Motya (Krischen, 1941, 34-5 and fig. 33-35). Fig. 19 gives a schematic reconstruction of the wall on the basis of our present knowledge.

This description of the wall must however be modified by reference to important features existing in certain parts of it, and we must discuss separately the main sectors making up the defences in this region: the Town Wall east of the South Gate, the gate itself, the western section of the Town Wall, the bastion and casemate, and the Tower flanking the channel.

The Town Wall East of the South Gate

At the eastern limit of the excavations Tr. 4a dug in 1955 (cf. *PBSR* 1958, 10 fig. 5, our Pl. 11 : 2) against the inner face of the city wall, shows a clear distinction between the upper part of the defences (above the offset covered by the filling (11) (loc. cit.) and what is below. The upper face is obviously of the kind proper for a free-standing wall, whereas below, under a belt of very small rubble, highly irregular courses of rough stone placed above a spread of even rougher boulders are encountered. This lower part looks as if early masonry has been reused for a foundation, and apparently this wall was intended from the start to be hidden below ground level by means of an adjoining earth filling (11). Further west, however, in Rooms 28-9 the smooth facing of the city wall descends right down to foundations level (cf. section H'-H', Plan VIII); here, immediately beside of the gateway, the filling banked up against the lower wall in Tr. 4a was evidently not intended to be put in though a fill was in fact dumped inside Room 28 when that structure was built. Similarly on the outside of the Town Wall, Tr. 4b (1955) (Isserlin in *PBSR* 1958, 10, fig. 5, and Pl. 11 : 3 in the present volume) shows that the offset above foundations was meant to be seen, and the face above, though weathered, is well finished. The gateway and the outside of the wall appear thus to have arisen from the shore level; whereas a little distance inside the Gate, where the Town Wall succeeded earlier work, it was apparently connected with a higher ground level from the time of its inception.

The Gateway

As our trenches show, the foundations of the walls flanking the gateway to the right and left were placed on disturbed rubble crossed by some robber trenches, which had originated from the levelled walls constructed in Phase IIA. This rubble was in turn covered by a bed of clay, found in a somewhat disturbed condition owing to many pits (cf. Section I-I, Plan VIII). This clay level may originally have carried paving, though Whitaker found none when he excavated in the gateway (1921, 182). However a limited sounding outside the south-west corner of the gate revealed an arrangment of flat slabs immediately adjoining the corner, one of which is tied into the masonry at the angle of the gate (cf. Plan III). These slabs look like the remains of paving just in front of the Gate, the main paving inside the gateway having presumably been removed at the time of the siege, when the gate was barricaded (1921, 182). As Whitaker also noticed, the narrowing of the gateway leaving only a restricted central entry (1921, 178—cf. our plan, and Pl. 8 : 3) is a late feature which may not long have preceded the fall of the city. The central threshold stone looks, in fact, as if it had been taken from a house such as those found by Soprintendente Tusa in the centre of the island (cf. *Mozia* V, fig. 4). The somewhat irregular layout of the gateway, implied in Whitaker's sketch plan, deserves to be noticed.

Room 28, a ruined structure trapezoidal in plan, built of rubble with ashlar corners and set back ca. 1 m from the north east corner of the Gateway (cf. Plan III, and Pl. 10 : 2) is not bonded into the city wall and its eastern end is founded on a sloping filling (Section H'-H' (25), (26)-Plan VIII) which seems to correspond to layer (10) in Trench 4a. It looks like a secondary addition not provided for in the original plan. In contrast to the good outer face of this construction, the inner side of the walls was left rough: they were evidently not meant to be seen, or even perhaps never intended to be free-standing but rather to retain a filling. Perhaps Room 28 formed the base for some stairs giving access to the "chemin de ronde" from the gateway. Entrance to it might conceivably have been gained from the west side of the trapezoidal Room 28 (visible, Pl. 10 : 2) where there is a big threshold stone: however, this is well above the level of the threshold of the gateway proper. Alternatively steps or other means of access would be required of which no trace remains; Room 28 was perhaps built at a time when a good deal of rubbish had collected in the gateway, and thus fairly late in the history of the city.

The Western Section of the Town Wall

This is everywhere superimposed on earlier constructions attributable to Phase IIA. The inner face of the wall stands on earlier house floors and wall stumps: in Trench 5a the foundation trench for the wall clearly penetrates into layers associated with Phase II (Section E-E (22), (8), Plan VII). The wall face rises from a level approximately the same as that to the east of the South Gate. A noticeable feature is an internal salient which begins ca. 4.5 m from the gateway and projects 2 m northwards before the wall turns west. The lower parts of this salient are probably in part derived from domestic structures (wall V is incorporated into it); the upper portion comprises large ashlar blocks and a column laid endways, which may have come from some public building, and were put to this secondary use when the City Wall was erected (cf. Pl. 12 : 2). The south face likewise overrides the stumps of the building with casemate-like rooms, attributed to Phase IIA, though denudation has made the evidence less clear and defined than on the north side.

The Western Bastion and Casemate

The western bastion juts out from the southern face of the Town Wall. It is not well preserved, and part of it has been robbed down to the lowest courses. What remains it essentially a stone socle, in places preserved up to a top level formed of large slabs; the mud-brick top which must once have crowned it has gone (cf. Pl. 9 : 1; Section K-K, Plan IX). This bastion is backed up against the Town Wall, which here includes a casemate (Room 22) now partly denuded, and blocked by a filling of mud-brick. The line of division between bastion and wall runs along the westward prolongation of the outer face of the Town Wall. This suggests that the bastion may be a secondary addition to the wall, a supposition perhaps strengthened by the use, mostly, of large slabs of schistose grey stone, in its construction, in contrast to the yellow limestone of the casemate wall. Furthermore a window-like opening of ashlar (found smashed by stone robbers working from a pit above) is placed where its splayed opening could have acted as an arrow slit in a wall face of earlier date than the bastion on the above mentioned alignment. The bottom of this "window" (Pl. 14, 5) is set 40 cm above the casemate floor; it is 32 cm wide at its narrowest, but more outside, and still stands to a height of 40 cm; its original height is unknown. However, the present outer face of the casemate is bonded to the stonework of the bastion, and if the Town Wall was originally a separate construction preceding the bastion the distinction has been obliterated. Within the latter a small sounding showed the existence of a layer of rounded yellow boulders immediately below the top layer of large slabs; but the sounding was not carried deeper. The casemate comprises an access corridor (Room 22a) and the main room (Room 22). Entrance from the city was gained by a door, 1.25 m wide, through the inner face of the Town Wall: jambs consist of several pieces of ashlar set on edge; there is no threshold stone but only footings of small rubble and boulders, on which the jambs were set (Pl. 15 : 1,2). When found, the doorway was blocked with rubble, the rough inner side of which retained a brick filling founded on débris in which a triangular arrowhead was imbedded. From the door the passage, Room 22a, led in, giving access to the main casemate, Room 22 (ca. 4.20 by 3 m) after having turned west at right angles. The walls of the corridor and of the room, where preserved, consist mainly of small stones, but include good ashlar carefully laid, some of it perhaps in secondary use. All the walls are apparently bonded into each other. Well coursed mud-brick topped the stone: there are no indications that the casemate had been roofed over. The floor consisted of well laid flags (originally part of the construction of Phase II) covered by a layer of clay (cf. Pl. 15 : 2). The main room of the casemate was found badly ruined; the northern side is denuded almost down to floor level. Since we did not clear the mud-brick filling down to the floor everywhere, we can only describe the upper parts of the surrounding walls where they were revealed by digging. Of these the best preserved northern wall (which forms part of the inner facing of the Town Wall) does not survive to the top of the casemate door immediately adjoining it on the east. The top part of the existing facing is poorly made, and includes some very irregular patches of rubble, besides a piece of cavetto cornice in secondary use. Perhaps we are here dealing with the results of some late repairs. Five metres to the west of the casemate door the inner facing of the Town Wall ends in a jagged edge. This is ca. 50 cm. short of the point where the Town Wall would originally have joined the tower. The junction has obviously been removed by stone robbing. In his sketch plan (1921, 186 Plan E) Whitaker shows the tower as jutting out from the wall; it is difficult to say to what extent this may represent the actual state of things he found (with the junction of Tower and wall still intact) rather than a reconstruction on paper. At present the wall facing, where broken off in a jagged edge, is seen to rest on two large blocks of stone which in their turn are bedded on the layer of yellow-brown clay forming part of the rubble streaks originating in the destruction deposits of Phase IIB. The west wall of the casemate seems likewise to be founded on these stones, and the outer western wall of the bastion is also superimposed on the layer of debris associated with Phase II.

The Tower

Whatever the shape or function of this building in Phase II may have been (v. supra, p. 55), the Tower in its final shape was a solid structure, the core of which was filled with layers of clay and rubble, roughly coursed to give it strength (Pl. 16 : 1 top left). At the apex of this filling there are a few slabs of schistose grey stone of the same kind as that used in the Town Wall bastion. Possibly the Tower received its final shape when the bastion was built. Nothing survives of the upper part of the structure to give a clue to its special defensive function: however from Whitakers sketch (1921, 186, Plan E) it seems likely that it was one of a pair guarding the entrance to the Cothon channel on its eastern and western flanks.

The Houses North of the Town Wall

Phase IIIA saw the reconstruction of the built-up area inside the city defences on lines not radically different from previous plans. To this was now added the space on top of the dump. There were several sub-phases connected with reconstructions of the buildings (for a panoramic view, see Pl. 11 : 1).

A first stage, recognizable in the area of Rooms 7-20 is associated with floors immediately above the "black flecked" filling (11) (Sections A-A, B-B, Plans IV, V and Pl. 11 : 1). Pits and other later disturbances dug from higher levels have, however, left sizable gaps in ground-plans of the buildings. Denudation has likewise removed floors, especially on the west, as seen in Section B-B (Plan V). In part of Room 15 the floor is lost, but its position can be defined by the upper surface of layer (11) (black flecked). In Room 12 a plastery streak only survives. In Room 14 the floor is missing in part, in Rooms 18, 19 and 20 the floors are wholly missing. Floors of this period are well preserved next to the town wall in Rooms 17-17a (Sections B-B, D-D, Plans V, VI) and in Room 10 (Sections C-C, D-D, Plans V, VI over layer (21), where they abut on the foot of the Town Wall at a corresponding level. Well W2 in Room 10, a cistern into which water was led by carefully laid clay pipes from the town wall, was now in use; we cannot be sure, at present, whether it also existed in Phase II.

Walls attributable to this first sub-phase are XXIV and XXV (Section C-C, Plan V), XXVIa and XXIX (Section B-B, Plan V), XXXV, XXXVI-VII, XXXVIII and XXXIX (Cf. Section A-A, Plan IV). (Other walls of this phase may exist, but our limited trenches have not revealed them.) The same phase is apparently also represented over most of the zone just north-west of the South Gate, where we noted the existence of a large building in Phases I and II. Here an intermission between Phase IIIA and the preceding IIB is hinted at, since the walls of Phase IIIA, while mostly on the same alignment as before, rest on earth or débris covering earlier masonry, even though these intervening layers are not substantial. Thus Wall IIC in Room 6 is placed on a layer of débris above earlier work; Wall VII which now divides the courtyard Rooms 5 and 6 is founded on the same debris; Wall VC, is also partly founded on earth. However, Wall XII (Section D-D, Plan VI) is directly superimposed on wall XIII without an intervening deposit, the change of direction between XIII and XII is probably due to the wish to join the later wall to the Town Wall salient. The cross wall Va dividing up the lane constituted by Rooms 8 and 9 was put in now, or possibly later—perhaps indeed as late as Phase IV. What remains of the floor belonging to this phase is probably mostly the make-up rather than the top dressing. It is represented by layers consisting largely of yellow clay, such as are found in Rooms 3, 3a, 4, 5 and 6 (cf. Sections A-A, D-D, F-F, Plans IV, VI, VII, and cf. Sections F′-F′, G′-G′, Plan XI). Grey floors also link the complex just discussed with walls VI and IX beyond the lane, Rooms 8-9 (cf. Section D-D, Plan VI). Originally such clay layers may have been capped in places by pebble pavements, and in Room 2 parts of such a pavement survive, west of Pit A, on top of the clay into which the pebbles are set (Cf. Section A-A, Plan IV, with Section G′-G′, Plan XI).

This complex of rooms offers at this stage rather more clues as to its architectural nature than were available for earlier stages. The double-faced rubble foundations bonded with clay mortar carried mud-brick walls which, to judge by surviving fragments were originally faced with white plaster; in one or two places fragments of bright red plaster were found which may have come from living rooms in an upper story. A central door in Wall VIII (heightened) between Rooms 3 and 4 is now discernible; to Rooms 5, and 6, now divided by Wall VII, Room 6a is now added in the north. To the east of Wall II, in Room 30, there was a well (W 4); so that the room was probably a courtyard delimited on the east by a robbed wall XXII, traces of which were encountered in Trench 21, Plan III.

The existence of the Siceliot Greek roof-type made up from flat tiles, the joints between which were covered by ridge tiles of semicircular section, (Lawrence, 1957, 108, fig. 58) is confirmed by the existence of numerous flat and curved tile fragments and nails found among the debris.

A number of wells or cisterns in this urban complex deserve notice, though their locations do not seem to follow any obvious plan. None of the wells shows signs of an original waterproof plaster coating on the inside, and since in antiquity the sea level was apparently lower than now, the ground water which they tapped (Well W2 when found still contained water at the bottom) may have been rather less contaminated by salinity than at present. (The deep well now in use near Villa Whitaker draws brackish and undrinkable water). Well W2, however, was made to receive rainwater from the Town Wall, through a carefully constructed system of terracotta pipes: so it may also to some extent have functioned as a cistern. The preservation and use of rainwater must in fact have been of great importance at Motya. Well W2 was provided with a terracotta cover of Greek type, which could be reconstructed and is described in Vol. II.

The existence of a stone water spout which projects slightly from the town wall in Room 10, next to the point where the clay pipe originates deserves notice. It belongs to the house of Phase IIA now partly engulfed in the Town Wall. Where the water for this earlier installation came from we cannot say without additional excavation.

In spite of much destruction caused by later events (and in particular the digging of Pits A and B) it is now possible to discern at least the outlines of some urban planning in this zone. On the east, there seems to be an *insula*, made up of houses meeting back to back along the east-west wall III. Well W4 probably was situated in the courtyard of the more northerly of these two houses. To the west, this complex was bordered by a narrow lane (Rooms 7-9/9a), which was later subdivided by transverse walls. A second *insula* seems again to have comprised two houses built back to back, along Wall XXVII. The courtyard of the more southerly house included the well, W2 while the more northerly building was served by Well W1. There may have been a third complex still further west. Pit B has obliterated whatever there may have been near the town wall, but Rooms 19 and 20 seem to have formed part of a house divided from its eastern neighbour by the lane (Room 18) between Walls XXXV and XXXVI. (No special road construction, or make-up, however, seems to have been applied to this lane, which was apparently simply an open space, as Section AA (Plan IV) shows).

While this urban pattern shows some vague and general form of planning, the houses themselves, as far as we can tell, are individually laid out without any close adherence to a standard pattern. The elements making up the plan of buildings in Phase IIIA are shown on Plan X; while Fig. 20 opp. p. 64 gives an artist's impression of the settlement in the excavated zone at this stage. Evidence of the existence of a secondary sub-stage within Phase IIIA can be discerned in the zone just north of the Town Wall, made up by Rooms, 9, 9a, 10, 15, 16 and 17a. Here, as Sections B-B, D-D (Plan V, VI) show, a second plaster floor occurs (above layer 15) though this is robbed near Well W2 and further east; Wall X above IX ties in with this floor and wall XI further east seems also to relate to it by level; the latter wall forms the limit beyond which this stage cannot now be traced eastwards. Westward features belonging to this secondary stage have been truncated owing to the digging of Pit B. To the north, as Section B-B indicates, erosion has likewise removed the floor, except for a narrow band adjoining wall XXVII on its northern side (cf. Section B-B, Plan V). In Room 13a the bottom-half of a Punic store jar (type 703) was found where it had stood in a hole in the floor, but the plaster floor itself had been largely eroded. It is visible in Pl. 10:2. Room 15 contained the lower part of a round clay oven but its upper part above floor level was likewise obliterated by erosion. Similarly, Walls XXXVI-XXXIX are reduced to stumps and Well W1 lost its top through robbing.

Date

Evidence for dating this phase is much more plentiful than for earlier ones. Some of it comes from rooms and trenches already referred to, but to these can be added Rooms 10-20 in the western half of the zone, where levels belonging to this stage were excavated. They represent mostly make-up, or fillings below the floors of Phase IIIA. While there is still a good number of items which had originated in the 6th or even 7th centuries B.C. (especially in the region of the "dump" below Rooms 10-20) the significant pottery belongs to the 5th century, and particularly its last quarter. In Room 4, sherds nos. 284-5 from Attic lekythoi, of a type which is elsewhere attributable to the late 5th century, come from the make-up (10) of the floor of Phase IIIA, (Section F-F, Plan VII). In Room 5 the corresponding make-up for the floor of IIIa (10) (shown in Section G′-G′, Plan XI) has furnished sherd no. 205 (Siceliot imitation of Attic lekythos of ca. 425 B.C.); nos. 215, 223 (fragments of Attic and Siceliot cup-skyphos, late 5th century); no. 262 (lamp, ca. 475-425); no. 298 (fragment of crater, ca. 470 B.C.).

In room 7, sherd no. 217 from a Siceliot vase imitating an Attic cup-skyphos of ca. 500-480 B.C. belongs again to the floor make-up (10). In Room 30, the presumed packing round the shaft of Well W4 produced sherd no. 157 (Attic skyphos, ca. 425-400).

In Rooms 16-17a-17b a very detailed stratigraphic sequence comprising, as we saw, two subphases illustrated in section B-B, D-D, Plans V and VI, has produced the following dating evidence. Disregarding a number of earlier sherds we find that the make-up (16) below the main floor of IIIA in Room 16 is dated by sherd no. 147 (Attic skyphos of ca. 425-400). The floor between (16) and (15) directly above the layer just referred to, contained, in Room 17a, sherd no. 156 (Attic skyphos ca. 430 B.C.) and in Room 17b, sherd no. 184 (handleless bowl, ca. 425 B.C.). From layer (15) make-up of the final floor of Phase IIIa came, in Rooms 17a and 17b, sherd no. 146 (Attic skyphos, ca. 425-400). From all these it seems likely that the main stage of building construction in Phase IIIA should go back to ca. 430-425: even if we assume that some of the sherds may have been trodden in when the floor was in use, we should be inclined to place the beginning of the phase well after 450 B.C. The locally attested secondary stage began perhaps not many years before the fall of the city in 397 B.C.

As regards the construction of the Town Wall, sherd No. 310 (from an Attic skyphos of the later part of the 5th century B.C.) came from mud-brick *in situ* near the Casemate, Room 22, and sherd no. 292 (apparently from a Siceliot or Campanian feeding-cup of the later 5th century) was found in the filling of the Tower (Room 21). This evidence seems to indicate a date similar to the one suggested earlier for the construction of the buildings within the fortifications.

Lastly, outside the South Gate, in Trench 6 (30) and (37)—the shallow water or beach-layer immediately north and south of the fragmentary wall XLVIII—a number of Attic sherds as well as bones and other rubbish were found. These include No. 111 (Siceliot, 7th century?) no. 144 (Attic skyphos, ca. 425-400); no. 300 (Attic fragment, later 5th century). Evidently this litoral fringe was liable to be used as a waste zone where rubbish from the city was discarded, more especially during the last phase in the city's history.

Phase IIIB

This phase covers the great siege of 397 B.C. and its immediate aftermath. Since we are here (and in the final Phase IV) dealing with surface deposits which have been much disturbed and often largely removed, it is not always easy to come to definite conclusions. Our analysis must therefore remain somewhat tentative.

We begin east of the South Gate, in the neighbourhood of Room 29 and Tr. 4a outside Room 28 (illustrated in Sections H-H, H'-H', Plan VIII). In our 1955 Report (Isserlin in *PBSR* 1958, 11-12) we took the layers (4) and (5) of Tr. 4a to represent the surface at the time of the great siege. On reconsidering the position in the light of fuller evidence, we feel that the surface assignable to that period should probably be layer (10/9) of Tr. 4a. This would conform satisfactorily with the presence of a number of arrowheads in (10).

In the gateway, we have nothing to add to Whitaker's observations, in particular concerning the late narrowing of the entry referred to (1921, p. 182). However, concerning the date of the curving revetment wall XIX we have changed our view (originally expressed in ALUOS, IV, 1962-3, p. 116-7). This structure is built above the broken stump of Wall XIXA. A continuation of XIX B (of period IIA) apparently once existed, for layers heaped up against it in Section G'-G' (Plan XI) were found to be continued by similar layers further south-west. This wall was breached when Pit A—more exactly A1, v. infra, was dug, and subsequently a narrower revetment wall was built on the stump to retain the filling of the pit. A horizontal joint in the wall roughly at the level of the threshold stone int he Room 28 (shown on Pl. 10 : 2) may indicate the position of a door allowing passage from the Gate towards the city across Wall XIX: the correspondence is not exact. On the other hand, the purpose of the wall appears to be connected with retaining the very considerable filling in Pit A. Its date would in that case depend on that of the filling.

As the section G-G, Plan VII, and Pl. 12 : 1 show, the filling in Pit A can really be divided into two, there being an upper pit A2 within a lower pit. The upper pit contains coins of the 4th century B.C.; the lower pit contains no material which need be later than the fall of the city. It would appear to be one of a number of large excavations where stone and other materials were hurriedly obtained for the massive filling required in the gateway and elsewhere in order to block them against the Greek attack. The pits were thereafter filled in and the revetment wall would in that case belong to the time in which Whitaker originally placed it (1921, 183-4), close to the great siege.

Further westwards, in the region of the domestic complex northwest of the Gate, it looks as if the houses had been razed to floor level: yellowish or reddish clay layers appear to have been spread over the stumps; however these disrupted and indistinct layers may, in part, belong to a later time (Phase IV). Indications of robbing and filling over the ultimate floors further west may likewise be ascribed to phase IIIB (or sometimes IV). The cistern or well W2 in Room 10 was filled and covered over with large pieces of stone (Pl. 14 : 1). Similarly, perhaps the top of the well casing of Well W1 in Room 12 was also robbed at this time. Still further west, north of the city wall in Rooms 21, 21a, 21b-c-d, 17b, a second big pit (B) interrupts the sequence, and stretches some way northwards round the tower, where its limits have not been determined. Like Pit A, it can be divided into an earlier, lower pit B1 and a later, upper pit B2. This pit has removed a considerable amount of the buildings of Phase IIIA, and makes it hard to envisage them as coherent entities. Like Pit A, Pit B was probally dug in order to obtain hastily needed materials to strenghten the city defences, and it may have been for the same purpose that the buildings just behind the walls were razed to the ground. This kind of process is attested elsewhere in antiquity (cf. e.g. Isaiah, Ch. XXII, verse 10).

Date

Datable material associated with this phase is far more plentiful than for any of the earlier stages. Some of it is associated with the floor deposits which had accumulated in rooms before the final siege.

From the eastern half of the housing complex we cite, from Room 3 (0) (Section F-F, Plan VII) sherd no. 181 (S. Italian handleless bowl); from Room 4 (0) (on the same section) sherd no. 287

(lekythos of the late 5th century B.C.); from Room 5 (0) (Section G′-G′, Plan XI) sherd no. 152 (Attic skyphos of the late 5th century) and no. 226 (Siceliot imitation of a very late 5th century cup-skyphos); from Room 7 (0) comes no. 140 (Attic skyphos of the late 5th or early 4th century) and no. 296 (from a very late 5th century crater); Room 11 (0) (Section G′-G′, Plan IX) has furnished fragment no. 303 (end of the 5th century B.C.).

In the western half of the excavated region we cite from Room 12 (0) (sections A-A, B-B, Plan IV, V) sherd no. 302 (from the very end of the 5th century), from Room 15 (0) (section B-B, Plan V) no. 180 (fragment of an Attic bowl of ca. 425-400), and from Room 16 (0) (Section D-D, Plan VI) fragment no. 196 (from an Attic cup of the late 5th century). In Room 17a (0) (Section D-D, Plan VI) was found no. 293 (from a similarly dated Attic oinochoe). Room 16 also contained, in layer (0) or (15) the Motyan coin no. 1963 (12) (trias of Motya, 420-397 B.C.); another (1963 (10)) turned up in Room 12 (0). From Room 18 (Section A-A, Plan IV) came sherd no. 202 (Attic cup, very late 5th century). Room 19 (0), (section A-A, Plan IV) contained sherd no. 143 (Attic skyphos, turn of 5th-4th century B.C.) and the S. Italian sherd no. 316 was found in the same room, layer (10).

With the final siege itself are to be associated the contents of the filled-in Wells W1 and W2, and the deposits below the filling in the blocked casemate (as well as finds in the sealing layer above), and also the material found in Pit A1 and B1. Of all these, however, only the contents of Well W2 can be treated as a closed group: elsewhere we are dealing with fills where sherds from the same vase may occur scattered throughout several layers.

The contents of Well W2 include no. 171 (part of a small handleless bowl of ca. 425-400 B.C.), and no. 195 (a sherd from an Attic cup comparable to one in the Tomb of the Lacedaimonians, dated 403 B.C.). Sherd no. 230, from the same well, seems to be datable near the turn of the 5th-4th century. Dealing next with the casemate (Room 22 and 22a) deposits found below the filling included sherd no. 232 (a fragment from an Attic plate from the end of the 5th century), no. 246 (Siceliot imitation of an Attic lekanis of ca. 400 B.C.), no. 167 (from a small handleless bowl of the middle or latter part of the 5th century) and no. 169 (from the same type of vase, but dateable ca. 425-400 B.C.). Below the blocking of the actual entrance was found sherd no. 257 (from an Attic bolsal of ca. 430-410 B.C.).

Pits A1 and B1 contain plentiful sherd material which is likewise datable from the time up to the fall of the city, but no pottery which would compel us to attribute the digging of these pits to a later time. Detailed discussion of the evidence seems superfluous: it will be sufficient here to list the later sherds and refer for particulars of dating (or otherwise) to the chapter on Greek pottery in Volume II. Neglecting earlier items, we can list, from Pit A 1, nos. 141, 142, 149, 150, 162, 172, 178, 181, 197, 200, 219, 222-5, 228, 229, 236, 243, 289, 291, 303, 324, 326, 329, 332. For Pit B1, the list includes nos. 163, 191, 233, 235, 319.

There is less certain associated evidence in the remainder of the excavated area, which suffered considerable destruction.

The conclusions, suggested by all the finds listed above, are quite coherent and unambiguous. Everything points to a final urban occupation at the end of the 5th century and the very beginning of the 4th. There is on the other hand no indication compelling us to assume that such occupation went beyond that time. The few items which might by themselves have been taken as a sign of this (such as the South Italian sherds—see Vol. II) could fit a settlement ceasing at the traditional date of the siege and destruction of Motya, 397 B.C. In any case these few sporadic items cannot be deemed sufficient to prove the continued existence of parts of a real city in this region of the island after that date. Yet while all this is true, some difficulties in detail remain. As is well known, Motya was besieged twice in two successive years. The great siege of 397 B.C. was followed in 396 by the countersiege mounted by the returning Carthaginians against the Greeks who were still occupying the city they had conquered. Archaeological evidence is not at present sufficient to allow us to distinguish the results of these two separate assaults. One might perhaps feel inclined to assign some of the ruthless pit digging and levelling to the later siege rather than the earlier one; the ruins of the city captured in 397 B.C. would presumably have mattered less to the Greek conquerers than the city before its fall did to the Phoenician defenders, who probably hoped to continue living there. Similarly, the casemate (Room 22) might have been filled up with bricks in anticipation of the Greek assault; or after it, in 396, if the arrowhead found on the casemate floor originated from the assault in 397. It could even have been filled in later still, and the prevention of accidents to straying animals might in that case be regarded as the reason for the blocking. The question must at present be left open.

Phase IV

While the Italian excavations have now definitely proved the existence of a small settlement in the Cappiddazzu region for several centuries after the events of 397 B.C. (cf. Tusa, in *Mozia*, II, 22; III, 10), our own work in the region of the South Gate did not bring to light remains of any buildings to be assigned to the period after the fall of Motya. Some rough boulder patches encountered sporadically in the surface layers (e.g. in Rooms 1a and 4) might have come from hut foundations; if so, they had been ploughed out and no sign of a coherent plan was noticed. The only other sign of activity is offered by the digging of Pits A2 and B2, probably also by stone robbers (as in the Tower near the Cothon channel, of which very little remained intact when we uncovered it).

The main process recorded in the stratification is, however, the laying down of strata of detritus, partly derived from material fallen from the town wall. These denote the end of active life in this part of the island. Later, only fields and vineyards existed here.

Date

The much disturbed top layers to be assigned to Phase IV contain, generally speaking, pottery of the same types and range as those found in deposits originating during Phase IIIb. Coin evidence would assign Pit A2 to the middle of the 4th century (coins 1961; (1-10), 1962: (1-11), 1963: (3-4), 1965: (1-3), all of ca. 344-336 B.C.) For Pit B2 there is no corresponding evidence (it contained only a medieval coin, no. 1964 (1)). Fourth-century coins are found scattered elsewhere (in Room 18, top layers (no. 1964, (4)); in Room 19 (0)—(1964, (5)). After the 4th century there are only a few stray finds, like coins from widely separated periods, indicating nothing more than the presence of the occasional visitor.

CHAPTER EIGHT

THE NORTH GATE EXCAVATIONS

General Topography

During the final and best discernible phase of Motya's existence, a traveller who approached the ancient city along the causeway from the mainland near Birgi would have been faced with a scene of the following general aspect:

Passing the boat harbour with its small quay described in Chapter 3, he would find that the roadway, on reaching the island, widened into a fairly monumental, though not over-carefully constructed, paved area averaging about 9 m in width (cf. Plan XII, and Pl. 19 : 1). This area was flanked on the west by a little temple (Pls. 22-24) with the altar in front of it (Pl. 21 : 2), both set within a rectangular, walled enclosure, of ca. 11.5 m. by 10 m. (as far as the present very incomplete ruins of its wall permit a judgement). To the east, another fragmentary *temenos* wall enclosed a structure, also apparently sacred and comparable in area (cf. Pl. 19 : 2). Some three metres southwards the traveller would pass between the two big quadrangular bastions fronting the North Gate; the road which they flank ascends very slightly, bending to the west before the visitor enters the outer and inner gateways proper. Beyond this the monumental road leads into the interior of the city (cf. Pl. 20 : 2).

The basic features of this region were described and discussed by Whitaker (1921, 163 ff.), as far as they were then known. His account should be studied for much additional detail not referred to here.

Our own energies were concentrated on the open ground outside the bastions and city wall, though some trial trenching between the bastions was also undertaken. In describing our results, we follow the tripartite division naturally suggested by the presence of the roadway, and the eastern and western sacred areas flanking it, and we begin with the last of these three, which was the first to be investigated. Mr Coldstream's description of the work he undertook here in 1961-2 was published in *ALUOS*, IV, 1962-3, 105 ff.

We reproduce it here with such adjustments as have been made necessary by subsequent research.

The Western Sanctuary

"In the course of the 1961 and 1962 campaigns, an area 16 m. (N-S) by 7 m. (E-W) was opened, extending from the city fortifications to a point very near the ancient shore, and only 3 m. short of the modern coastline before Whitaker's excavations (cf. 1921, 140, n. 1 and 166, plan C, showing the coastline at *ca.* 14 m. outside the western bastion. More than 10 m. have been added to the foreshore in the course of subsequent excavations by Whitaker and ourselves). This area was extended in later years, especially towards the east.

"We begin with a brief description of the various structures within this area, as they appear on the plan (Plan XII); and then, with the help of stratigraphical evidence, we consider their relative and absolute dating.

"The most interesting and surprising feature of this excavation was the discovery of a small monumental building (Pl. 23 : 1) which came to light in 1961 and was completely cleared in 1962. None of the masonry remains *in situ* above the foundations, which are approximately square (3.93 m.

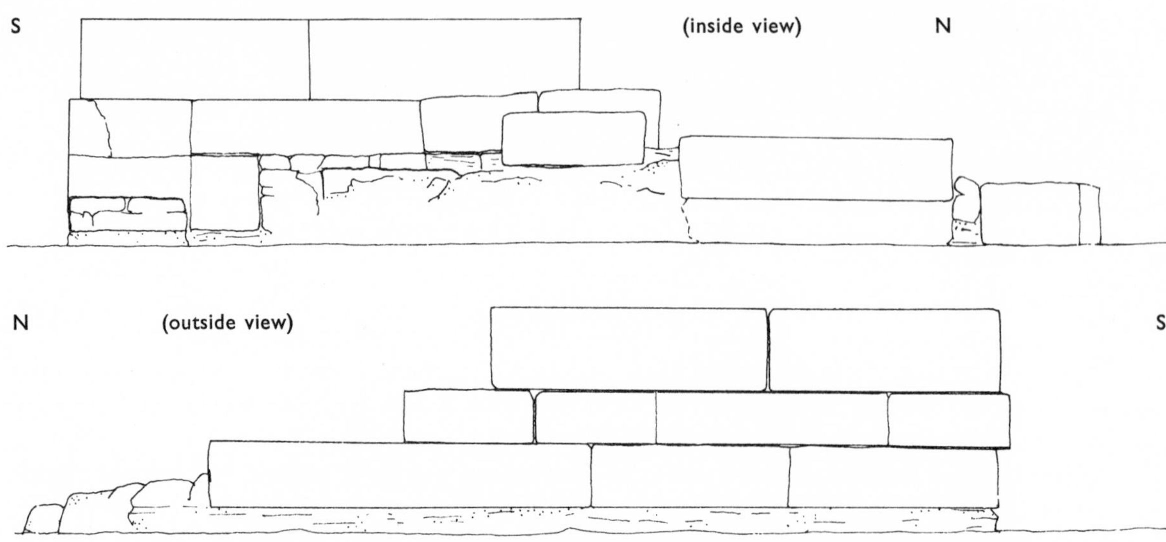

Fig. 21. Details of masonry of the Western Sanctuary outside the North Gate.

× 4.11 m.). Their lowest course is formed of huge irregular boulders, set into the natural sand at about the modern sea-level, and lined with a sticky yellow clay. The upper foundations consisted of a rubble core faced with dressed blocks.

"On the western face, three ashlar courses of well-squared poros blocks are preserved (Pl. 22 : 1; Fig. 21). The uppermost course, which projected 0.11 m. above the modern surface, is 0.30 m. high: three of its blocks appear in Whitaker's plan C, (1921, 166) but only two survive. The height of the other two courses are 0.19 m. and 0.28 m. respectively. These blocks had been well dressed on all their surfaces; their careful preparation is in striking contrast to the slapdash manner in which they were laid in position. On the western face, the overhang of the two upper courses shows that the foundations were never properly dressed *in situ*, and that the blocks are probably re-used.

"The foundations of the eastern part of the building had been much more throughly plundered; enough, however, survives to demonstrate that the exterior masonry was treated in a different manner from the courses on the western side. Three blocks remain *in situ* at the north-east corner, approximately on a level with the lowest of the three western courses; a fourth, presumably from a higher level, had toppled off the eastern face. All four are dressed only on their outside surfaces; their interior edges are irregular, and bond in roughly with the rubble inside.

"Five more blocks of this type among the rubble foundations form a north-south line at a point 1.40 m. east of the western edge (x-x^1) (Plan XII); to the west of this line there is a gap in the foundations. This striking feature, when considered in conjunction with the difference in the style of masonry between the two sides of the foundations, invites the conclusion that our building passed through two stages: more precisely, that the western section, with its carefully squared blocks, is a later addition to an earlier rectangular structure, of which the western edge originally stood at x-x^1. Such an interpretation, as we shall see later, is consistent with such stratigraphical clues as we were able to recover from the immediate vicinity.

"So much for the masonry preserved *in situ*. The evidence for the superstructure is confined to three fragmentary capitals which had fallen upside-down near the foundations. All are of great interest, but their precise position on the building must remain a matter for conjecture.

"The first fragment A (Pl. 24 : 1; Fig. 22A) which was found at the foot of the northern foundations, is of archaic Doric type. It preserves about one quarter of the circumference of a very flat echinus,

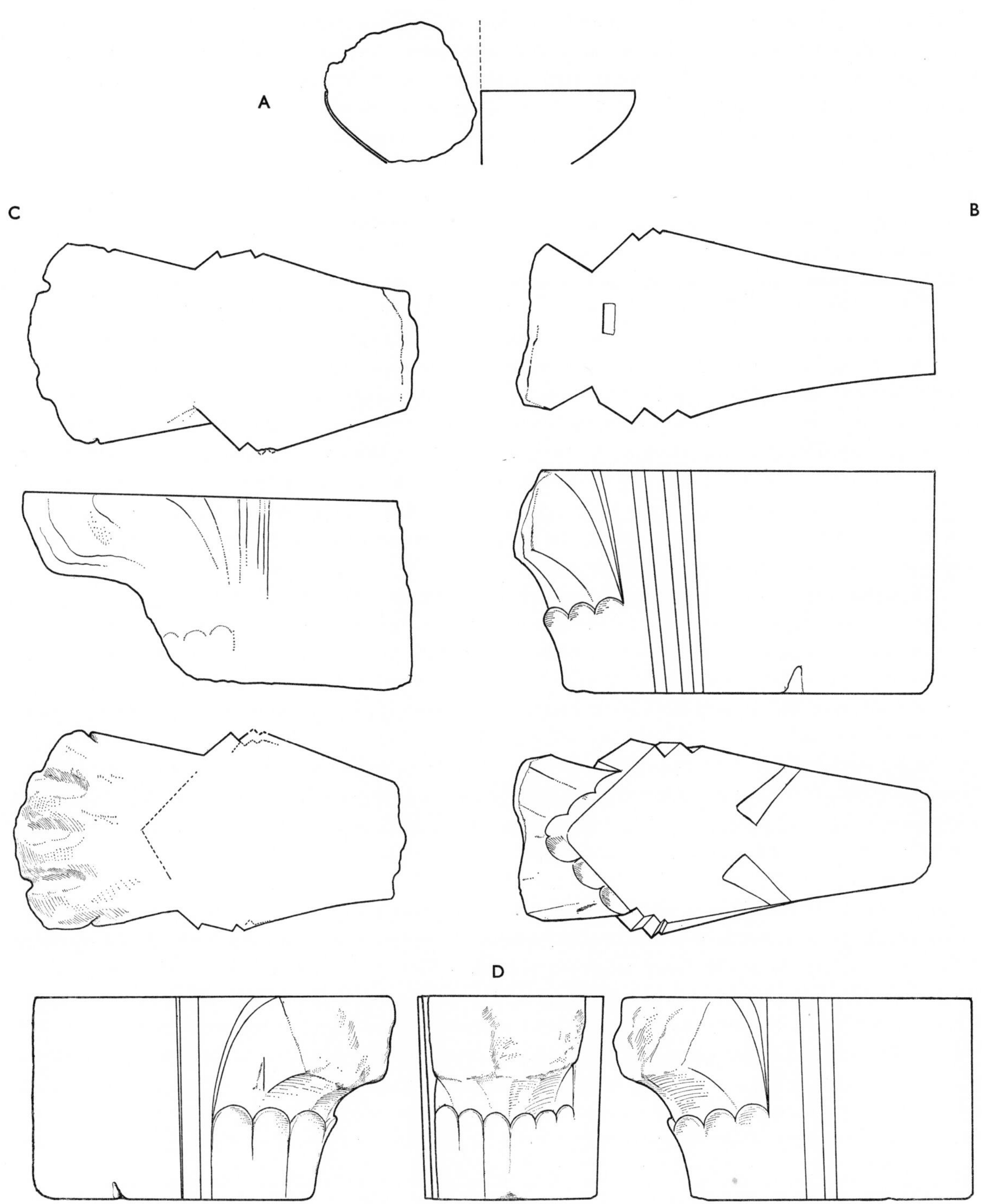

Fig. 22. Details of Capitals A, B, C and D found near the Western Sanctuary.

whose upper and lower diameters are *ca.* 0.66 m. and *ca.* 0.40 m., respectively; part of the abacus also survives, hewn out of the same block. Here and there traces of a stucco coat are preserved; the usual three neckrings at the base of the echinus were rendered only in stucco, and not modelled in the stone beneath. If we may compare small things with great, the profile has its nearest equivalent in the capitals of Temple F at Selinus (cf. Koldewey & Puchstein, 1899, 119, Fig. 95), a building of the late 6th century; our fragment thus provides the earliest known evidence of Hellenic influence on the architecture of Motya. To judge from its position and style, it must have belonged to the earlier, rectangular structure. If it adorned the northern facade, a frontage of only 2.52 m. would hardly allow any arrangement more ambitious than a single column *in antis*, or two columns prostyle. (For the popularity of this arrangement in later Punic shrines, see Lézine, 1961, ch. 2.)

"The other capitals, B and C (Pl. 24 : 2, 3; cf. Fig. 22 B-C) were found near the south-west and north-west corners respectively, in the debris accumulated from the final collapse of the building; they must therefore, be associated with the later, western extension. Unlike capital A, their character is wholly oriental. Both are engaged capitals, pentagonal and wedge-shaped in section, and almost identical in design; their shape would have been suitable for crowning the corners of the building near which they lay. Decoration is confined to two of the shorter sides whose lower edges meet approximately at a right angle. On these two faces, heavy floral volutes emerge from a row of incised calyx leaves, and are flanked by one or two rough vertical flutes. Capital C is the more complete of the two, although its surface is badly worn; on B, the projecting volutes have been broken off, but the calyx leaves and the flutes are in better condition.*

"The purpose of our building is still somewhat obscure, but we are reluctant to believe that it was entirely secular. It is too small, and too dangerously exposed, to have served either as a private house or an official building. The size and shape of the foundations may be matched in the Phoenician homeland by the small harbour shrine at Amrit (Marathus) (Dunand & Saliby, 1961-2, 3 ff., pl. 1-3; cf. Lézine, 1961, figs. 14-15), as well as by several later shrines in the Carthaginian territory. Furthermore, in front of our building, i.e. at a distance of ca. 1.5 m. to the East, was a construction of roughly-trimmed coursed rubble, very nearly square in plan with sides averaging 1.75 m., aligned approximately on the E-W axis of our building: this rubble construction appears to be the stone base of an altar, the upper, mud-brick part of which has now disappeared. A small number of votive objects were also found in the surrounding area, and will be discussed below.

"At a point 2.70 m. south of our supposed shrine, and on the same east-west alignment, we came upon the rubble foundations of a hitherto unknown wall, about 1 m. thick (Pl. 25 : 1; this is marked I on the plan). Its surface, which is well levelled, evidently provided the base for a mud-brick wall whose debris showed clearly in the layer lying immediately above. Its construction would have been too flimsy for a fortification and its alignment suggested some relation to the shrine, perhaps as an enceinte. This was confirmed in 1964, when its eastward continuation was found to return northwards towards the sea. The entrance to the enclosure seems to have been near the north-east corner where a carefully laid, roughly square stone construction may represent the remainder of a gate structure, the details of which elude us. One certain fact, however, emerges from a consideration of the surroundings of wall I: its destruction must provide a *terminus post quem* for the building of the west bastion, which would have been rendered useless by the existence of a wall standing immediately in front.

"At the southern limit of our excavation, our attention was especially directed to the re-entrant where the city wall, with its handsome ashlar facings, abuts on to the west bastion. By examining the foundations of these two structures (Pl. 25 : 2), we were able to form some tentative conclusions on their relative chronology. The bastion lacked a true foundation trench; instead, rough masonry had

* A fourth capital, D, was later found in disturbed ground east of building. It resembles B, but since its dimensions differ it may come from another context. See Fig. 22, bottom. B.S.J.I.

apparently been piled into a V-shaped cutting. The only datable sherd from among these foundations was a small crumb of late Attic black-figure, after rather than before 500 B.C. The city wall, on the other hand, proved to have a fine footing in a row of poros blocks 0.60 m. high, projecting outwards 0.30 m. from the overlying courses; furthermore, near the western limit of our area, a regular foundation trench contained no pottery later than early "Ionian cups" of *ca.* 600 B.C. We were thus driven to the assumption, paradoxical at first sight, that the ashlar wall is considerably earlier than the bastion on to which it abuts (for a contrary view, see Whitaker (1921) 142, 166). There was, however, a considerable disturbance at the point where the two structures meet. Here all trace of the foundation trench had vanished; the footing of the wall was in poor condition; adjacent to the rubble foundations of the bastion, only a fragment of the original block survived; this had been tilted from its original position, and left without adequate underpinning. All this seemed to indicate that the ashlar wall had at some time been breached, and then hastily repaired after the addition of the bastion. No certainty, however, can be reached on this issue until the area has been explored more fully.

"So much for the structures visible on the plan. We now pass on to consider the stratification, as illustrated in our two sections N-N, O-O (Plan XIII). After a few sporadic traces of prehistoric occupation, our area was continuously inhabited throughout the life of the Phoenician colony. The Phoenician period may be divided, with reference to the architectural features, into the following four stages:

1. Before the building of the ashlar city wall.
2. The time when the city wall and the first shrine were built.
3. The period when the first shrine was in use, down to its destruction.
4. The period when the second shrine was in use, down to its destruction.

Prehistoric Occupation

"No trace of pre-Phoenician occupation came to light above the modern sea-level—a circumstance which greatly hampered the investigation of these early strata. To the north-west of the shrine, three wooden stakes were found embedded in a black mould (Section N-N (9), Pl. XIII) just above the virgin sand (Pl. 22 : 2); these may perhaps have served as piles for primitive huts, but no pottery was found in association with them. (For identification of the stake see Appendix 3, p. 106.) The same black mould, at the same level, was encountered two metres outside the ashlar wall. Here we discovered scanty traces of a pre-Phoenician burial, which had evidently been disturbed by the incoming tide; all that remained was a human tooth, part of a native prehistoric vase (Vol. II, Chapter 2) and the impression of a Naue II iron sword (Vol. II, Chapter 4) preserved in a shelly marine concretion.

Stage 1

"Immediately above this black mould a layer of sandy-grey clay (Section N-N, (6) Plan XIII) produced the earliest Greek sherd found in our area (no. 67), the rim of a geometric skyphos of the late 8th century B.C. From this stratum (found mainly just north of the city wall to the west of the western bastion) none of the pottery was later than the 7th century: imports included a few scraps of linear Protocorinthian, and the rim of an Etruscan bucchero kantharos. In the area examined by us there is at present no sign of any permanent structure belonging to this period.

Stage 2

"All the material of this stage comes from a continuous layer of sandy grey clay lying around and underneath the foundations of the shrine and Wall I ((5) in Sections N-N, O-O, Plan XIII). At the north end only *ca.* 0.15 m. of this stratum had been left undisturbed; but near Wall I it survives to a depth of *ca.* 0.50 m., interrupted only by thin sandy streaks which probably represent the walking-levels at different times.

"Some of the pottery in this layer (including Protocorinthian of the early 7th century B.C.) must belong to the previous stage. Near the city wall and western bastion, in particular, a renewed study of the stratification has now identified a deposit of this stage, including no finds later than the 7th century B.C. It was, in fact, through this deposit that the builders of the city wall drove their foundation trench ((7) in section N-N, Plan XIII). Elsewhere, however, much later pieces have appeared including many "Ionian cup" fragments of a more advanced type than those from the foundation-trench of the city wall and these may be dated to the middle of the 6th century, or shortly after. In view of this, we should now revise our dating of the construction of the city wall relative to the western sanctuary and wall I, and attribute both to stage 2 (mid 6th century B.C.), though there may well have been an interval between the time when the city wall was built, and the time when the sanctuary with its surrounding wall was erected. For the city wall the pottery found in the foundation trench ((7) in Section N-N, Plan XIII) provides a *terminus post quem* of *ca.* 600 B.C.; our stratigraphical evidence thus supports the conclusions of Whitaker (1921, 174, 208) and Dunbabin (1948, 332) that Motya was an open city until the 6th century. If we must look for an emergency or crisis that might have induced the Motyans to fortify their island for the first time, this must surely have been the attempt by Pentathlos of Knidos in *ca* 580-70 B.C. to found a Greek colony at Lilybaeum, which was foiled by the Phoenicians and the natives of western Sicily (Dunbabin, 1948, 328-9, 332 with references). A date of *ca.* 550-20 for the erection of wall I and the first shrine is consistent both with the profile of capital A and the current dating of "Ionian cups".

Stage 3

"In our west section, this phase is represented by an accumulation of earth up against the south side of Wall I (cf. Section N-N (4), Plan XIII) and its end is marked by the overlying stratum of mud-brick debris left by its destruction. Neither deposit, regrettably, contained any datable pottery. Layer (3), however, lies in the same horizon as a layer of crushed poros chips, clearly visible in the western section opposite the shrine, but absent from all other parts of our site; these are surely the trimmings from the squared blocks of the shrines western extension. The contents of this layer must therefore date the remodelling of the shrine; once again, unfortunately, the pottery is too scrappy to yield a precise date; the only item we can point to is a small piece of an Attic black-glaze handle, which is unlikely to be earlier than the 5th century B.C.

"At the end of this phase, the destruction of Wall I and the rebuilding of the shrine seem to have been only two symptoms of a general upheaval which also left its mark upon the city fortifications. We have already mentioned the evidence for the breaching of the ashlar wall, followed by the hasty erection of the west bastion. The early 5th century black-figure sherd discovered in the foundations of the bastion must also provide a rough dating for the destruction of wall I. It may not be too fanciful to connect these disturbances with the aftermath of the Carthaginian invasion of Sicily in 480 B.C., when the tide of war may have recoiled upon the Phoenician settlements after the battle of Himera; in this context it is worth remembering the statement of Pausanias that a dedication at Olympia commemorated a victory over Motya by the Acragantines (Pausanias v. 25·5; Dunbabin, 1948, pp. 430-1).

Stage 4

"Apart from an almost sterile layer of grey soil in the west section (Section N-N (2), Plan XIII) which must be contemporary with the use of the second shrine, all the deposits of this phase are connected with the siege and sack of Motya in 397 B.C. (cf. Section N-N (1), Plan XIII). According to Diodorus, the army of Dionysius I came across the causeway; the shrine would therefore have been in the thick of the battle. Just below the topsoil, an almost uniform layer of hard light brown earth (Section N-N (0), Plan XIII) yielded large quantities of Greek arrowheads, whose greatest concentration lay just outside the city wall. The same layer passes over the shrine foundations, where it includes much stone debris. We were unable to tell whether the shrine was destroyed by the invaders, or (as seems more likely) dismantled by the defenders; but the immediate sequel to the siege is illustrated by a deep pit dug down to sea level to the north of the shrine—a massive attempt to plunder what may have been a rich votive deposit. At all events, the only precious object found by us was a piece of badly corroded copper with some traces of silver, apparently part of a bracelet. A terracotta mask representing a face with orientalising features (see Vol II, chapter 2) was also found near the altar. The violence of the sack may be gauged by the circumstances in which some Attic red-figured skyphos sherds (fragments nos. 135, 139, cp. 136-8) came to light; some of the joining pieces were found among the debris above the south-west foundations of the shrine, while others emerged from the bottom of the plunderers' pit 7 m. to the north.

"The pottery from the siege deposits included a plentiful sprinkling of Attic red-figure and black-glaze fragments, many of which are datable to the turn of the 5th-4th centuries B.C. The most interesting find, however, came from the topsoil just to the south of the shrine: two fragments of a Greek limestone relief, showing a battle scene. The better-preserved piece (Pl. 25 : 3) shows the legs of a striding warrior, advancing to the left; the right leg of a second warrior in a kneeling position; and in the corner, a fine representation of a Corinthian helmet.

"After the sack of 397, there is no trace of any subsequent occupation in our area. The only later finds are a few sherds of roughly-glazed medieval ware from the robber trenches, which are much in evidence all over the foundations of the shrine."

The Road

Whitaker (1921, 164) noted that the causeway and the road leading into Motya were closely connected with the North Gate. But he was uncertain about the relative and absolute dates of these features. In what follows we give the results of our own investigations.

Varying in width from circa 10 m., *extra muros* to 7.60 m. between the bastions, the road is surfaced by large irregular paving stones (cf. Pl. 19 : 1; Pl. 20 : 1). Some of these stones in the gateway reach 80 cm. in width, while others outside the gate are even bigger. The stones are laid in a disorderly fashion, and often with considerable interstices, though there are occasional alignments. These aligned stones may be intended to give greater stability to the road surface. Such stabilisation, in a more regular guise, is still in use for cobbled roads in Sicily. There is no regular camber in the gateway (cf. Section S-S, Plan XIV) and only a doubtful one outside it, (cf. Section P-P, Plan XIII). Outside the city walls, the foundation of the walls enclosing the Eastern and Western Sanctuaries serve as kerbs. A filling of loose stones bordering the road near the north-west angle of the eastern bastion may have been intended for drainage.

Many of the paving stones show deep rutting suggesting a very prolonged use of the road surface (cf. Pl. 20 : 2), and detailed investigation by Mrs. Pike in the Gateway (Appendix 4, p. 107) indicated that there was two-way traffic. A raised stone slightly off centre in the trench ZL between the bastions (Section S-S, Plan XIV) may have been part of a boundary between these traffic streams.

To make up or repair the road surface a cover of coarse gravel, set in a matrix of a very stiff grey clay was added in irregular patches. Part of this clay may have been deposited by rainwash (cf. Section P-P (19), Plan XIII).

West of the road a fine pebble surface (in trench ZE) was encountered outside the carriage-road. This probably served as a walking level near the entrance to the *temenos* enclosure. East of the road, on the other hand, the paving continued as a strip *ca.* 3.5 m. wide set at a right angle to the main road in front of the eastern bastion; it was spattered with arrowheads from the final siege, and then covered with mud-brick debris fallen from the tower (in trenches ZQ, ZG and ZP; cf. Section R-R (34) Plan XIV). Between the bastions the main road level is similarly covered with patches of debris, including boulders from the walls and mud-brick, though it could still have been used for occasional traffic by the small population which continued to occupy the Cappiddazzu ruins for several centuries after 397 B.C. No later made road has been noticed, and in fact the choked entrance must have been found inconvenient. The modern track making for the island from the causeway deflects and enters the city near the postern described by Whitaker (1921, 159, and fig. 13) and this arrangement may have been in force for a considerable period.

A little to the north of the destroyed end of the Eastern Sanctuary, the road was broken off, leaving an irregular edge (cf. Plan XII, Section P-P). Measures taken immediately before the great siege to divide the city from the causeway (a natural line of access for the attacking Greeks), storm action by the sea at a time when the water level may have been higher, or stone robbing after the fall of Motya, may all be regarded as possible causes for this break. Similarly a rough alignment of stones discernible just north of the Eastern Sanctuary, and running across the road (Wall VII), may perhaps be a last remnant of some hurriedly thrown-up barricade dating from the final siege. Two skeletons of young persons buried in shallow graves in the East Sanctuary (cf. Pl. 21 : 1) may be battle casualties, or possibly linked with some later events: part of a Punic amphora placed over the skull of one of them, was the only accompanying object.

To investigate the earlier history of the road two test trenches were dug across it: one, Trench ZA (Section P-P, Plan XIII) at the spot just referred to, where the road was broken; the other, Trench ZL (Section S-S, Plan XIV) in the entry between the bastions. Supplementary information was obtained in Trenches ZE, ZF, ZG and ZQ flanking the eastern and western edges of the road.

As Trench ZA (cf. Section P-P and Pl. 19 : 3) showed, the final road surface (III) rested on a bed of brownish-bricky earth and sand (Section P-P (19)). This covered a sandy layer (20), either intentionally laid down or else possibly partly wind-blown (and so perhaps indicating a period of reduced activity). This layer in turn covered a second, lower road surface (II) made up of stones rather smaller than those in the upper pavement and set very irregularly with wide interstices into a bed of greyish-brown clay (21). This lower road, rather badly preserved, was narrower than its successor, but, like it, bordered on both sides by kerb-stones. Again, there is no definite camber discernible. No signs of wheel-ruts were noticed in the small portion uncovered. Perhaps it served for pack animals and humans only, cart traffic not yet being admitted to the city. A walking surface of pebbles and small stones bordered Road II on the east (cf. Section P-P); on the west, Sections ZE and ZF likewise show fine pebble pavings, apparently representing old walking-levels. Below this there was an even earlier paved surface or walking-level (I) likewise made of big slabs of stone very irregularly laid and set in natural grey sand (Section P-P (22)). Only a very small amount of this was cleared. Some areas of rough, loosely-set stone cobbling, encountered near the altar of the western sanctuary at the same general level, may go with this first road.

We may now turn to the results of the trial section ZL cut across the road between the bastions (cf. Section S-S, Plan XIV). Here, below the paved surface of the final road (III), there are no street levels of rough paving such as was encountered in the two earlier roads (I and II) found in Trench ZA. Heavy traffic was apparently not expected to proceed beyond the city walls before the final period in the city's history. There is, nevertheless, a succession of four earlier pebble pavements, some of them very good. Going by general stratigraphic considerations (v. infra, p. 79) it may be permissible to link both the pebble pavement between S-S (2) and (35) and the one between layers (36) and (37) with the period when road II was in use in area ZA. The earlier pebbled walking-levels between S-S (37) and (38), and between (38) and (39) might then be presumed to be contemporary with the earliest road or walking-level (I) in section ZA. These earlier walking-levels are very little known; if we can go by the limited evidence provided in sections ZL and ZQ, the road area was bordered to the east by walling which may have served as a kerb, though it might have belonged to a different kind of structure.

The Eastern Sanctuary (cf. Plan XII)

This complex of walls enclosing a roughly rectangular area on three sides is imperfectly preserved and somewhat puzzling. On the west is a rubble wall (Wall III) lying roughly south to north, and bordering the uppermost road level (Road III): this is doubtfully continued by a layer of disconnected rubble underlying the ashlar kerb (Wall V) which makes up the south side of the rectangle, and borders the paved area fringing the eastern bastion. This kerb is made up of four large slabs placed end to end, set on top of an area of rubble but continues eastwards beyond the rubble walling to terminate inconclusively, apparently robbed. The third, eastern rubble wall (Wall VI) turns off from it northwards, and continues for some 5 m.; again it is partly thrown down and only the lower footings are in position. At its northern end this wall is broken by erosion and its expected continuation seawards is lacking; nor is there any trace of a wall running East-West to provide the fourth side of an enclosed area. Within these rubble walls there is an ashlar kerb (Wall IV) running N-S *ca.* 80 cm. E of the kerb of Road III; its southern end is indicated by a slab placed on end, at right angles to the wall: the northern end is eroded. It may conceivably have served as a step to some higher level now gone: this complex of walls and the layers filling it give the impression of being only the lowest part of a structure, the upper portions of which have been removed.

The stratigraphic sequence in this region is as follows. The earliest levels are only known from the deep trial trench ZB (cf. Sections Q-Q, R-R, Plan XIV), levels (33) and (32), topped by the black sand (31) overlying the natural subsoil; (31) probably represents the decayed vegetation on the beach, which was also met below the Western Sanctuary (Section N-N (9), Plan XIII). There follows, in ZB, sand with iron pan (30), topped by grey sand (29), the upper surface of which, containing charcoal, appears to represent an old walking-level. This layer of grey sand represents open ground without any special features, sloping down towards the east.

The grey sandy layer is covered by layers of light or darker red sand and sandy to bricky earth, ZB (28), (27); they correspond in level to Road II in Trench ZA (cf. Section Q-Q, R-R, Plan XIV and P-P, Plan XIII).

The rubble wall acting as a kerb for Road III was sunk into the top of these layers. Next to it, a row of amphorae was inserted bottom upwards into the sandy-bricky earth ((27), Section Q-Q, Plan XIV), between the road kerb and the inner ashlar kerb (cf. Pl. 19 : 2). Originally, they probably contained votive deposits, but they were found empty, their bottoms having been smashed. Three of them survived almost entirely, while a fourth (marked ⊗ on the plan, Plan XII) further north was fragmentary.

A further phase, linked with the smashing of the amphorae, is attested by a level of grey-brown clay and sandy earth, intermixed to the south with rubble ((26), Sections Q-Q, R-R, Plan XIV). It finishes above with a walking surface and into it was set the ashlar kerb (Wall VII) running parallel to the kerb of Road III (Wall VI). Considerable quantities of broken pottery were found in the level above this floor, especially in ZB. They include rough saucers fired so soft that they were unsuitable for ordinary use. Some others served perhaps as saucer lamps of Phoenician type (see Vol. II Chapter 2). All these items are most probably ritual. Part of a broken Phoenician glass bottle apparently of 5th century type was found in the make-up of the floor in Trench ZD (see Vol. II Chapter 7). Nearby a pit was dug from a higher level to bury a sheep and its young.

These features represent the final phase of the Eastern Sanctuary before the fall of Motya. Its character and functions are ill-defined and difficult to understand because the plan of the structure is incomplete, and only its lowest foundations are extant. The amphorae and ritual pottery hint at some sacred purpose. The plan with its interlacing of walls of ashlar and rubble (the former ending in one place with a slab placed on edge transversally) recall to some extent the tophet of Sulcis (Pesce, 1961, 69-70, fig. 17).

We have, however, at Motya no stelae or other ritual objects (though they may have been removed): perhaps our structure had a different religious function (see below, chapter 11 f).

The siege of Motya, indicated as usual by stray arrowheads, was followed, in this region as elsewhere, by the digging of numerous pits (as in ZD, and especially in the north-east corner of the rectangular eastern sanctuary enclosure where late deposits go down in depth, and the walling is missing). Reddish drift sand, and brick-wash from the decaying city walls and bastions finally covered the ancient site.

The Fortifications

It was not our intention to make a systematic study of the fortifications near the North Gate. Useful information about them was collected none the less during our work in this region. We present these results, hoping that at a later date it may be possible to undertake a more complete excavation of the defences of this part of the city.

Work outside the western bastion has shown (p. 73) that the main isodomic ashlar wall of the city dates from the 6th century, and more particularly from the time after the raid by Pentathlos of Knidos (*ca.* 580-70). It has also been shown that the western bastion was apparently added hurriedly to the city wall later than 500, and possibly following the battle of Himera in 480 B.C. (p. 73-4).

On the plan given by Whitaker (1921, 166, Plan C—where a distinction is made between the isodomic wall, now ascribed to the 6th century, and the bastion and related walling) it is made clear that the fine ashlar now fronting the isodomic wall is the facing in front of a thick filling. Ocular inspection of Whitaker's trench shows this to be correct, for a solid mass of mud-brick lies behind the ashlar. Whether this is later than the isodomic ashlar, or whether the latter was added later is not apparent, and would need further investigation.

Work done since 1963 on the road levels near the eastern bastion has confirmed the late date of that structure. The foundations of the bastion in Trench ZL (Section S-S, Plan XIV) are at and above the level of the final paved road surface, and rubble stones banked up against the footings of the bastion act as a protective cover for them. Since the lower foundations of the bastion appear also to be an adaptation of earlier work for secondary purposes, it looks as if the bastions in their final shape are considerably later than the paved road surface, and their construction may not be too far removed from the final threat posed by the impending siege of 397 B.C.

That the wheel ruts in the road surface are at an angle to the bastion, and so belong to an earlier phase, lends support to this. Indeed our findings both in Trench ZQ and Trench ZL suggest that, as far as the eastern bastion is concerned, earlier structures probably preceded the present fortifications. In this connexion we may note that Soprintendente Tusa (in *Mozia I*, p. 40, note 1) indicates that an earlier tower of good ashlar work is encased in the present eastern bastion; and that the bastion includes a re-used architectural fragment from the Cappiddazzu among its building materials (*Mozia IV*, 15).

The Historical Development of the North Gate Region

We can now discuss the various phases of development in the region outside the North Gate. For this, it may be useful to take as a fixed standard of comparison, the sequence worked out in detail for the area around the Western Sanctuary (p. 73). It is of help in this discussion that, as our sections show, the original ground surface in the North Gate region appears to have been fairly level, and this tended to be reflected by a fairly level run of strata higher up.

Of the pre-Phoenician or native occupation, which was attested by a disturbed burial and by the wooden stakes driven into mud in the Western Sanctuary (p. 73) no traces have been found elsewhere, although native sherds have been found in later levels, especially in the region of the Eastern Sanctuary, and a few scattered human bones in Trench ZG (35) might have come from a disturbed burial. The same muddy or sandy base level found by Mr. Coldstream has, however, been encountered elsewhere, sometimes also with black mud on top, as in Trench ZB (Sections Q-Q, R, R-R, (31), Plan XIV).

The *Stage 1* levels in the Western Sanctuary may be equated with levels in a number of other localities. The earliest road or walking-level in Trench ZA (Section P-P (25), (22), Plan XIII) and in Trench ZL (Section S-S (38), (37), Plan XIV) should belong to this period. Proceeding westwards from Trench ZA we would associate the cobbles below the altar platform (Section 0-0 (18), (17), Plan XIII) with this stage, while eastwards in the region of Trench ZB, Layer (29) in Sections Q-Q, R-R (Plan XIV) should be equated. The general picture of our zone is that of a stretch of fairly level open ground, traversed by a path or walking level leading towards the seashore from habitations which in this part of the island were probably situated inside the later city wall. Comparing the sequences, Stage 1 at the North Gate was open ground during Phase I at the South Gate.

With *Stage 2* we are on firmer ground, and a much fuller picture emerges. In addition to the Western Sanctuary with its altar and the wall surrounding it, and to the first Town Wall, we must assign to this stage the construction of Road II in Trench ZA (Section P-P, (21), Plan XIII) and probably also, as we saw, (p. 77) the two early walking-levels surfaced with pebbles in Trench ZL (Section S-S, pavements between (2) and (35), and between (36) and (37), Plan XIV). Fine pebble paving in near-by Trench ZQ should also belong to this period. Eastwards from the road, layer (28) in Trench ZB (Sections Q-Q, R-R, Plan XIV) corresponds to Trench ZA, level (21)—the construction level of Road II (cf. Section P-P, Plan XIII). There is no definite sign of any sacred structure yet, though it seems possible that this area east of the road already possessed a sacred character. Otherwise, Stage 2 introduced to the region outside the North Gate its two main distinguishing features- the road and the western sanctuary, just as it also witnessed the construction of the Town Wall, though not yet the present gate bastions which were preceded by buildings about which we know very little, as yet. Moreover, as we saw, (p. 29) the road by now probably connected with a causeway to the mainland.

Stage 2 at the North Gate may be broadly compared with Phase IIA at the South Gate; and so at both this period is shown to have been an active and flourishing one.

North Gate *Stage 3* appears to correspond to South Gate Phase IIB—both being concerned with use and destruction of buildings. In the Western Sanctuary a sandy layer (Section N-N (3), Plan XIII) was assigned to this stage, which invites correlation with the stratigraphically analogous sandy layers (20) in Trench ZA (Section P-P, Plan XIII) and Trench ZB (27) (Sections Q-Q, R-R, Plan XIV. The association with stratum (12) in Section 0-0 (Plan XIII) is less certain. In fact the sandy character of these layers would be in place particularly in Stage 3B, a time of partial intermission—since wind-blown sand would then be less mixed with trodden mud than at times of intensive human activity.

Stage 4 (which in this zone began with the remodelling and use of the Western Sanctuary) is mainly attested in the sequence by layer (2) in Section N-N (Plan XIII). This should correspond to the third road-body (19) in Trench ZA (Section P-P on Plan XIII); to layer (2) in Trench ZL (Section S-S,

Plan XIV); and to the deposition of layer (26) in the Trench ZB region (Sections Q-Q, R-R, Plan XIV). The present remains of the Eastern Sanctuary also date from this stage and so do the bastions of the North Gate, which, as we saw (p. 78) may have been erected not very long before the fall of Motya. Stage 4a thus corresponds to Phase IIIA at the South Gate; both terminate with the siege of 397 B.C., with which Stage 4b and Phase IIIB are associated in their respective regions. Arrowheads are a prominent feature in the deposits of this time in both zones. In the North Gate region our excavations revealed no signs of constructional activity after that event: the only entries in the chronicle of the years to follow concern the two burials possibly linked with the great siege, much long-continued robbing of stone and pit digging, and the slow crumbling and decay of the once mighty defences which was to lay a blanket of debris over the traces of so much earlier activity.

Absolute Dating

In the preceding paragraphs we have tried to correlate the stratification of the North Gate region as a whole with that of the area of the Western Sanctuary, in which absolute dates for a number of stages first became available. The evidence offered by datable finds from other parts of the region seems to fit fairly well with the stratigraphic equations proposed by us, though it must be admitted that far more evidence is available for the final phase of the sequence than for those which go before.

For Stage 1 we depend partly on the few datable pieces of Greek pottery discovered in the vicinity of the Western Sanctuary, especially the Corinthian kotyle fragment no. 18 (Vol. II, Chapter 1) from N-N (6), Plan XIII and the Siceliot skyphos no. 67 from the same location.

Stage 2 is largely dependent on Mr. Coldstream's trenches for dated Greek pottery—especially such items as the Corinthian skyphos No. 59 (from 0-0 (14) or (13), Plan XIII) and the Ionian cup no. 113 (from the lower part of 0-0 (5)); to which must be added the Doric capital A. The other parts of the region have not furnished datable material of similar value, though in Trench ZB (28) (Sections Q-Q, R-R, Plan XIV) a rim fragment of a Punic amphora was found which would suit a 6th-century dating (Vol. II, Chapter 3) and there are some other fragments of Punic pottery similar in date elsewhere.

For Stage 3, good dating evidence is scarce everywhere. The small piece of an Attic black-glaze handle from the Western Sactuary (p. 74) is definite, but not good enough to be included in the list of selected items published in Vol. II, Chapter 1. The same is true for the early 5th century black-figured sherd found in the foundations of the western bastion (p. 74). In the eastern half of the excavated area the amphorae between the kerbs of the Eastern Sanctuary belong to this stage but are not of very great value for dating. Stage 4, on the other hand, is rather more fully documented. Near the Western Sanctuary there are a number of items of late 5th- or early 4th-century date (p. 74-5). Others were found on the road surface, like the Lucanian sherd, no. 315. In the Eastern Sanctuary, the top layers (26) (27) (Sections Q-Q, R-R, Plan XIV) contain the ritual bowls (p. 77) which would also fit this context. Layer 4b, the layer directly connected with the great siege of 397 BC, is everywhere demarcated and clearly distinguished by plentifully scattered arrowheads. Two coins of 4th century date (1964, nos. 10 and 11) found in different places on the road surface, are among the scant traces of later activity here.

CHAPTER NINE

EXPLORATORY TRENCHES IN THE INTERIOR OF THE ISLAND

In conjunction with the resistivity measuring programme described above, two series of long exploratory trenches were dug in the interior of the island. The first was at the cross-roads between the path from the Villa to the Tophet, and the path towards the causeway; the second was placed in the centre of the "dip" and some way up its eastern slope (cf. map, Plan II).

1. *The trenches near the central cross-roads* (A on Pl. II; for plans, see Plan XV)

The first of these was a trench, 18 by 1 m. parallel to the northern edge of the road from the Villa to the Tophet at a distance of 1 m; and extending westwards from the beginning of the field wall bounding the path to the North Gate on the east. At the cross-roads, this trench was widened and extended southwards by 3 m. and an offshoot 50 cm. wide continued eastwards along the road towards the Villa for a distance of 6.80 m. The second trench began east of the boundary wall against which the first trench was set, and continued for 27.6 m.; it was mainly 1 m. wide, but its middle portion was extended to 2 m. Some offsetting was made necessary by local conditions, and the final 7 m. was only 50 cm wide.

The western trench contained, near the boundary wall, part of a building, the west wall of which was solidly built in the style called by Italian archaeologists *a telaio*, i.e. of upright pillars set between stretches of rubble masonry. The foundations of a partition wall branched off eastwards, near the northern edge of the trench, and was flanked on either side by the remains of plaster pavements. The N-S wall seems to have had two construction periods, the earlier of which corresponded to levels below the plaster floors; substantial masses of tumbled rubble lay at the foot of the wall at the western side, i.e. outside the building. The ground was badly disturbed by pitting, but a second building appears to have begun ca. 3 m. further west. Its eastern face had gone, but part of a longitudinal wall and the beginnings of two cross-walls extending northwards could be discerned. The western part of the building was, however reduced to shapeless tumble; it appears to have been erected during the second phase of the eastern building, for its foundations do not reach below the later plaster floor, and to have been built over an open sandy space, part of which apparently survived as a lane between the eastern and western structures. There were no signs of paving or any made surface. Among the rubble lying at the southern end of the lane was a large stone with a cup mark; pieces of iron slag were found near it, and it might have been used in iron smelting. A very large roofing tile, 66 × 46 cm, rested on the western building.

The second main search trench, east of the boundary wall, went through a building complex which is probably part of the one on the west. While again there appear to be two periods, only the later one was uncovered. Badly mauled in its eastern part it yet shows a series of rooms or courts with plaster floors divided by rubble wall-foundations, which, no doubt, once carried mud brick upper work. A space between walls may be a lane, but its floor shows no special characteristics beyond the common plaster, and further evidence is needed to determine its character. It should be noted that none of the walls found here was of the *a telaio* style with pillars between stretches of rubble work.

From associated finds it would appear that the upper phase in all the trenches—the only one extensively uncovered—belonged to the last period in the city's history (5th-4th century B.C.). There is evidence from pottery that the earlier stage goes back at least to the 6th century. The trial trench no. 1, dug in 1955, forms part of the same complex: its location is shown on the plan, Plan XV.

2. *The exploratory trenches in the central valley*

The second set of trenches (B on Plan II), located along the southern boundary of the field-path traversing the central valley or dip in an E-W direction, was laid out in a straight line, except for a slight curve near its east end made necessary by local conditions. It was mostly 0.7 m wide, and 51 m. long and revealed two phases, but here again, except for sondages, only the later phase was uncovered. Evidence began on the upper slope to the east of the valley bottom, where there was a disturbed area only partly investigated; a road was forecast here by resistivity survey, but more investigation is needed to prove its existence. Lower down the slope to the west there was a complex of walls and cross-walls belonging to a domestic structure or structures. These included parts of a room or court with a plaster floor containing holes probably intended for store jars; a plastered courtyard, which was in existence in more than one phase with a slope intended to draw rain water into a cistern; and fragments of a well-head of terracotta, similar to the one from the South Gate (cf. p. 64). There were also tile drains, and a drain cut into the ashlar of a wall-foundation. A paved area here may have formed a courtyard. Lower down, the built-up area with good plaster floors ceased, and this was apparently a zone of backyards or gardens. At the bottom of the dip what seems to have been a section of a fairly crudely made minor road was encountred. Laid out between kerbs, it was surfaced in its final stages with a mixture of gravel including many potsherds; its history, attested by a number of earlier layers of plaster and other materials, appears to go back some time. The original surfacing was laid over the brownish *terra rossa* found in various parts of the island above natural rock. Terraces or gardens also extended up the western slope and an increasing profusion of potsherds at a higher level revealed the proximity of buildings (not yet reached) balancing those on the eastern hill. This region seems to have been a domestic quarter and to have included a good deal of open space.

Associated finds showed that the final phase of these constructions belonged to the 5th-4th century. Earlier sherds of the 6th and 7th century attest occupation in previous periods.

PART THREE

OVERALL RESULTS AND COMPARISONS

CHAPTER TEN

MOTYA: THE OUTLINES OF DEVELOPMENT ACCORDING TO PRESENT INFORMATION

A Classical account preserved by Stephen of Byzantium, who took it from Hekataios, would link the eponymous founder figure in the story of Motya with the exploits of Heracles: that is, by implication, approximately with the 13th century B.C. The older scholars were inclined to accept this tradition. Thus Massa (1709, II, 114) assumes that the city was founded some 100 years before the fall of Troy, since it is linked with the life of Heracles, who according to learned calculations died 77 years before that event. A similar view was still held by Coglitore (1884, 27-28) who was inclined to date the foundation of Motya from the late 13th century B.C. However, more recently, the antiquity of this story was questioned by Dunbabin (1948, 330) who would ascribe it to the time of Pentathlos' expedition.

A later date for the foundation of Motya in the 8th century B.C. is accepted by Pace (1935, 218), Tusa (*Mozia*, I, 15), and others; while Dunbabin (1948, 327), Rhys Carpenter (1958, 42 ff.) and Culican (1961, 48) are among those who would prefer an even later date of foundation. Still more recently, opinions have perhaps swung back a little. The recent discovery of the "Melqart of Sciacca"—a figurine of Phoenician type assignable to the 12th-9th century B.C. according to S. Chiappisi (1961, 65), to the 12th-11th century according to Tusa (1967, 52) but before according to Harden (1962, 222 note 53), may indicate the fairly early presence of traders from Phoenicia in waters not far from Motya. Even then, they might well have selected the island as a place where they effected occasional landings or stayed for short periods, as they did much later at Sabratha (Ward-Perkins, 1953, 379); or founded a "factory" or "baglio" before creating a town proper, as they did in the 8th century B.C. at Toscanos in Spain (H. G. Niemeyer and H. Schubart, 1969, 123). We may here recall somewhat analogous opinions recently expressed in more general terms by Moscati (1968, 196), and by Bisi (1967, 57-8) who makes the point that early settlements by the Phoenicians on the mainland in the Marsala-Birgi region may still await discovery. However, there is at present no proof of anything of this sort. No trace of such early activity at Motya, other than prehistoric sherds, has, indeed, been discovered up to now, and the 8th century foundation-date must, therefore, for the time being be accepted for the Phoenician settlement at Motya (Cf. now also Tusa, *Mozia* VII, 53 ff.). For reasons which emerge from the review of the Greek pottery (pp. 53, 73 above) a later date of foundation for the city does not seem acceptable. It did not at once extend over the whole island; thus near the South Gate, Phase IA began only in 650 B.C.

Motya was at first a Phoenician trading town, but it later came increasingly under Carthaginian influence which in the end made her a Carthaginian base—a dichotomy recently underlined by Bisi (1967, 54 ff.). Its history during the first and second stages of its existence is only fitfully and indirectly illustrated by historical records, and a good deal depends on conjecture as to the way in which certain political events might have affected it. Thus the threat posed by the expedition of Pentathlos (580 B.C.) has been assumed to have resulted in the (somewhat later) construction of the first ring of fortifications around the town (Dunbabin, 1948, 332). However, according to recent findings by Tusa (*Mozia* VII, 55 ff., 79) the construction of the first town wall on the northern side of the island might go back to the 7th century and have continued into the sixth. On the other hand the removal of the threat was apparently reponsible for considerable development, including probably the construction of the causeway and the shifting of the necropolis to the mainland. The renewed Greek threat under Dorieus (510 B.C.), as well as the preparations for the Carthaginian campaign which ended disastrously at Himera in 480 B.C., may be presumed to have been responsible for renewed interest in, and strengthening of, the fortifications of the city, while the general weakening of Carthage's position after 480 should have brought in its train a long period of stagnation. The renewed military effort by Carthage, successful for a decade beginning in 409 B.C., should on the other hand, be reflected at Motya by greater activity in military engineering and perhaps in other fields.

That the year 397 saw the destruction of the city was stressed by all writers up to, and including, Coglitore and Whitaker. In spite of the recent discovery of traces of continued occupation in the Cappiddazzu region (Tusa in *Mozia* III, 85 ff.), it is worth keeping in mind the fact, stressed by Coglitore (1884, 170) that writers like Polybius, Strabo, Pomponius Mela, and Pliny the elder, well informed about Sicily in the centuries after 397 B.C., do not mention Motya. The existence of a hamlet or even village would presumably not have interested them, though the presence of a true city could hardly have been passed over by all of them.

All this amounts to something less than an outline of the true history of Motya: it is not even a complete list of the catastrophes which affected her, for there may well have been others besides those which arose out of contacts with the Greeks. It seems possible, even in the present very incomplete state of excavations at Motya, to arrive at a somewhat more definite picture by considering the evidence made available by archaeology.

If we do this, then it will become apparent that, while little activity is so far attested in the 8th century B.C. and not much for the 7th, though the fortifications and perhaps the Tophet began then (Tusa, *Mozia VII*, 79), the 6th century B.C., and more particularly its second half, was a period of great importance: in fact it may well have been the most flourishing period in the life of Motya. This was the time when the causeway to the mainland seems to have been built; the existence of fortifications on at least part of the perimeter is attested: the city defences had expanded into the region of the former necropolis in the northern part (Whitaker, 1921, 208); to the south, settlement near the South Gate now covered a zone only partly built over before; the Cothon channel and basin were probably constructed late in the century.

Near the North Gate, the Cappiddazzu temple (Tusa in *Mozia*, IV, 13), the Tophet (Ciasca in *Mozia* II, 47-8) and the small sanctuary outside the North Gate were all erected. To this time the best sculptures in the Tophet belong (Garbini in *Mozia* III, 50), although there was still considerable activity in the early part of the following century (Garbini in *Mozia* IV, 62). This period of activity may still be linked with the early part of the 5th century. After that there appears to have been a decline, probably as a result of the battle of Himera (480 B.C.). The second part of the 5th century saw the construction of the fortifications near the South Gate, and probably elsewhere in their present form. However, except for the Tophet, which continued to receive attention (Ciasca in *Mozia* II, 50), and perhaps a rebuilding of the Cappiddazzu temple (Isserlin, 1958, 14), life in Motya during much of this century seems to have been comparatively stagnant. Certain modifications of the defences, such as the wing walls over the Cothon quays, are probably attributable to the late 5th or the beginning of the 4th century. It is worth noticing that in the later stages of the city's existence new constructions often made use of earlier materials, indicating a decline in prosperity: this is true, e.g., of the structures flanking the road leading in from the North Gate, and of the bastions, where materials from the Cappiddazzu temple—apparently no longer in use—were employed (Tusa in *Mozia* I, 39). Similarly it may be significant that Whitaker found the area of the presumed *agora* employed for drying unbaked pottery amphorae, and that a kiln was erected there (Whitaker, 1921, 173-4). Thus the city which fell to Dionysius would have been well past its zenith, although, as Diodorus attests, even at that stage Motya was rich and militarily not negligible.

CHAPTER ELEVEN

SOME SPECIAL PROBLEMS

(a) Town Planning

When dealing with the results of our excavations we had occasion to notice within the urban framework of Motya the existence of certain important constructions such as the main road leading into the city from the North Gate, the *agora* partly dug by Whitaker, the important temple near-by, the Tophet, and the Cothon. We had reason to assume that different areas within the city had different functions, and also that, though there was regular town planning near the centre the peripheral buildings tended to follow the direction of the shoreline in their alignments. We must now see whether the *constituent elements* and the *urban lay-out* at Motya can be usefully compared with those at other, and in particular other Phoenician or Punic, sites: whether, in fact, it may be possible to speak of specially Phoenician types of town, or town plans, and, if so, to what extent the result can elucidate the urban arrangments at Motya. In doing this, we take into account earlier studies in this field, and in particular the important essay by Barreca (1961, 27-43).

That in Roman times, at least, the educated public could appreciate a difference between a Greek and a typically Phoenician town can be assumed from the well-known passage in Strabo (III, 4, 2). Here the Phoenician character of Malaka in Spain is contrasted with the typically Greek layout of near-by Mainake: we might add that such a distinction should have originated well before the time when Strabo wrote, since tendencies in the Mediterranean world were then moving towards greater uniformity rather than increased diversification. If ancient Malaka, usually located at modern Malaga, was archaeologically explored and the elements of its urban planning known, we should be in a position to appreciate what Strabo's Φοινικικὸν τῷ σχήματι implied. However, there is at present practically no information about this matter. We must thus follow the alternative course of considering jointly the archaeological and textual information available for those sites in the Phoenician world about which something *is* known. This may afford some idea about the features which may be expected in a Phoenician town. (Under Phoenician we shall subsume Carthaginian, since insufficient criteria to separate them are at present available.) We review the comparative evidence under two headings: I The main constituent urban features, and II Urban planning.

I. (a) Certain cities are said to be characterized by very tall multistorey houses. This is reported, for instance, about Aradus (Strabo, XVI, 2, 13), Tyre (id., XVI, 2, 23) and Carthage (Appian, *Libyca*, ch. 128). At Motya tall houses are mentioned by Diodorus Siculus (XIV, 51, 1, 5-7), but, as is stated in chapter 4 (p. 33), the available archaeological evidence renders their presence likely only near the North Gate, and not among the buildings in the humbler quarter near the South Gate. Tall houses may have been restricted to the "urban centre" at Motya.

(b) As has been pointed out by Barreca (1961, 37) an acropolis was a feature of a number of Phoenician and Carthaginian cities in Sardinia such as Tharros, Nora, Monte Sirai, and perhaps Cagliari; the existence of an acropolis (Byrsa) in Carthage is of course well known. Greek cities, however, after the archaic period more rarely included an acropolis. At Motya a likely place to look for something of the sort would be the high ground near the Villa Whitaker, for reasons set out in chapter 4 (p. 33), but this can be clarified only by excavation.

(c) A main road leading from the town entrance (often in the harbour region) towards a piazza or agora is attested at a number of Phoenician and Punic sites, such as Nora, Leptis Magna (pre-Roman period) and Sabratha; buildings of a public character sometimes adjoined the forum, as at Leptis Magna (Theresa Howard Carter, 1965, 130-131) and Carthage (cf. Gsell, 1920, II, 78-79). Important sanctuaries were situated in a number of Phoenician and Punic towns next to the piazza, such as Carthage (see Appian, Historia Romana, *Libyca*, 127), Nora, and Monte Sirai. Monte Sirai and Motya are, indeed, very similar in providing the same sequence of main gate, main road, piazza and sanctuary if we remember the piazza partly cleared by Whitaker near the Cappiddazzu temple at Motya (Whitaker, 1921, 173) and the sacred character of the "Mastio" near the piazza at Monte Sirai in its second phase (Barreca, *Monte Sirai* II, 39). The planning at Motya, as far as is known, seems more regular, but further evidence is required about it and the buildings near by.

(d) At a number of Phoenician and Punic sites the main road continued across the city, as a *cardo*, as at Selinunte during the Punic phase after 409 B.C., and later at Solunto, or at Nora and Tharros in Sardinia. At Carthage the main road leading from the forum to the acropolis was flanked by two others (Appian, *Libyca*, ch. 128): this arrangement may perhaps be illustrated concretely at the North African Greek site of Euesperides, as mapped and interpreted by Wright (cf. Goodchild, 1952, 210, fig. 1 and Kraeling, 1962, 44, fig. 6, and 43). At Motya we cannot say whether the main road entering by the North Gate continued across the city as a *cardo*: Pace assumed that it did (1938, 365-367) but Lehmann-Hartleben apparently doubted it (1926, 183). Nor can we at present decide whether there may have been three main roads, as at Carthage. Both of these questions must be left to excavation.

(e) Tophets or sacrificial areas intended especially for burnt offerings of infants are known from a number of Phoenician and Punic cities (cf. Harden, 1971, 86 ff.). Usually they appear to be situated near the outskirts of the city. Those at Tharros, Monte Sirai and Nora are on the northern side of the town, while the one at Carthage (like the tophet at Jerusalem) was to the south of the city nucleus. In this matter Motya compares with the Sardinian sites and not with the North African metropolis.

(f) Cothons or artificial inner harbours are known or assumed to have existed in Phoenician cities, and a number have been tentatively identified. (Cf. Harden, 1971, 235 note 157.) Recently current assumptions of many years at Motya and elsewhere have been questioned (Mingazzini in *Mozia*, IV, 105 ff; 1968, 137 ff). Since investigations are in progress at the presumed "Cothon" at Motya, it seems best to leave this matter in abeyance until more is known, when comparisons can be made with greater profit.

II. We may now consider whether, in addition to the existence of certain main constituent elements in the city which are known to have existed in other Phoenician towns, Motya can be shown to have been arranged on a general plan which can be explained by reference to Phoenician, Greek or other types of town plan. As shown in chapter 4, the peripheral buildings near the shore at Motya seemed to be laid out without reference to a common system of alignment, following rather the direction of the coastline while nearer the centre of the island we thought we could detect elements of a grid plan. Now the distinction between a peripheral belt, where buildings follow the direction of the town wall, and a centre where this alignment is not followed, are known in the Middle East in the first millennium B.C., e.g. at Tell Beit Mirsim in Palestine, where attention has recently been drawn to this type of plan (Lampl, 1968, 38-9). In this respect, the plan of Motya may go back to oriental prototypes. However, at Motya, we found indications that this central part was denoted by *regularity*, involving apparently a grid plan and perhaps an axial main road. This is not so in the eastern examples. Regularity of planning was of course known in the Ancient East and occasionally applied there in the first millennium B.C., as at Megiddo in Period III (Lamon and Shipton, 1939, 62, and figs. 71-2) and the unfinished town of Zernaki Tepe in Anatolia, which was laid out with a truly astonishing regularity

(Burney and Lawson, 1960, 185 ff.). Similarly, the idea of axial roads was known in 6th-century Babylon, and elsewhere. However, it is doubtful whether we should be justified in citing Near Eastern prototypes, especially where a regular grid is concerned. There are, indeed, examples of Phoenician and Punic towns which possessed plans denoted by rectangular blocks of houses set in a regular network of roads intersecting at right angles. We may mention Umm el Amed in Phoenicia (Dunand and Duru, 1962 *Texte*, 89 fig. 20, *Atlas* LXXXIX), T. Megadim near Athlit (as yet unpublished; I have to thank the excavator, Mr. Broshi of the Israel Museum for sending me a copy of the plan), Lixus at the other end of the Phoenician world (Tarradell, 1960, 106) and Carthage itself, at least in some parts of the urban territory, as recent excavations have shown (cf. Harden, 1971, 124 and bibliography referred to there). However, all these instances belong to a period when Greek influence was very probably at work, and must be reckoned as being affected by Hippodamian ideas of town planning. At Motya Greek influence is the more likely if, as we suggested, a planning module of ca. 35.40 m. can be assumed, for this corresponds very closely to an *actus* of 120 Attic feet of 29.6 cm. It should be added, perhaps, that the city of the Phaeacians in Homer's Odyssey (Books VI, ff.) approached by a causeway against which ships are drawn up, and where the visitor, on entering the city, is confronted by a temple and a market place, seems likewise to show some similarities with the type of plan encountered in the northern part of Motya. Thus in town-planning as in other spheres, Greek-Phoenician cultural contacts may have had a long history.

The orientation of the presumed grid at Motya—roughly NE by SW—may be paralleled at a number of Greek sites. However it is perhaps significant that it was also, so far as can be seen, the grid orientation at Carthage, as Cintas has recently pointed out (1968-1969, 59).

Taking the urban plan of Motya as a whole, the suggestion that elements inherited from the common Phoenician tradition may have been combined with Greek ideas of regularity is perhaps not unlikely: but we must await further exploration before we can justify deductions based on the very partial knowledge of ancient Motya which is at present available. It would also appear, from the comparisons given above, that, where urban features are concerned, parallels are closer with other Phoenician and Punic cities in the central Mediterranean (Sicily, Sardinia) than with Carthage.

(b) Fortifications

Whitaker, after describing the various types of fortifications at Motya, added a brief comparative section about the defences of Phoenician cities known at his time (1921, 152-3), and Pace (1938, 388) drew attention particularly to similarities between the fortifications at Motya and those at Eryx/Erice. Since then a more detailed comparison between the defence works at Motya and Erice has been made by Krischen (1941, 34-5 and pls. 20, 45, Abb. 33, 34). He saw no indication that the town walls at Motya were raised to any great height—which was indeed not required, since it was sufficient that they were higher than ships approaching from the sea; nor did he assume the existence of upper storeys in the towers, or of arrow slits or windows, the provision of platforms for artillery being adequate for defence purposes. A rampart walk provided with a simple cornice and water spouts, and a parapet crowned by battlements with semicircular tops were, however, elements regarded by him as essential parts of the defences. Since Krischen wrote, there has been further detailed study of the walls of Erice based on excavation by Bisi (1968, 103 ff.), who distinguished, above lower layers of megalithic stone construction attributable to the Elymians and datable from the 8th (?) to the 6th century B.C. (*loc. cit.*, 105), a constructional phase which she ascribed to the Carthaginians (first part of 5th century B.C. to the first half of the 3rd). This, according to her, comprises the upper parts of the towers and curtain walls, including the posterns, and is typified by pseudo-isodomous masonry (loc. cit., 106) which to us seems to recall Whitaker's types A and C at Motya.

Constructional similarities have also been noted between the walls of Motya and those of Monte Sirai and Nora in Sardinia (Barreca, in *Monte Sirai* I, 16), though here Whitaker's type B is referred to. The walls at Monte Sirai are attributed to the 6th century and presumably would compare with older constructions at Motya rather than with those at Erice. This indicates common techniques employed in the building of fortifications in the Phoenician and Punic settlements of the central Mediterranean during the 6th and 5th centuries B.C. The relationship is evident also in the existence of similar gate-plans (with polygonal bastions) at the North Gate at Motya and on the acropolis at Monte Sirai (cf. Whitaker, 1921, 166, plan C, with Barreca, *Monte Sirai* II, fig. 1).

When we wish to pursue inquiries further we are faced with considerable difficulties. The section of a town wall recently uncovered in the small Phoenician colonial settlement at Toscanos in Spain (A. Garcia y Bellido, H. Schubart, H. G. Niemeyer in Barreca and others, 1971, 151 ff.), which according to the excavators should reflect the methods of fortification in use in large, early Phoenician colonial establishments such as Gades, shows in its technique some analogies with the supposedly Phoenician type of walling at Samaria and Megiddo, Ramat Rachel, and Assur. This wall dates from the 7th century B.C. (Barreca, 1971, 155). The stretch of very fine walling at Motya uncovered by Whitaker (his "type D"—1921, 150) now dated to the 7th or 6th century by Tusa (*Mozia* VII, 55 ff., 79) may be a later descendant of this type of masonry though affected by Greek techniques. In Phoenicia itself, however, our information about the town walls is insufficient to guide us. The megalithic defences at Arvad are presumably late (Poidebard and Lauffrey, 1951, p. 81) although an earlier dating has been suggested (H. Frost, 1966, 13-28). Furthermore, there is no evidence of a general continuation in the overseas settlements of defence features that are presumably to be expected in the Phoenician homeland; in particular, the Phoenician colonial towns so far excavated offer no example of a common Asiatic types of gateway well known in lands bordering Phoenicia and presumably used in Phoenicia also. There is however one feature—battlements with semicircular tops—which seems to have been a traditional Phoenician characteristic. This, like much else in Phoenician architecture, was originally derived from Egypt (cf. the representations of Egyptian fortresses of the Middle and New Kingdoms, discussed by Emery (1960, 7-10 and plan IV), who assumes continuation of the type into the first millennium at Buhen). As Nicholls noted (1958, 110 and note 160), battlements of this type are shown on the towers of the town featured on the Amathus bowl which is ascribed by Gjerstad to the 8th century (1971, 10, 16-18). In addition to the examples from Motya, the existence of the type has been reported at Tharros (Pesce, 1964, 138) and such battlements are also apparently depicted on the defences of the city represented on a tomb painting from Djebel Mlezza in Tunisia (reproduced by Harden, 1971, 99 fig. 31b).

Representations by Assyrian artists of towns in the Phoenician homeland do not show this type of battlement. This may be due to inaccuracy, or to the representations being conventional and meant to apply to the Syro-Palestinian region as a whole.

The comparative lowness postulated for the town walls of Motya has also been assumed in the case of a number of other Phoenician cities, as at Tyre in the time of Sennacherib (Barnett, 1960, 18), Sidon in the 4th century B.C. (Harden, 1962, 133), at Erice (Krischen, 1941) and perhaps, in the Dj. Mlezza painting where the walls seem to be equal in height to two-storied houses. As against this, the statements of Arrian about the walls of Tyre at the time of Alexander the Great (*Anabasis*, II, XXI, 4), and the description by Appian (ch. 95, cf. Gsell, 1920, II, 22 ff.) of the defences of Carthage before they fell to the Romans would seem to hint that with the passing of time ideas on defence changed. Such changes may well have occurred also in other respects, especially under the impact of Greek military technology.

Greek influence on the Phoenician fortifications at Motya had been noted for some time, more particularly in their later stages. We can instance the strengthening of the City Walls with ashlar of

Greek type, described by Whitaker (his types D-E, 1921, p. 146-151), or the parallel in plan between the outer North Gate at Motya and the Athenian Dipylon Gate observed by B. Pace (1915, 432).

Greek influence, however, seems to have been at work before this. The art of fortification in early classical Greece shared with the Orient one technique of town defence, the use of a mud brick wall supported on a stone socle. The stone socle, which sometimes consisted of properly built facings with a packing of earth or rubble in between, as in 5th to 4th century Corinth, resembles in principle the constructions near the South Gate (Rhys Carpenter and Bon, 1936, 48, 54, 77. and see also especially Parsons, ibid., 87, discussing the east long wall there), or Mantinea (Fougères, 1898, 135 ff., esp. 146 fig. 22). An even greater similarity, however, is noticeable between the fortifications at the South Gate of Motya, and the technique of city-wall construction evolved somewhat later in the Greek cities of southern Italy and Sicily. This is the type of wall where the stone facings were carried up to the full height of the curtains, completely masking the earth and rubble filling, a type fully discussed by Säflund (1935, 97-8). The defences of Motya are basically of this kind. We should also note that the towers of Greek city defences before Hellenistic times were solid up to the rampart walk, like the tower near the Cothon channel, as were indeed oriental models (Winter, 1971, 173). At the same time we must however point out certain differences in construction between Greek and Phoenician town wall. Both in Corinth (Parsons, 1936, 282) and at Mantinea (Fougères, 1898, 146) foundations of the city wall were set in clearly defined foundation-trenches. The one at Mantinea is stated to have been 1½-2 m. deep. Nothing of this kind has been observed by us at Motya, where there is no indication of a foundation-trench on the inside of the city defences by the South Gate, though there may have been a shallow foundation-trench in some places on the outside, and though the recently discovered foundation-trench, found by Tusa on the north side of the island, must be borne in mind (*Mozia*, VII, 55 ff.).

Lastly, there seem to be certain parallelisms between constructional details in the town defences of Motya and those of certain early Italian settlements. Thus Prof. Bisi has recently identified a first, Elymian, stage in the defences of Erice, marked by the employment of megalithic technique and datable from the 8th (?) to the 6th centuries B.C. (Bisi, 1968, 105). The megalithic style of walling in use in the North Gate bastions at Motya may be derived from such prototypes. Even more interesting, perhaps, are certain analogies with continental Italy. The curtains flanking the South Gate at Motya consist of a wall backed on the inside by a deep filling arranged in layers, while on the outside the stretch of wall east of the Gate, at least, was free standing above the footings which were placed in a low bedding of soil. This recalls the methods employed in the city walls of Veii (Ward-Perkins, 1959, 45) which on the inside, were backed up against a substantial filling, and on the outside had their footings covered.

The resulting picture shows that at Motya of a limited number of original Phoenician traditions were retained, but there is also some evidence of an interrelation with Greek, and local Italian (Sicilian and Etruscan) techniques; such techniques being shared to some extent with other Phoenician or Punic towns in the central Mediterranean. Historically, such a state of things would not be surprising, though more evidence is desirable.

(c) Houses

As Prof. Tusa has observed (in *Mozia* V, 7 ff.) much less is known of domestic architecture in the city of Motya than could be desired. Nevertheless, if we review the evidence from excavations by Whitaker, the Italian expeditions and ourselves, certain basic facts can be stated, and comparisons can be made with houses at other Punic and Greek sites in Sicily and elsewhere.

At Motya, the existence of several types of house is archaeologically attested. The most elaborate is represented only by one example, the House of the Mosaics, excavated and described by Whitaker (1921, 194 ff.), and recently discussed at some length by Tusa (in *Mozia* III, 88 ff.). Tusa believes it was built after the fall of the city, well into the second half of the 4th century (*Mozia* III, 93). This seems possible, though further excavation is desirable to settle the point. Parallels to this type of structure in the Hellenistic Greek world are of course well known and are fully discussed by Tusa, and the Greek origin of the type is not in doubt.

A second variety is apparently represented by at least two examples. The first of these is the house at the south-eastern staircase. This building, perhaps partly revealed by Schliemann (cf. p. 108) was excavated and fairly fully described by Whitaker (1921, 159-160 ff; plan B, 162). Its construction is marked by the employment of large upright sandstone blocks set at ca. 1 m. intervals, the spaces between them being filled with rubble walling. This method of construction is styled *a telaio* by Italian archaeologists. There is a second specimen of the type near-by.

When excavating the House of the Mosaics, Whitaker noted (1921, 194) that it was erected above the ruins of an earlier building, and it is clear from its extant remains that this earlier structure must have been similar to the house at the south-eastern staircase. Tusa provides a new detailed plan showing both the older building and the overlying house of the Mosaics (in *Mozia* III, fig. 11; sections, fig. 12). A comparison of this plan with that of the house at the south-eastern staircase shows that the two buildings, so far as they are known, are remarkably similar both in lay-out and dimensions. It is not easy to reconstruct the complete plan of either house, since both are so incompletely preserved, but each may have included a central *cortile*.

No other example of a house built on a similar plan by similar constructional methods is known at Motya, but houses and other structures incorporating masonry of *a telaio* type are known on the island in a number of localities. The houses flanking the main road leading into the city from the North Gate are thus built, and such masonry is also found among the house ruins overlying the Cappiddazzu (Tusa, in *Mozia* II, 22-23; fig. 5), in buildings near the centre of the island, uncovered by Tusa (cf. *Mozia* V, 11, 22), and in some walls in the Tophet (Ciasca, in *Mozia* II, 34-5). We found a wall stump constructed in this fashion in our exploratory trench (A) at the central cross-roads (cf. Plan XV). Other examples occur in constructions backed against the town wall.

The majority of these examples appear to date from a late stage in the history of the city, or after its fall. The walling on both sides of the main road by the North Gate employs much re-used material (cf. also what Tusa says (*Mozia* I, 39) about the dating value of this, when discussing the adjoining north-west tower.) The ruins of the house over the Cappiddazzu belong to the second phase (*Mozia* II, 23) and the walls in the Tophet are dated well after 397 (*Mozia* II, 53). Tusa is inclined to give a fairly late date to the structures recently recovered by him near the centre of the island (cf. *Mozia* V, 18, 32). The walling found by us at the central cross roads appears to belong to the 5th or early 4th century; no indication of later use was found in our trench. These suggested dates are worth keeping in mind when we turn to the early houses near the south-eastern staircase, and below the house of the mosaics, the dating of which is at present uncertain. Whitaker believed that the former belonged to the earlier rather than the later period of Motya (1921, 160) but he does not say what was found there: Schliemann, who appears to have begun the excavation of this structure, favoured a 5th-century date for the ruins found on the strength of certain fragments of painted Greek vases (see below, p. 109). A 5th-century date is, indeed, perhaps the most likely, both for this structure and for the ruins below the House of the Mosaics.

Outside Motya, we cannot, apparently, point at present to any plans of Phoenician and Punic houses that are genuinely analogous. The style of masonry called *a telaio* is however widely known. It occurs in the Punic ruins at Selinunte which date from after the Carthaginian conquest of that city in 409 B.C. (cf. Di Vita, 1953, 39-40); at Solunto (Tusa, *Mozia* III, 144; Di Vita, 1953, 43); in Sardinia at Cagliari (Di Vita, 1953, 44) and at Nora (Pesce, 1961, 75). We may also refer to similar constructions in Africa, especially at Carthage (Harden, 1971, 125). It is worth noting that these examples tend to belong to the 4th century B.C. or later, rather than before; but the technique was not unknown earlier, as occasional examples at Tell Abu Hawam III and II show. (ca. 538-332, Stern, 1968, 218-9; cf. Hamilton, 1935, 2, 6). This style of building was, indeed, frequently employed in Israelite Palestine but does not seem to have become popular with Phoenician builders until the later period.

A third type of house is known from the upper strata in the South Gate area. This is a house of the courtyard type, sometimes with a pebble-paved *cortile*. The masonry is not constructed *a telaio*; walls are of rubble with occasional large ashlar blocks laid lengthways. This system also appears to have been employed in the ruins found in the exploratory trench (B) in the central "dip". A feature of the house remaining in this trench was the plastered floors set on a slope so as to collect water in cisterns occasionally topped by terracotta well covers (as fragments found show). Terracotta drainpipes and tile drains also occurred; and roofing was of the Siceliote tile type. In fact this type of house may be said to be related to Sicilian Greek houses, as at Himera (E. Joly in Adriani, 1970, 237-315, cf. Graham, 1972, 300-1), though our buildings have none of the more civilised amenities attested in the Greek *pastas* house. The buildings near the centre of the island, excavation of which was begun by Tusa (in *Mozia* V, 19 ff.) may prove to be of this type; walling *a telaio* is however, occasionally employed there, and the only structure that has been excavated to any considerable extent includes unusual features (*Mozia* V, 23-4).

We next come to the oldest constructions found near the South Gate. The large building of Phase IA found just north of the gateway appears to be similar, both in its general plan and in its dimensions, to the large building C, dated ca. 700 B.C., which was discovered recently in the Phoenician colonial settlement of Toscanos near Malaga in Spain (A. Garcia y Bellido, B. Schubart, H. G. Niemeyer, in Barreca and others, 1971, 153 ff.). This building is interpreted by the excavators as a public building, namely the commercial headquarters or counting house of the settlement. Ours might well have fulfilled a similar function. The building at Toscanos is assumed to have been completely roofed. We found no evidence of roofing in the central Room 1 of our building and interpreted it as a courtyard, but of this there is no definite proof. The analogies with certain store buildings in Palestine, as at T. en-Nasbeh and Beth Shemesh, to which the excavators of building C at Toscanos draw attention (1971, 153), would also apply to ours and it should thus belong to a more widely-found type, the presence of which in early Phoenician settlements is not without interest. A related type of building in Palestine, in which the central room is not divided from the rooms flanking it by walls but by rows of stone pillars, has recently been dealt with by Pritchard (1970, 268-276) who points out that the floor of the central room which may have been an unroofed court open to the sky was generally plastered, while the rooms flanking it were provided with paving (loc. cit., 272 and 276, note 41). This type of house has also been discussed more in detail by Shiloh (1970, 180 ff.). Pritchard's observations may help in interpreting our building, though its very incomplete state makes it difficult to come to definite conclusions. Room 1 was, perhaps, rather wide for roofing, and we have tended to regard it as a court. Rooms 5 and 6, where a pebble pavement was found, we interpreted in 1963 as a courtyard because it contained a hearth and a handmill (*ALUOS* 1962-3, 115) but it remains possible that it was a room.

We may conclude by turning our attention to a type of house known from literary evidence to have existed at Motya—the high multiple-storied house referred to in Diodorus (XIV, 48, 4, and 51, 1; 5-7). Little direct evidence about this type is available from excavations. However, a review of all the house remains at present excavated in various parts of the island brings out the fact that the walls of the buildings flanking the main road which enters the city by the North Gate are more solidly built and seem more capable than most of supporting the weight of upper floors. In addition, both the historical accounts and archaeological evidence make it likely that this is where the Greek besiegers launched their main attack and where the high houses referred to in the account of the siege must thus have stood. We have little information about the planning of these buildings, but we can note that the method of construction employed is again the one called by Italian archaeologists *a telaio*.

(d) Roads

Since a street is essentially a road flanked by houses, we include in this comparative study both roads and streets, whether made up, paved, or not. In seeking for analogies our main attention will be focused on examples from the Greek and from the Phoenician or Carthaginian world.

Comparative material within the Phoenician-Carthaginian sphere is of some interest, since certain classical authors assert that Carthage preceded Rome in the art of road-construction, more particularly in building paved roads. The relevant passages in classical authors, all of them well-known, are referred to by Forbes, (1934, 115-118).

Archaeological evidence in the Carthaginian homeland, especially at Carthage is disappointingly scarce. Certain stretches of road surface and well-drained streets, bordering *insulae* of houses, have come to light at Carthage (cf. Harden, 1971, 124, and 236, note 163), but these apparently formed part of the last city immediately before the destruction by the Romans in 146 B.C. and are, for purposes of comparison, too late for us, as they belonged to a town already much affected by Hellenistic influences.

Our best comparison in Punic settlements is probably to be found at Sulcis in Sardinia. Here Barreca (1961, 38-9) has recently cleared and briefly described the remains of three superimposed lengths of road surfaces forming part of a circumvallation road. The oldest of these (ascribed by Barreca to the 7th or 6th century B.C.) is roughly, though solidly, built, and consists of a layer of small irregular stones, ca. 20 cm. thick, but the second road which he ascribes to the 4th-3rd century B.C. is well constructed of small stones cemented together with mud, presenting a fairly flat surface. The third road is of Roman date, and does not concern us here. Where the natural rock crops out both the first and second road layers are missing, leading the author to the hypothesis that the roads of Punic cities, like those in Greek towns, made use of the natural rock surface wherever possible. This would have been improved where circumstances required it with a spreading of small stones more or less accurately laid, depending on the period in question, and the importance of the road concerned. Other pieces of road uncovered in or near Punic settlements in Sardinia, as at Monte Sirai (Barreca, in *Monte Sirai* I, 56-7) or at Monte Nai (Barreca, in *Monte Sirai* IV, 110) consist largely of rock surfaces showing deep wheel-ruts; the width of the road at Monte Nai is given as ca. 3 m. (Barreca, in *Monte Sirai* IV, 110).

None of these roads showed any marked indication of camber, drainage, or proper kerbs, though at Monte Nai, walls flanking the road served as boundaries.

In the Phoenician homeland, Tell Abu Hawam II shows city roads indifferently paved with stone, pebbles, or compressed mud laid on a rubble bedding (Hamilton, 1935, 3). A somewhat more solidly constructed stretch of paved road of the Persian period—late 6th to early 5th century B.C.—has been unearthed recently at Shikmonah near Haifa in Israel, (cf. Elgavish, 1968, 13).

Turning to roads in Greek cities in Sicily, we are confronted at Tyndaris by construction methods rather like those in Phoenician towns. There, the oldest (4th century B.C.) phase of a road recently investigated shows a walking surface of beaten sand over a thin layer of pebbles and potsherds, although the circumvallation road was somewhat more solidly constructed (F. Barreca, 1958, 149).

Greek road-work in the homeland seems on the whole to have been primitive, especially in the older periods, as is apparent from what Forbes says (1934, 101 ff.). Occasionally, better roads were made; such as one at Corinth (Rhys Carpenter and Bon, 1936, 59 ff.) attributed to the 5th century B.C., which consisted essentially of a bedding of loose small blocks of poros stone and chalk-like limestone covered by a coating of much smaller stones and heavy soil to make up the road surface. It is bounded by walls, and in places it is flanked by a flat expanse of hard-trodden clay, which might, but need not, have served as a side walk for pedestrians. The whole arrangement bears some resemblance to conditions outside the North Gate at Motya.

The general Near Eastern, and perhaps more particularly Assyrian-Babylonian tradition in making paved roads must also be kept in mind (Forbes, 1934, 70 ff.). The Phoenicians appear to have been in active contact with Babylonian road builders, as the presence of paving slabs from Lebanon on a stretch of the great processional street in Babylon goes to show (Forbes, 1934, 79). The basic method of road-construction, employing clearance and laying down of a road body was in any case more widely known in the ancient Orient. It is referred to e.g. in Isaiah (XL, 3) and in the Mesha inscription, though, as has been pointed out (Brown, Driver, Briggs, 1951, 700 s.v. מסלה) none of the examples of the use of this term for a built-up road body apply to a street in a city, but rather to a highway outside.

Taken together, our comparative material is at present too incomplete to allow us to say much about the antecedents of the type of road construction discovered at Motya. We must await the results of future research.

(e) Metrology

Note: No absolute agreement exists concerning the metric equivalents of ancient (Near Eastern and Greek) weights and measures. In what follows we shall therefore use figures given in the following widely accepted works of reference: *Handbuch der Klassischen Altertumskunde*, ed. I. Müller, I, 1892, p. 833 ff. (Chapter by H. Nissen); *Suppléments aux Dictionnaires de la Bible*, vol. V, Paris, 1957, (s.v. "métrologie biblique", article by J. Trinquet); or the *Interpreter's Dictionary of the Bible* (New York and Nashville, 1962), vol. IV, (article "Weights and measures" by O. R. Sellers, pp. 836-838).

The question of the weights and measures in use at Motya is of interest. Satisfactory data about weights are as yet insufficient to allow of statistical analysis, but on the other hand, there appears to be enough information about standards of measurement for us to attempt to determine those that were in common use.

Since Motya was a city inhabited by Phoenicians and Carthaginians, but also under strong Greek influence, we must be prepared for the possible existence of Greek standards of measurement as well as others that may be derived from Asia or Africa. The Greek system was essentially based on the foot (the most commonly used being the Attic foot of 29.6 cm); and frequently-employed fractions including the quarter and half foot (7.4 cm. and 14.8 cm. Attic), while the cubit of 1½ feet (44.4 cm. Attic) and the half cubit (22.2 cm. Attic) were also known. Of larger units the plethron of 100 ft. (29.6 m. Attic) were frequently employed. The Asiatic and Egyptian systems, on the other hand, were based on the cubit, the foot being unknown. There was a general tendency for the cubit to exist in two forms, a shorter "common" and a longer "royal" cubit. In Egypt the royal cubit was made up of 7 palms equalling 28 fingers while the common cubit of 6 palms equalled 24 fingers. The length of these cubit was 52.5 and 45.0 cm. respectively, and the half cubits (spans) were 26.25 cm. (for the longer) and 22.2 cm. (for the shorter cubit), the palm of the short cubit being 7.50 cm., and the finger 1.875 cm. in length. In Asia the older Babylonian cubit approximated to 49.5 cm.; Phoenician cubits of 49.7 cm. (long) and 41.25 cm. (short) are also mentioned. In Israel the cubit standards may have been slightly smaller than the Egyptian, 51.829 cm. for the royal cubit and 44.424 cm. for the common cubit; these were again divited into 7 or 6 palms respectively, equalling 28 and 24 fingers and differing little from their Egyptian counterparts. Among larger units a measuring rod of 6 cubits is referred to in ancient Israel and it was known also in Babylonia. In Israel, the long rod would have been ca. 3.10 m., the short one ca. 2.66 m. On the same principle, the Phoenician cubits would produce units of 2.982 m. and 2.475 m. respectively. The corresponding Egyptian standards would have been 3.15 m. and 2.70 m. respectively.

Before considering Motyan measurements in detail, we may recall some brief published observations about Phoenician-Carthaginian measurements. In Carthaginian North Africa, Gsell (1920, IV, 189) reports the frequent employment of the Egyptian cubit of 52.5 cm., while the general use of a cubit of 44.4 cm. in Carthage and also in Carthaginian Sicily is assumed by Nissen (1892, 883).

When we try to determine what standards were in use at Motya, we can begin with two suppositions. The first is, that in the laying out of buildings, roads, etc., the use of simple units, or very simple fractions, seem most likely on common sense grounds (e.g. a building might be 10 × 6½ units): a consideration of a good number of such measurements, taken in buildings where exact workmanship seems to have been used, should identify the unit. This method has been employed with some success elsewhere. Our second supposition is that it would be highly significant if certain individual measurements recurred in striking quantity in a number of smaller items, such as stelae, carved stones, architectural members, etc. We must, of course, keep in mind that different standards might have been used for different kinds of public or private buildings. The available data come from Whitaker's book, from the Italian reports (*Mozia*, I-VII), and from our own excavations. Numerous measurements of the stelae in the Tophet, given in the Italian reports (*Mozia*, I-IV), as well as the figures given for architectural members in the Cappiddazzu are particularly useful.

Turning firstly to large-scale public planning there seem to be a number of features which were planned in Attic feet. We may instance the diameter of the Cappiddazzu, which, as we saw (p. 87) seem to represent a planning module; its length, 35.4 m., equals very nearly an *actus* of 120 feet Attic (35.52 m.). Attic feet appear also to have been used in the layout of part, at least, of the town wall and bastions. Thus the length of the eastern bastion (Whitaker, 1921, 156, plan A) is 10.93 m., or almost exactly 37 ft. Attic, and it juts out 6.52 m., equalling 22 Attic feet. The piece of fine ashlar walling between two towers, described by Whitaker (1921, 146-147, fig. 9) measures 30.20 m. or 102 Attic feet. Near the South Gate, the distance between the bastion at the south-west corner of the island and the bastion flanking the Cothon channel on its eastern side is very nearly 29.6 m., or 100 Attic feet; however, the distance between the two bastions flanking the South Gate is 31.6 m., but planning is here disturbed by an acute angle between the western bastion and the Town Wall; had the junction been a right angle this distance would be diminished to something like the length of the fine ashlar walling between two towers (see above). From this it appears that distances more or less approximating to 100 Attic feet between towers or bastions were, at least sometimes, in the planners' minds. Reference to Whitaker's plan, or ours, makes it appear likely that this unit (or multiples of it), was also adopted in planning other sectors of the town wall. There are, however, places, e.g. the length of town wall flanking the east bastion on its northern side, where the *actus* unit of 120 Attic feet (35.52 m.) may have been intended. The Attic foot is perhaps also the unit of measurement employed in the layout of the Cothon channel. Here the narrowest sector is 5.30 m. wide—very nearly 18 Attic feet—and the average depth between the paving of the channel and the surface of the quay is 1.78 m. (or 6 Attic feet), while the length of the sides of the quay flanking the narrowest part is 7.50 and 7.40 m. respectively, measurements which seem to imply 25 Attic feet (7.40 m.). However, some of these measurements could also be regarded as approximations to measurements in cubits of 52.5 m. Lastly, in the planning of the inner unit of the North Gate, a structure of Greek type as Pace recognised (1915, 434), we find further detail implying measurements in Attic feet. Here the width of the eastern passage is given as 2.67 m, that of the western one as 2.37 m. (Whitaker, 1921, 169)-measurements corresponding almost exactly to 9 and 8 Attic feet. The measurements of the central pier, 3.70 m. in length and 1.20 m. in width (Whitaker, 1921) correspond closely enough to 12½ and 4 Attic feet.

The employment of Attic measurements is however less obvious in other parts of the city defences, such as the gates.

The maximum (northern) width of the South Gate gate, 5.41 m., is very nearly 11 Phoenician long cubits, while the minimum (southern) width, 4.97 m., is almost exactly ten such cubits. Perhaps this implies that the Phoenician standard rather than the Attic foot was used. Elsewhere it looks as if reference to the Egyptian longer cubit of 52.5 cm. or perhaps a slightly reduced version of it (51-52 cm.) would explain much. The main road entering the city from the North Gate is 7.80 m. wide (Whitaker, 1921, 170)-that is almost exactly 15 cubits of 52.5 cm.; the newly discovered road in the centre of the island is 5.50 cm. wide (Tusa, in *Mozia* V, 19) which is fairly near to 10½ cubits. This standard also seems to have been used in some public and private buildings although not all buildings known seem to lend themselves to analysis by this or, for that matter, any other standard. Thus in the casemate in the city defences west of the South Gate the width of the door is 1.25 m., just short of 2.5 cubits; the length of the entrance passage is 2.50 m., or ca. 5 cubits; the length of the angle turn is 2.20 m., or a little above 4 cubits; the pillar west of the entrance is one cubit 52 cm. wide and a little more than three cubits long. The length of the casemate is ca. 8 cubits, and its width was apparently the same.

At the other end of the island, the doorway of the Phoenician house near the south-eastern staircase (Whitaker 1921, 159 ff.) provides a chance for obtaining some accurate measurements of the cuttings intended to take the wooden door frame and lock visible on the photo (Whitaker, 1921, 161, fig. 14). Here the horizontal cutting for the lintel is 1.32 m. long or 2½ Egyptian cubits; the width of the wooden door frame between outer edges is 1.05 m., or exactly two cubits; the inner width is 92 cm. or 1¾ cubits. The height of the door appears to have been intended to be 3⅓ cubits (1.75 m.).

The width of the wheel ruts in the North Gate, 1.56 m., equals 3 cubits almost exactly.

Lastly, when we analyse measurements given for stelae, architectural carvings, etc., we note some which occur frequently: 8 cm. (a little large for an Egyptian palm, but ca. $\frac{1}{6}$ of a Phoenician large cubit); 9 cm. ($\frac{1}{5}$ of a cubit of 45 cm.); 10 cm. ($\frac{1}{5}$ of a diminished large Egyptian cubit); 11 cm ($\frac{1}{4}$ of a cubit of 44 cm.); 12 cm. ($\frac{1}{4}$ of a diminished Phoenician cubit); 13 cm. ($\frac{1}{4}$ of a large Egyptian cubit); 16 cm. (a little large for two palms). The impression received is that cubits of 44-45 cm., 49 cm., and 52 cm. may all be represented here; connexion with feet, Attic or others, seems less likely. The cubits of 52.5 and 49.7 cm. have been encountered before; perhaps the hint that a standard of 44.4-45 cm. was also used at Motya may prove useful as more measurements become available through excavation.

We may conclude with a negative note. Recently, Graham (1972, 300) has drawn attention to the use made by the Greeks in Sicily of the Doric foot of 32.6 cm, and he thought the employment of this standard of measurement could be demonstrated at Himera. We have not, up to now, found sufficient indications that this unit was used at Motya, but it is of course not impossible future work there may demonstrate that it was on occasion employed there also.

(f) Religion

Few facts relating to the religious beliefs and practices of the ancient Motyans have come to light in our excavations and we did not find a single inscribed object with a divine name. We are not yet therefore, in a position to say much about religion. This may be left for later, when it is hoped additional data may permit a systematic study. Nevertheless some remarks about the religious significance of some of our discoveries seem apposite.

We may divide our subject into the domains of private and public cult. Among objects connected with private cult we may cite the phylactery described by Dr. Snodgrass (vol. II, chapter 4). This belongs to a class of object well attested in Phoenician and Punic archaeology (see now especially Leclant, 1968-9, 99) and probably not without relation to the ancient Israelite phylacteries. Better attested, however, are the small domestic altars or *arulae* (Cf. vol. II, chapter 3). These, as is well known, are not Phoenician, but are common in Greek Sicily and southern Italy (Van Buren, 1918, 15 ff.) and their presence, therefore, attests that domestic cult practices must have been affected by Greek ideas and forms. The same applies to ritual cake stamps (see vol. II, Chapter 3). For evidence relating to public worship, we may look to the West Sanctuary just outside the North Gate and to the fragmentary sanctuary to the east nearby. We might, indeed, add that the main road through the North Gate appears to aim straight at Mount Eryx with its famous ancient sanctuary. Perhaps the siting of the causeway from Motya to the mainland on this alignment, rather than across the shortest stretch of water between the present landing stage on the island, and the mainland near Palma (Spagnola) may itself to some extent be due to considerations of a religious nature.

The Western Sanctuary in its final shape may, as Mr. Coldstream has pointed out, have borne comparison with other Phoenician sanctuaries in the homeland and N. Africa. One may recall that the position for the altar indicates a W-E orientation with the adyton on the west side, a tradition shared with the Cappiddazzu temple at Motya and with certain other Phoenician or Phoenician-built sanctuaries, such as the temple at T. Taiyinat, or the Temple in Jerusalem.

It is harder to make any useful comment about the Eastern Sanctuary because of its extremely fragmentary condition. The construction and arrangment of the surviving walls show perhaps certain analogies with the Tophet at Sulcis in Sardinia (cf. Pesce, 1961, fig. 17) and possibly also with the much ruined neo-Punic sanctuary at Menzel Harb in Tunisia (Foucher, 1966, 119-121). The ritual bowls resemble in character inscribed cult bowls from the Temple at Tas-Silg in Malta (Garbini, *Malta* III, Pl. 39 : 7, 12; Pl. 40; Pl. 41 : 4) although the Motyan ones bear no inscriptions.

Of the multitude of ritual deposits mentioned at Sulcis, such as betyls, cippi, and figurines (Pesce, 1960, 69) we have no trace, although we cannot say what may have been contained in the vanished upper layers of what is now only a truncated stump. The urns of Sulcis are paralleled to some extent by the three urns deposited between the inner and outer kerbs of our building. However, perhaps the analogies do not lie entirely with the Punic sites: the extramural sanctuary devoted to the chthonic deities, recently discovered at Bitalemi near Gela (Orlandini, 1966, 8 ff.), offers similar features, including buried deposits.

Our knowledge of Phoenician religion at Motya is still fragmentary. As, however, the Italian excavations in the Tophet and in the Cappiddazzu have shown, ancient oriental ideas and practices were preserved, though the advent of Greek civilization might modify their expression. This applies to our finds also. If some of the temples at Motya, which were sacred to deities worshipped by both the Greeks and the Phoenicians (Diodorus, XIV), are ever located and excavated our knowledge of this aspect should receive a significant augmentation.

In any case, a considerable variety of religious structures is now known in the city, particularly since the apparently sacred installations in the complex of buildings excavated by Soprintendente Tusa near the centre of the island (in *Mozia* V, p. 23) must now be added to the list of religious buildings. One may, with due caution, also consider whether a sacred character might have been intended for the building north of the Villa, which was partly dug by Whitaker, and more of which was recently cleared by Soprintendente Tusa (in *Mozia* V, 10 ff.). The planning, so far as revealed (a square room, descent into which is made by a flight of steps from a higher level, and provided with a central pillar; the whole apparently surrounded by other rooms), recalls sanctuaries of the type with a central pillar recently identified at Shechem (Tananir) and Amman (cf. Boling, 1969, 82 ff.; Hennesy 1969, 155-157 ff.) These two buildings date respectively from the Palestinian Middle Bronze II (ca. 1600-1543) and Late Bronze Age (just before 1400 BC to some time in the 13th century B.C.), but Wright (1968, 9-16) has drawn attention to the existence of somewhat analogous temples in the Near East during the Iron Age. This type of sacred edifice could thus have extended to the Phoenician sphere at that time. The deposit of jars in the building, noted by Tusa, would then be sacral, and comparable to ritual deposits of pottery, including store jars, at Selinus during the period of Punic occupation (Tusa in *Mozia* II, 147).

APPENDICES

1. NOTE ON MOLLUSCA FROM OUTSIDE THE SOUTH GATE

The report received from Mr. C. P. Nuttall of the British Museum (Natural History) in London, given below, refers to material from digging location Tr. 60 (7) which corresponds to Tr. 6 (37) in our present notation. Several species from this layer, ca. 1.30 m below land surface, differ from those found by the underwater survey of Dr. Wilkinson given in Appendix 2; however both workers agree that the fauna analysed here is "typical present-day Mediterranean".

Provisional report on a collection of Mollusca from the island of Motya, near Marsala, Sicily, made by the Department of Semitic Languages and Literatures, Leeds University

Sample T.R. 60, Black sand and shells—MTR 60(7) Coll. 10.7.64 by R.M.

Gastropoda

Fragments of several different trochids several *Rissoa* (at least two species)
25+ *Cerithium vulgatum* Bruguière
5 *Cerithium rupestre* Risso
1 *Muricopsis* cf. *blainvillei*
1 *Nassarius corniculum* (Olivi)
2 *Nassarius (Cyclope)* cf. *neritea* (Linné)
2 *Nassarius* cf. *costulatus* (Brocchi)
1 *Pyrene rustica* (Linné)

Bivalvia

1 *Cardita trapezia* (Linné)
6+ *Lucina (Loripes) lactea* (Linné) (mainly fragments)
1 *Cardium edule* (Linné)

Most of the sample was washed and sieved to extract the shells from the sand. The residue includes many small pebbles and a certain amount of poorly preserved plant remains which gave the sand its dark grey appearance.

Dr. Kathleen Chesters, one of the palaeobotanists in this Department, has examined the plant remains and reports that the material includes one grape seed. The bulk of the fragments also appear to belong to land plants but they are quite indeterminate. They could easily have been washed into the water.

Several other molluscan species were found which have not been listed as they are either small or broken. The whole fauna, with one possible exception (discussed below) is of shallow-water marine molluscs and is strongly dominated by the two species of *Cerithium* and by *Lucina lactea*. Although many shells are broken, I think, because of the large number present, that many of the specimens of these three species are likely to have lived close by, and were not transported from some distance after death.

This sand would have been formed in shallow sea-water. It seems possible that conditions were moderately sheltered, as in a bay or natural harbour. On the other hand it is equally possible that this sample comes from the strand line of a fossil beauch.

One small fragment of shell about 6 mm. × 2 mm., and bearing a pale brown stripe, may well be of a holicid land snail (the family that includes garden snails). It seems rather more fresh than the rest of the material and might not be contemporary. In any case it could have been washed out into the water quite easily. It forms such an insignificant proportion of the whole collection that its presence has no bearing on the conclusions reached.

2. DISTRIBUTIONAL STUDIES OF MARINE MOLLUSCA IN WESTERN SICILY

by Cristopher Wilkinson
Department of Biological Siences, Portsmouth Polytechnic

Synopsis

This paper gives details of sampling methods and identifications of the marine mollusca collected near Is. Motya (San Pantaleo) and Is. Favignana, W. Sicily. It compares the distribution of species occurring in the shallow water of a lagoon with that of species occurring in deep exposed water.

Introduction

A team of underwater divers from the Imperial College of Science and Technology, London, went to Motya, Western Sicily in the summer of 1962. They assisted with underwater aspects of the excavations carried out by the Institute of Archaeology; identified animal remains from these excavations and carried out the following investigation into the present distribution of marine molluscs.

Survey 1. Motya (27.VII.62)

Collecting was carried out in the shallow lagoon which surrounds Motya (see Map, fig. 5.) Distribution of mollusc species is typified by the results of the first transect carried out from the south east shore of Motya. It extended horizontally from above extreme high water mark to 45 feet beyond extreme low water mark where the deepest depth was only 1′7″. Random quadrats were sampled further out into the lagoon, thus providing specimens occuring down to 3′. The water marks were some distance apart. Bearing in mind the lack of tides the following horizontal distances indicate the shallowness of the gradient.

E H W — N H W — 6′; N H W — N L W — 6′-14′; N L W — E L W — 14′-15′.

Corresponding with these water marks the transect was divisible into three zones, of which the last only is concerned in this paper.

1. Isopod zone from 8′ below E H W to the existing water level.
2. Burrowing Polychaete zone below E H W from 10′8″-15′.
3. *Posidonia oceanica* extended from 15′, i.e. E L W to cover almost the entire lagoon.

Six quadrats 10″ square and 2′ apart were sampled at every 15′ interval. All fauna and flora falling within the quadrat was removed and placed into labelled bags for later sorting and identification. Collecting had to be carried out by wading in the water. The molluscan results are as follows:

TRANSECT I

1. Horizontal distance from E L W — 15′.
Depth of water from N W L — 6″.
No. of quadrats containing molluscs — 4/6.

Species present:

Quadrat 1 (R1)
4 (2 juv.) *Rissoa (Zippora) paradoxa* Monterosato.
4 (2 v. juv.) *Cerithium vulgatum* Bruguière.
Quadrat 2 (R2)
4 *Rissoa (Zippora) paradoxa* Monterosato.
Quadrat 3 (R3)
1 *Rissoa (Zippora) paradoxa* Monterosato.
1 (v. juv.) *Cerithium vulgatum* Bruguière.
2 (1 v. juv.) *Conus mediterraneus* Hwass.
Quadrat 4 (L1)
2 *Rissoa (Zippora) paradoxa* Monterosato.

2. Horizontal distance from E L W — 30′.
Depth of water from N W L — 1′1″.
No. of quadrats containing molluscs — 5/6.

Species present:

Qadrat 1 (R2)
1 *Alvania reticulata* (Montagu).
4 (v. juv.) *Mitra cornicula* Linné.
1 *Pusia tricolor* Gmelin.
1 (v. juv.) *Cerithium vulgatum* (Bruguière).
2 (v. juv.) *Haminea hydatis* (Linné)?
Quadrat 2 (L1)
1 *Tricolia tenuis* (Michaud).
1 *Mitra cornicula* Linné
1 *Pusia tricolor* (Gmelin).
1 (juv.) *Haminea hydatis* (Linné).
1 (dead) *Diodora graeca* (Linné).
2 *Cerithium vulgatum* Bruguière.
1 *Conus mediterraneus* Hwass.
Quadrat 3 (R1)
2 *Conus mediterraneus* Hwass.
Quadrat 4 (L2)
1 *Conus mediterraneus* Hwass.
Quadrat 5 (R3)
1 *Cerithium vulgatum* Bruguière.

3. Horizontal distance from E L W — 45′.
Depth of water from N W L — 1′7″.

No. of quadrats containing molluscs — 4/6.

Quadrat 1 (R1)

1	*Mitra cornicula* Linné.
2	*Cerithium vulgatum* Bruguière.

Quadrat 2 (R2)

1	*Rissoa (Zippora) paradoxa* Monterosato.
1	*Cerithium vulgatum* Bruguière.

Qudrat 3 (L1)

4 (v. juv.)	*Cerithium vulgatum* Bruguière.

Quadrat 4 (L3)

1	*Conus mediterraneus* Hwass.
1	*Cerithium vulgatum* Bruguière.

Beyond the transect line further collections were made from six quadrats placed at random in 2-3′ of water.

2	*Chiton olivaceus* Spengler.
1	*Acanthochitona communis* (Risso).
1	*Lepidopleurus cajetanus* Poli.
1	*Pusia tricolor* (Gmelin).
3 (2 juv.)	*Rissoa (Zippora) paradoxa* Monterosato.
4	*Columbella rustica* (Linné).
4	*Tricolia tenuis* (Michaud).
1 (dead)	*Persicula miliaris* (Linné).
4	*Alvania reticulata* (Montagu).
8	*Cerithium vulgatum* Bruguière.
5	*Cerithium sp.*
5 (2 juv.)	*Conus mediterraneus*
1 (dead)	*Venerupis aureus* (Gmelin).
1 valve	*Diplodonta rotundata* (Montagu).
1 valve	*Cardium lamarcki* Reeve.

Species of Gastropoda from the Motya Survey in order of frequency

Species	*Total Number Collected*	*Number of Occurrences*
Cerithium vulgatum	25	10
Rissoa paradoxa	15	6
Conus mediterraneus	12	7
Mitra cornicula	6	3
Tricolia tenuis	5	3
Alvania reticulata	5	2
Columbella rustica	4	3
Pusia tricolor	3	3
Haminea hydatis	3	2
Persicula miliaris	1	1
Diodora graeca	1	1
Venerupis aureus	1	1
12 species	*Total* 81	

Survey 2. *Favignana*

Near Is. Favignana two deep water transects were carried out at Scoglio Correnti and Is. Galeotta from 0 m-30 m. It was also hoped to carry out more extensive transects at Secca del Toro, but rough seas prevented more detailed work, other than to make general surveys and random collections down to 40 m. It is an area worthy of further study. The method used for these transects (No's II and III) has already been described by the author (1966 & 1967). Samples were taken at 5 m intervals with 100 cm² quadrats; profiles are as in Figs. 1 and 2 and the molluscan species found are given in the tables below.

TRANSECT II
Sc. Correnti
12°17′ (E. side of 2nd island out). Cf. fig. 23, p. 105.

Depth in metres below sea level	*Number*	*Species*
0 m.	No samples taken.	
5 m.	1 (v. small)	*Chiton* sp.
	1	*Modiolus barbatus* (Linné)
	1 (v. juv.)	*Cerithium* or *Murex*
10 m.	1	*Pusia tricolor* (Gmelin)
	1 (dead)	*Pleurotomoides purpurea* (Montagu)
	28	*Rissoina variabilis* (Mühlfeld)
	2	*Philbertia linearis* (Montagu)
	1	*Mitrella scripta* (Linné)
	3 (juv.)	*Alvania montagui* (Payraudeau)
	9 (juv.)	*Bittium reticulatum* DaCosta.
	1 (juv.)	*Calliostoma conulum* (Linné)
	1 (v. juv.)	*Monodonta sp.?*
	1	*Mitrolumna olivoidea* (Cantraine)
	2 (1 juv.)	*Fusus leucozona* (Philippi)
	1	*Alvania lineata* Risso
15 m.	20 (2 v. small)	*Rissoina variabilis* Mühlfeld
	7 (var. st.)	*Columbella rustica* Linné
	14 (var. st.)	*Bittium lima* Bruguière)
	3 (juv.)	*Mitrella decollata* (Bruguière)
	1 (juv.)	*Mitra savignyi* (Payraudeau)
	8 (var. st.)	*Alvania montagui* (Payraudeau)
	1 (juv.)	*Philbertia linearis* Montagu
	1 (juv. valve)	*Barbatia barbata* (Linné)
	2 (v. juv.)	*Calliostoma conulum* (Linné)
20 m.	12 (dead) (3 juv.)	*Cerithium vulgatum* Bruguière
	1 (juv.)	*Calliostoma conulum* (Linné)
	2 (v. juv.)	*Murex cristatus* Brocchi
	1 (juv. valve)	*Barbatia barbata* (Linné)
	3 (2 dead 1 v. v. juv.)	*Bittium reticulatum* DaCosta
	1 (juv.)	*Triphora perversa* Linné
	2 (dead)	*Mitrella scripta* (Linné)
	1 (juv.)	*Cantharidus exasperatus* (Pennant)

Depth in metres below sea level	*Number*	*Species*
25 m.	1	*Vexillum (Uromita) ebenus* (Lamarck)
	2 (v. small)	*Chiton* sp.
	1 (juv.)	*Cerithium pulchellum* Philippi
	3	*Musculus discors* (Linné) attached to calcareous algae.
30 m.	4	*Mitrella scripta* (Linné)
	1 (juv.)	*Murex cristatus?* var. *inermis* Philippi
	2 (dead)	*Mitra savignyi* Payraudeau
	4 (valves)	*Barbatia barbata* (Linné)
	2	*Cantharidus exasperatus* (Pennant)
	2 (juv.)	*Fissurella* sp.
	2 (juv.)	*Haminea* sp. ?*hydatis* (Linné)

Transect III

Is. Galeotta

12°18′ (profile facing west). CF. fig. 24, p. 105.

Depth in metres below sea level	*Number*	*Species*
0 m.	145 (v. v. juv.)	*Rissoina variabilis* Mühlfeld
	2 (dead)	*Columbella rustica* (Linné)
	1 (dead)	*Cerithium* sp. 1 fragment.
	1	*Pleurotomoides purpurea* (Montagu)
	7 (juv.)	*Calliostoma* sp. (after comparison with Norman Coll. they might be any of several spp.)
5 m.	2	*Columbella rustica* (Linné)
	2	*Rissoina variabilis* Mühlfeld
	4	*Alvania montagui* (Payraudeau)
	1 (v. juv.)	*Chlamys ?varius* (Linné)
	1 (v. juv.)	*Lima ?inflata* (this sp. is attributed to Chemnitz but his names are not normally accepted)
	2 (juv.)	*Bittium reticulatum* DaCosta
	1	*Nassarius costulata* (Renieri) var. *pulcherrima* Buquoy, Dautzenberg & Dollfus
	1	*Musculus discors* (Linné)
10 m.	11	*Rissoina variabilis* Mühlfeld
	1	*Cerithium pulchellum* Philippi
	1	*Alvania montagui* (Payraudeau)
	2 (1 juv.)	*Bittium reticulatum* DaCosta

Depth in metres below sea level	*Number*	*Species*
15 m.	1	*Murex cristatus* Brocchi
	4 (1 juv.)	*Rissoina variabilis* Mühlfeld
	10 (s. juv.)	*Alvania montagui* Payraudeau
	7 (3 juv.)	*Mitrella scripta* (Linné)
	1	*Triphora perversa* (Linné)
	10 (s. juv.)	*Bittium reticulatum* Da Costa
	4 (juv.)	*Pleurotomoides purpurea* (Montagu)
	1	*Mitrolumna olivoidea* (Cantraine)
	1 (juv.)	*Fusus syracusanus* Linné
20 m.	4 (juv. valves)	*Barbatia barbata* (Linné)
	1 (dead)	*Diodora graeca* (Linné)
	1	*Persicula miliaris* (Linné)
	4	*Mitrolumna olivoidea* (Cantraine)
	1 (juv.)	*Bittium ?lima*
	1 (dead)	*Mitra tricolor* Gmelin
25 m.	1 (valve)	*Arca noae* Linné
	5 (3 v. juv.) (2 valves)	*Barbatia barbata* (Linné)
	1 (juv.)	*Chlamys varius* (Linné)
	1 (v. juv.)	*Cardium* sp.
	1 (juv. dead)	*Dentalium vulgare* DaCosta
	1 (v. juv.)	*Haliotis lamellosa* Lamarck
	1 (dead)	*Alvania montagui* Payraudeau
	1 (dead)	*Philbertia linearis* (Montagu)
	1	*Mitrella scripta* (Linné)
	1 (juv. dead)	*Triphora perversa* (Linné)
	1	*Rissoina variabilis* Mühlfeld
	2	*Rissoina bruguieri* Payraudeau
	1 (juv.)	*Bittium reticulatum* DaCosta
	1	*Pleurotomoides reticulata* Renier
30 m.	2 (v. juv.)	*Haliotis* sp.
	1 (v. juv.)	*Calypterea chinensis* Linné
	1 (juv.)	*Chiton* sp.
	1	*Cardium* sp.
	1	*Pusia tricolor* (Gmelin)
	1 (juv.)	*Lepidopleurus cajetanus* (Poli)
	1	*Persicula miliaris* (Linné)
	1 (dead)	*Rissoina bruguiere* (Payraudeau)
	1	*Calliostoma conulum* (Linné)
	1 (juv. dead)	*Haminea hydatis* (Linné)
	1 (juv. dead)	*Homalopoma sanguinea* (Linné)
	1 (juv. dead)	*Mitrella* decollata (Bruguière)
	1(juv. dead)	*Bittium reticulatum* Da Costa
	1 (dead)	*Pleurotomoides purpurea* (Montagu)
	1 (juv.)	*Cantharidus striatus* (Linné)
	1	*Parvicardium papillosum* (Poli)

v. juv. — very juvenile
s. juv. — some juveniles
var. st. — various stages of development.

The most common species of Gastropoda from the Favignana Survey in order of frequency

Species	*Total Number Collected*	*Number of Occurrences*
Rissoina variabilis	211	7
Bittium reticulatum	28	7
Alvania montagui	27	6
Mitrella scripta	15	5
Bittium lima	15	2
Cerithium vulgatum	12	1
Columbella rustica	11	3
Mitrolumna olivoidea	6	3
Calliostoma conulum	5	4
Philbertia linearis	4	3
Murex cristatus	4	3
Musculus discors	4	2
Mitrella decollata	4	2
Triphora perversa	3	3
14 species	*Total* 349	

Survey 3a

Marine Mollusca contained in a Roman Amphora found off Levanzo, Sicily 1962 in 100 feet of water.

1	*Vermetus* sp. or spp.
7 valves	*Spondylus gaederopus* Linné
1 juv. + 2 valves	*Venus verrucosa* Linné
2 juv. + 6 valves	*Lima lima* Linné
4 valves	*Arca noae* Linné
9 valves	*Barbatia barbata* Linné
4 valves	*Codakia (Jagonia) jagon* (Anderson)
5 (1 juv.)	*Haliotis lamellosa* Lamarck
1	*Astraea (Bolma) rugosa* (Linné)
5 valves	*Chlamys pes-felis* (Linné)
3	*Cypraea spurca* Linné
1 broken	*Murex trunculus* var *conglobatus* Michelotti
1	*Murex brandaris* Linné
1 broken	*Ocenebra erinacea* (Linné)
1	*Purpura haemastoma* (Linné)
2 valves	*Lima hians* Gmelin
1	*Crepidula unguiformis* Lamarck

Note: Most of the above were too encrusted and calcified to be associated with the female octopus found in the amphora.

3b. Strand-line collecting

1	*Cypraea spurca* Linné
2 (1 dead)	*Haliotis lamellosa* Lamarck
1 valve	*Venus verrucosa* Linné
1 (dead)	*Patella ferruginea* Gmelin

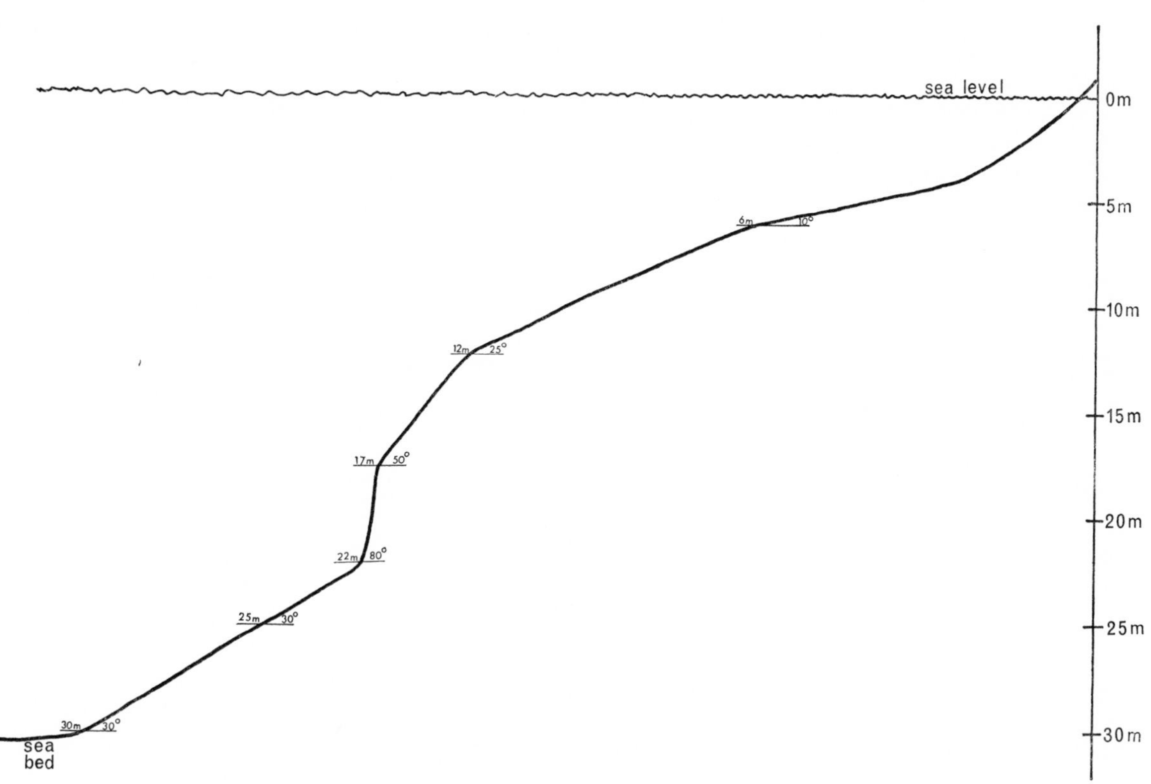

Fig. 23. Profile of Transect II. Sc. Correnti.

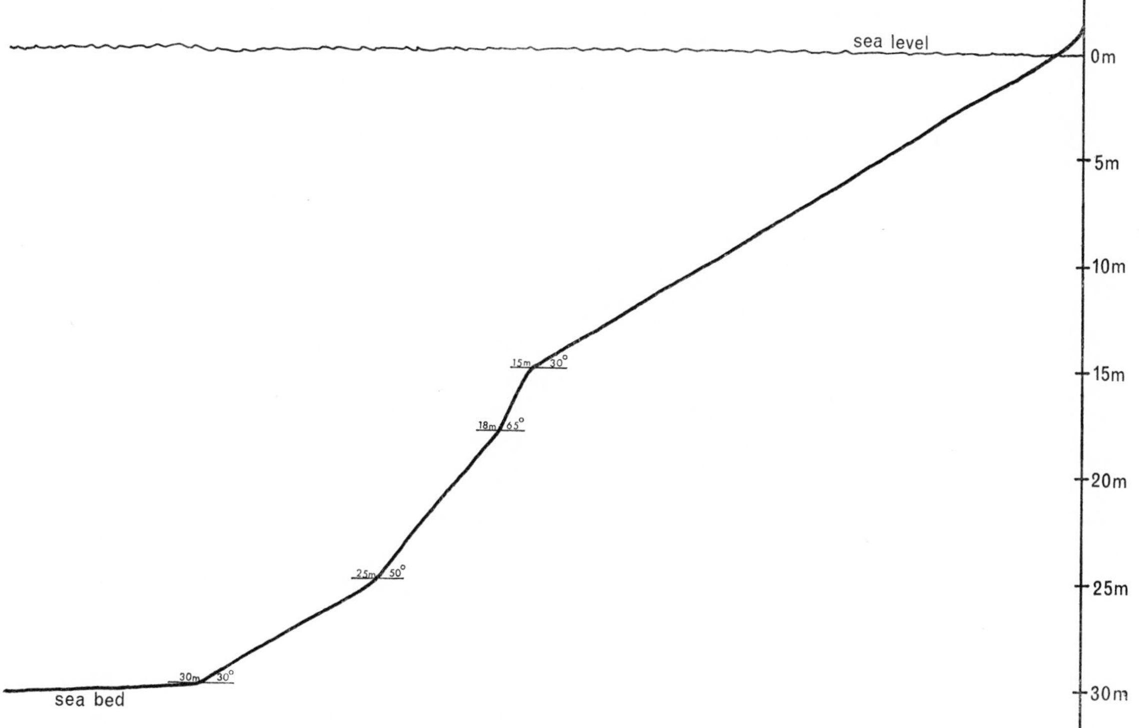

Fig. 24. Profile of Transect III-Is. Galeotta.

I am most grateful to the late Rev. H. E. J. Biggs for generously carrying out these determinations.

As in two previous papers (loc. cit.) it appears that *Rissoina variabilis* very often congregate together. Numbers of individuals found together were 145, 28, 20, 11, 4, 2 & 1. Thus it is the most common species in the deep water transects. It is, however, absent completely from the shallow lagoon transects.

At Om. Transect 2, the quadrat seems to have dropped on a very young "colony" or recently hatched batch of eggs. On the other hand, *Rissoa (Zippora) paradoxa* and *Mitra cornicula* seem to prefer the shallow lagoon distribution. *Columbella rustica* occurred in both surveys, but as reported for Malta, (loc. cit.) no examples were taken below 15 m. Although *Alvania reticulata*, *Tricolia tenuis* and *Conus mediterraneus* were only collected in the shallow water of Motya lagoon, the sampling is too small to draw any definite inferences. In fact, *Conus mediterraneus* has been collected on submarine cliffs in Malta down to 35 m., so its range of depth is comparatively wide.

Bittium reticulatum was common again at Favignana although not found at Motya. No transect yet shows it occurring above 2 m. Of the 15 examples of *Bittium lima* 14 were found in one quadrat, hence its higher position than might be expected on the frequency table. *Cerithium vulgatum*, *Pusia tricolor* and *Haminea hydatis* were found in both surveys, and the first being the most common species in Motya. The third most common species in the deep water transects—*Alvania montagui*—is unexpected since in Malta *Alvania cimex* Linné was more common. Again *montagui* has been collected mainly in small groups—10, 8, 4, 3, and 2 × 1. Is it replaced by *Alvania reticulata* in the shallow waters of Motya lagoon? *Mitrolumna olivoides* was collected in three quadrats whereas in Malta only two dead examples were found in the sponge *Calyx nicaeense* (loc. cit. 1967).

References

H. E. J. Biggs & Christopher Wilkinson, 1966, Marine Molluscs from Malta. *J. Conch.* 26: 52-65, 2 figs., 4 tables.

C. Wilkinson, J. Bevan, and C. Balaam, 1967, Distributional Studies of Marine Molluscs in Malta. *Underwater Association Report* 1966-67. 89-100 pp., 3 figs., 5 tables.

3. NOTE ON A TIMBER SPECIMEN FROM THE NORTH GATE REGION

The brief report by Miss C. Western given below was first published in *ALUOS* IV, 1962-3, 111-2. The digging location (Trench C 10) corresponds, in our present terminology, to layer (9) to the north-west of the Western Sanctuary outside the North Gate, as indicated above (p. 73).

Timber Specimen from Motya, North Gate Trench C 10 by Miss C. Western.

The specimen is part of a branch, its present diameter being 1¾ ins. and its length 5 ins. The wood was found wet, or at least damp, and probably the original diameter was about 2¼ ins.-2½ ins. A certain amount of bark remains intact. The whole piece was impregnated with Carbowax 4000 (polyethylene glycol), and then sections were cut by hand and expanded in water.

Despite some deformity the anatomical features of the wood bear a close resemblance to those of both *Phillyrea* and *Rhamnus*. *Phillyrea media* and *Rhamnus alaternus* are the only species of which comparative material is available to me, but since it is not usually possible to make a definite distinction between the woods of species within a genus this may not be of much importance. So far as can be ascertained from inadequate references *Phillyrea media* occurs in most of the higher altitudes near the coast of the eastern Mediterranean, as far south as Mt. Carmel and Mt. Tabor, and in Cyprus, and at lower altitudes (up to 300 m.) in Dalmatia, which is some distance further north. It is frequently associated with *Rhamnus alaternus* and *R. palaestina*. *R. punctata* occurs in the low-lying maquis in Cyprus, and also on Mt. Carmel. Surprisingly, neither *Phyllyrea* nor *Rhamnus* species are listed for either Greece or Yugoslavia, but species of both certainly occur in the maquis of southern France, and *Phillyrea angustifolia*, *P. decora* and *P. latifolia* are listed as of Mediterranean distribution. All are shrubs or small trees, evergreen or almost so, with small leathery dark green leaves, usually superficially similar to those of the scrubby evergreen oaks.

Since it is hard, by comparison feature by feature, to distinguish between the wood of *Rhamnus* and *Phyllyrea* one can only make a distinction by general appearance, and the specimen from Motya is in general much more like the specimens of *Phillyrea* available for comparison than those of *Rhamnus*.

4. TRAFFIC THROUGH THE NORTH GATE

The following report by Mrs. G. Pike is reprinted without modifications from *ALUOS* IV, 1962-3, 112-14.

The northern entrance from the seashore to the hinterland of Motya consists of a cutting, faced with heavy blocks of masonry, which extends some 750 m. behind the North Gate (Plate X, b). A wall of massive stone blocks divides the entrance into two roadways, 350 cm. in width, paved with rectangular stone slabs. The wall had obviously been built in order to separate ingoing from outgoing traffic, a simple but effective device which is not encountered on the Greek city and temple-sites of Sicily and Calabria.

Pairs of ruts, which, where they are well-preserved, show the sharply defined inverted trapezoidal section made by the passage of wheels shod with iron tyres, run down the centre of both halves of the dual carriageway. The distance between the ruts, taken from centre to centre, was 156 cm.

Except in Egypt, there are very few representations of vehicles other than the ubiquitous chariot, dating from pre-Roman times, in the lands bordering the Mediterranean Sea. It was not customary to bury the vehicles of transport and agriculture with the dead, as in other parts of the world, e.g. Ur, the Pontic Steppes of Russia after about 2000 B.C., and Central Europe during the Hallstatt period. The Mediterranean climate is unfavourable to the chance preservation of wooden objects. In particular, it seems impossible to find any trace of such vehicles in Phoenicia or any of her colonies, except tracks in rock or stone.

Some research has been carried out on the many tracks of vehicles still visible on the limestone rock, which can be related to definite sites or cultures, *i.e.* by Captain-Instructor H. S. Gracie in Malta, H. Rolland in the region covered by the Massiliote Greek traders in Provence, J. B. Ward Perkins in the Faliscan territory north of Rome. Something is also known of the Sacred Ways which connected the Classical Greek cities with the temple-sites, *e.g.* Athens-Eleusis, Sparta-Amyklai.

Whilst freely admitting that mankind is occasionally capable of incredible folly when relating the width of the vehicle to that of the draught animal or animals, I have found that in the West Mediterranean region today (Malta, Sicily, Etruria, South France), the distance between the wheels of a vehicle, taken centre to centre, varies in the great majority of cases from 170 cm.-145 cm. if drawn by two animals, and 140 cm. to 133 cm. if drawn by one. The most satisfactory width is about 170 cm. for a pair-drawn vehicle and around 135 cm. for a cart or waggon drawn by a single beast. The ancient tracks studied by the above writers and observed by myself, fall inside these limits. Great horses such as the English Shire Horse are not known in these regions, and it seems probable that the horses and oxen of antiquity were the same size or slightly smaller than those of today. The nature of the draught animal, where it is known, seems to have little effect on the width of the vehicle. It is suggested, therefore, that the tracks through the North Gate at Motya were made by a succession of pair-drawn wheeled vehicles. The "milestone" (the doorstop of the Phoenician gate) in the centre of the east roadway gives some confirmation to this theory. A single ox would find it an insuperable obstacle, and even a horse or donkey would have been seriously inconvenienced.

The possibility that the tracks might be of Punic origin makes it impossible to decide whether the vehicle used was a cart or waggon. The ultimate Phoenician origin of the Motyans precludes any deduction from the geographical situation of the island which lies in the Great Eurasian Cart Zone, stretching from Portugal along the north shores of the Mediterranean, across the Ukraine and Caucasus to India and Indo-China.

An attempt was made to date the tracks. They were certainly not made by the modern Sicilian carts which come to the island from Birgi every day, and have made a very definite pair of ruts 136 cm. centre to centre. The distance between the wheels of all Sicilian carts measured, including specimens in museums, varied within 2 cm. each way round a norm of 135 cm., which suggests that they were not made any later than the end of the 18th century A.D., when the Sicilian cart first appeared. It seems unlikely that the tracks are mediaeval since the Sicilian roads were so bad that the late Antonia Daneu of Palermo, an authority on Sicilian folk-art, believed that carts (and by inference waggons) were not used in Sicily until shortly before 1800. There is no evidence of Roman or Greek occupation on Motya, and it is hardly likely that the squatters who occupied a small portion of the island after its depopulation by Dionysius of Syracuse in 398 B.C. would use the North Gate to such an extent that definite ruts were made on stone slabs. So the tracks should be contemporary with the Punic occupation of the island and subsequent* to the building of the North Gate, *i.e.* 6th century B.C.-397 B.C.

5. PARTS OF SCHLIEMANN'S DIARY DEALING WITH HIS EXCAVATIONS AT MOTYA

The following entries in Schliemann's diary referring to his work at Motya are reproduced with the kind permission of Prof. Francis R. Walton of the Gennadius Library attached to the American School of Classical Studies at Athens. We are also grateful to him for helping with difficult readings in the English text, while for the translation of the Greek summary we are obliged to Dr. G. J. Papadopoulos. For further information about the diaries see Isserlin, 1968, 144-148.

Schliemann's Diary: English Text

Motya, 19th October, 1875

I arrived here yesterday, and after having carefully inspected the topography of this island, I decided to commence the excavations on the S.E. side on the very shore in a place where the latter is 4 meters above the level of the sea, and where a chamberpavement is visible in the slope of the shore at $2\frac{1}{2}$ m below the surface. Thus it is evident that in this place a certain portion of the island, with the circuit wall, has been washed away by the sea, and, by beginning the work in this particular place I would spare a great deal of time and labour. I had today 13 workmen, 10 men and 3 boys, payment to the former 2 to the latter 1 f. or 80 cents. We had not dug long before we laid bare the stone posts of a house whose architecture is curious, for to the right it has walls of sun dried bricks, to the left walls of small stones joined with earth; the front, as far as laid bare, has 4 quadrangular columns 2 m high 2 of which are *monoliths*. On 2 of the columns are *remains of the stucco* with which they had once been covered.

Motya 20th October

Fine weather; 17 workmen; excavations in the house on the shore continued; brought to light another chamber pavement consisting of a thick layer of chalk on which a coating of crushed brick and gravel sand, so that the pavement has a glazy appearance; one of the pavements yellow; other red. Just behind one of the base columns is a □ *stone box* 70 cms. high, 85 broad × long and 20 thick,

* (but cf. now p. 78 above. B.S.J. I).

weighing I think 200 kilo, having on its front side a horizontal cutting and also a deep cut in the midst of one of the upper sides, as it were that the superfluous water should run off by it; it is of rough chalkstone and rudely made. We constantly dig up large quantities of broken pottery, mostly of rude workmanship; some is of green, other of red clay but unpainted; the vases have mostly no neck. But fragments of very fine painted greek pottery are frequently found without being abundant. They all seem to date of the 5th century B.C. *Fluted* pottery is among them, contrary to the general opinion which gives to it only 200 B.C.

Motya, Thursday 21st October

Not having found anything at all in the excavations on the shore, I began already yesterday at 3 p.m. a 24 m long by 3 m broad trench on the highest part of the hill, and found here arrowheads. *γλωχίνοι* and one in form of a leaf, the former Syracusian, the latter Motyan, further several earthen painted *lamps*, *hand-mills*, similar to the Trojan of lava or trachite. 1 *whorl of green stone*, 2 of terracotta, a great many *copper* or *bronze nails*; a terracotta tablet with a *sphinx* in *bas relief*, painted potsherds.

The acts of the brigandage in Sicily are much exaggerated; *no* act of *robbery* brigandage has been committed in this province of Trapani, and no foreigner has ever been molested in any part of Sicily. The statement of Πολύαινος that the Carthagenians communicated from this western coast of Sicily with Carthage by means of telegraphic signs, which they read by means of δίοπτρα is a physical impossibility, on acct of the spheric form of the earth and the distance of 120 *miles* which separates Carthage from Motya, the *nearest point*. From here the mount near Carthage cannot be seen on acct of its little height, nor can Motya be seen from Carthage owing to its lowness. But if the island were 2000 m high and there were an analogous height at Carthage both mounts could see each other and telegraphic communication by signs would be possible by means of telegraphs, but since nature has made both this coast and that of Carthage level, seeing is quite out of the question. It is said that in very clear days the island of Pantelleria, which is not far from Carthage, can be seen, but on acct of its lowness it can hardly appear on the horizon no telegraphy by signs is of course possible by it.

Motya, Friday, 22nd October

I only continued the excavations on the top of the hill until breakfast, for we struck in 2 m depth the natural soil without finding anything, except a *fine arrow* in the *shape* of a miniature lance. I then began to excavate on the N. side of the island a 24 m long trench just through the ancient gate which faces the dam or dike which once connected the island to the coast. It is a strange fact that I *never found yet the slightest trace of archaic pottery*; indeed *no potsherds to which archaeology would give a higher age than the first half of the 5th century B.C. at the very utmost*. Of *copper coins* several were found, but only on 2 of them can be seen the *cancer* (Taschenkrebs) the rest is eaten by rust. The fragment of another terracotta sphinx was sold to me.

There being nothing to find and no historical riddle to solve I shall not continue the excavations. Great dirt and uncleanliness here. Good people; speak only the dialect which makes one greatest difficulty. The excavation in the gate gave only a few inches of artificial and then only pure virgin soil. I therefore gave it up and worked for a couple of hours on the top of the hill. But here only ½ m artificial and afterwards pure virgin soil. Some three coins were found here of which 1 with an *oxen* head, 1 with a cancer, both on the other side with a female head.

I afterwards worked with my 18 labourers for 1½ hours on the W side, but my efforts here seem equally unfortunate. At a foot below ground we struck a large house *floor pavement of chalk* and sand, but no object was founds save an arrowhead △ of pyramidal form without flutings. Below the pavement pure virgin soil. *It is important to remark that all the pottery here is made on the potters' wheel.* By continual intermarriage the inhabitants of this island have become all near relations, and the 19 families form as it were one single family. Each of them (h)as a small property which gives them a small living; for this reason there is an air of independence about them and they are certainly, with 2 exceptions, the worst workmen I ever had.

Greek Text (Translation)

On the western side of Sicily, opposite the city of Marsala, at the distance of only 2 miles from the shore, there lies a small flat roundish island, now called San Pantaleo, having a circumference of $1\frac{1}{2}$ miles, and which is covered by vines and inhabited by 19 poor countrymen, who through various intermarriages, became all of them relatives and who form, in a manner of speaking, only one single family. This island is the location of the famous Carthaginian city of Motya, which was once outstanding through the beauty of its houses and the riches of its inhabitants. Many thousands of pottery vessels covered over (by soil), two gates, and parts of the circumference wall are the only remnants of this people. This city was besieged in 397 B.C. by Dionysius the Elder, tyrant of Syracuse, who attacked it with an army of 80,000, and a powerful fleet; in this siege the catapult was put to use for the first time, which brought about in ancient warfare the same change which was brought about in the new by gunpowder. This gigantic machine, all by itself, terrified Himilko, who came to the aid of Motya with large Carthaginian forces, so that he went back and left the city to its fate. Thanks, nevertheless, to the heroism of the Greeks found in the army of Motya, the city resisted for a long time. When however it fell in the end, the rage of the tyrant was such that he ordered his soldiers to slaughter all the inhabitants, men, women, and children, and to crucify all the Greeks. According to the wish of Mr. Bonghi, the most learned President of Public Education and for the profit of learning, I undertook with 19 workmen, for one week, in many parts of Motya, trial excavations, which showed that the architecture of the city consisted generally of sun dried (mud) bricks. I also found by the south eastern sea shore the remainders of a large house, the walls of which consisted of rectangular pillars, and partly of bricks and partly of stone, covered with stucco, tied together with lime plaster. I also found some remnants of round pillars, but none in position. In all the houses the floorings of the rooms are made from sand and lime plaster. The depth of soil is only in a few parts $2\frac{1}{2}$ m, generally it does not exceed $\frac{1}{2}$ m. The pottery consists of two kinds: some of it is of excellent quality and structure, and is Greek, belonging to the good period artistically; and the other is unpainted and thick, and crudely shaped.

BIBLIOGRAPHY

Adriani, A. and others, 1970. *Himera I. Campagne di scavo 1963-1965.* Instituto di Archeologia, Università di Palermo. Rome.

Airoldi, A., 1793. *Raccolta di Scritture e documenti che riguardano le antichità e belle arti in Sicilia,* (MS 4 Qq. D. 42), (Palermo, Biblioteca Communale).

Almagia, R., 1944. L'opera geografica di Luca Holstenio. *Studi e Testi,* 102. (Città del Vaticano).

Barnett, R. D., 1960. *Assyrian Palace Reliefs* (London).

Barreca, F., 1958. Tindari dal 345 al 317 a.C. *Kokalos* IV, 145-150.

——, 1961, La città Punica in Sardegna. *Bolletino del Centro di Studi per la Storia dell' Architettura,* XVII, 27-43.

—— and others, 1971. *L'Espansione Fenicia nel Mediterraneo.* Relazioni del colloquio in Roma, 4-5 Maggio 1970. Consiglio Nazionale delle Ricerche, Centro di Studio per la Civiltà Fenicia e Punica presso l'Istituto di Studi del Vicino Oriente dell'Università di Roma. (Rome).

Bellido, A. Garcia Y, Schubart, H., and Niemeyer, H. G., 1971. in Chapter "Espagne", Barreca & others *L'Espansione Fenicia nel Mediterraneo* (Rome).

Bisi, A., 1967. L'Irridazione Semitica in Sicilia in base ai dati ceramici dei centri fenicio-punici dell'isola. *Kokalos,* XIII, 30-60.

——, 1968. Sondaggi alle mura Puniche di Erice. *Archeologia,* VII, 103-106.

Bochart, S., 1712. (edition) *Geographia Sacra, seu Phaleg et Canaan* (Lugduni Batavorum).

Boid, E., 1827. *Travels in Sicily, and the Lipari Islands,* in the month of December, 1824. By a naval officer (London).

Boling, R. G., 1969. Bronze Age Buildings at the Shechem High Place: ASOR Excavations at Tananir. *The Biblical Archaeologist,* XXXII, 82-103.

Brown, F., Driver, S. R. and Briggs, S. A., 1906. *Hebrew and English Lexicon to the Old Testament.* (New Impression 1951) (Oxford).

Buren, E. D. van, 1918. Terracotta arulae. *Memoirs of the American Academy in Rome,* II, 15-53 (Rome).

Burney, C. A. and Lawson, G. R. J., 1960. Measured Plans of Urartian Fortresses. *Anatolian Studies,* X, 177-196.

Bury, J. B., 1900. *History of Greece to the death of Alexander the Great* (London).

Carpenter, Rhys., 1958. Phoenicians in the West. *American Journal of Archaeology,* LXII, 35-53.

Carpenter, R. and Bon, A., 1936. *Corinth; Results of Excavations conducted by the American School of Classical Studies at Athens, III, ii. The Defences of Acrocorinth and the lower town* (Cambridge (Mass.)).

Carter, Theresa Howard, 1965. Western Phoenicians at Lepcis Magna. *American Journal of Archaeology,* LXIX, 123-132.

Chiappisi, S., 1961. *Il Melqart di Sciacca e la questione fenicia in Sicilia* (Rome).

Cintas, P., 1968-9. Urban Development: The Carthaginians in their City. *Archaeologia Viva* I, 2, 53-66, (Paris).

Cluverius, P., 1619. *Sicilia Antiqua* (Lugduni Batavorum).

Coglitore, I., 1883-4. Mozia-studi storico-archeologici. *Archivio Storico Siciliano, Nuova Serie,* VIII, 265-370; IX, 1-74.

Coldstream, N., 1964. The North Gate, 1961-1962; and The Greek Pottery. *Annual of the Leeds University Oriental Society,* IV, 105-111; 118-122.

Columba, G. M., 1906. *I porti della Sicilia. Monografia storica dei porti dell'antichità nell'Italia insulare.* (Rome).

Culican, W., 1961. Aspects of Phoenician settlement in the West Mediterranean. *Abr Naharim,* I. 36-55.

Denon, D. V., 1788. *Voyage en Sicile* (Paris).

Di Vita, A., 1953. L'Elemento Punico a Selinunte nel IV e III secolo A. C. *Archeologia Classica* V, 39-47.

Duhn, F. v., 1921, Italien 1914-1920. *Jahrbuch des Deutschen Archäologischen Instituts, Archäologischer Anzeiger,* XXXVI, Col 201-204.

Dunand, M. and Duru, R., 1962. *Oumm el-'Amed: Une ville de l'époque hellénistique aux échelles de Tyr* (Paris).

Dunand, M. and Saliby, N., 1961-2. Le sanctuaire d'Amrit. Rapport préliminaire. *Annales Archéologiques de Syrie,* XI-XII, 3-12.

Dunbabin, T. J., 1948. *The Western Greeks* (Oxford).

Elgavish, J., 1968. *Archaeological Excavations at Shikmonah* (Haifa).
Emery, W. B., 1960. A Preliminary Report on the Excavations of the Egypt Exploration Society at Buhen, 1958-59. *Kush*, VIII, 7-10.
Forbes, R. J., 1934. Notes on the History of Ancient Roads and their Construction. *University of Amsterdam, Allard Pierson Stichting, Archaeologisch-Historische Bijdragen*, III (Amsterdam).
Forbin, L. N. P. A., Le comte de, 1823. *Souvenirs de la Sicile* (Paris).
Foucher, L., 1966. Un sactuaire néo-punique à Menzel Harb. *Africa*, I, 119-121.
Fougères, G., 1898. Mantinée et l'Arcadie Orientale. *Bibliothèque des Écoles Françaises d'Athènes et de Rome, Fascicule* 78.
Freeman, E. A., 1891-4. *The History of Sicily from the earliest times* (Oxford).
Friedrich, J., 1951. *Phönizisch-Punische Grammatik* (Rome).
Frost, H., 1963. *Under the Mediterranean* (London).
——, 1966. The Arvad Plans 1964, a photogrammetric survey of marine installations. *Annales Archéologiques de Syrie*, XVI, 13-28.
——, 1971. Segreti dello Stagnone: Canali e relitti perduti intorno a Mozia. *Sicilia Archeologica*, XIII, 5-12.
Gesenius, F. H. W., 1829. *Thesaurus Philologicus Criticus Linguae Hebraeae et Chaldaeae Veteris Testamenti*, vol. I, (Lipsiae).
——, 1837. *Scripturae Phoenicae monumenta quotquot supersunt.* (Lipsiae).
Girolamo, A. di, 1898. *Sull'assedio di Lilibeo nella prima guerra punica* (Trapani).
Gjerstad, E., 1946. Decorated Metal Bowls from Cyprus. *Opuscula Archaeologica*, IV, 1-18.
Goodchild, R. G., 1952. Euesperides, a devasted city site. *Antiquity*, XXVI, 208-212.
Gordon, C. H., 1965. *Ugaritic Textbook*, III. (Rome).
Graham, J. W., 1972. Notes on Houses and Housing Districts at Abdera and Himera. *American Journal of Archaeology*, 76, 3, 295-301.
Gsell, S., 1920. *Histoire ancienne de l'Afrique du Nord*, I-IV. (Paris).
Hamilton, R. W., 1934. Tall Abu Hawam. *Quarterly of the Department of Antiquities in Palestine*, III, 74-80.
——, 1935. Excavations at Tell Abu Hawam. *Quarterly of the Department of Antiquities in Palestine*, IV, 1-69.
Harden, D. B., 1971. *The Phoenicians* (Pelican Edition) Harmondsworth.
Hennessy, J. B., 1966. Excavation of a late Bronze Age Temple at Amman. *Palestine Exploration Quarterly*, XCVIII, 155-162.
Hoare, Sir Richard Colt, 1819. *A Classical Tour through Italy and Sicily* (London).
Houel, J. P. L. L., 1782. *Voyage pictoresque des iles de Sicile, de Malte et de Lipari* (Paris).
Isserlin, B. S. J., and others, 1958. Motya: 1955. Report of the trial excavations at Motya near Marsala (Sicily) undertaken by the Oxford University Archaeological Expedition to Motya. *Papers of the British School at Rome*, XXVI, (N.S. XIII), 1-29.
——, 1964. Motya, a Phoenician-Punic site near Marsala, Sicily. *Annual of the Leeds University Oriental Society*, IV, 84-86, 114-118.
——, 1968. Schliemann at Motya. *Antiquity*, XLII, 144-148.
Jeffery, L. H., 1961. *The local Scripts of Archaic Greece* (Oxford).
Jenkins, G. K., 1971. Coins of Punic Sicily, Part I. *The Swiss Numismatic Review*, 50, 25-78.
Koldewey, R. and Puchstein, O., 1899. *Die Griechischen Tempel in Unteritalien und Sicilien*, I. (Berlin).
Kraeling, C. H., 1962. *Ptolemais, City of the Libyan Pentapolis.* (Chicago).
Krischen, F., 1941. *Die Stadtmauern von Pompeji und Griechische Festungsbaukunst in Unteritalien und Sizilien* (Berlin).
Lamon, R. S. and Shipton, G. M., 1939. Megiddo, I. Seasons of 1925-34, Strata I-V. *The University of Chicago, Oriental Institute Publications*, volume XLII (Chicago).
Lampl,P., 1968. *Cities and Planning in the Ancient Near East* (London).
Lane, W., 1893. *Arabic-English Lexicon* (London).
Lawrence, A. W., 1957. *Greek Architecture* (Harmondsworth).
Leclant, J., 1968-9. Magic-Egyptian Talismans in the Cemeteries of Carthage. *Archeologia Viva*, I, 2: 95-114.
Lehmann-Hartleben, K., 1926. Archäologische Funde in den Jahren 1921-1924. Sizilien. *Jahrbuch des Deutschen Archäologischen Instituts, Archäologischer Anzeiger*, XLI, col. 182-185.
Lézine, A., 1961. Architecture Punique. Receuil de documents. *Université de Tunis, Faculté de Lettres, Publications, Ière Série: Archéologie, Histoire*, 5 (Paris).
Luynes, A. de, 1855. Recherches sur l'emplacement de l'ancienne ville de Motya. *Monumenti Antichi e Bulletino dell'Instituto di Correspondenza Archeologica*, 92-98 (Rome).

Massa, G. A., 1709. *La Sicilia in Prospettiva.* 2 vols.
Meyer, E., 1931. *Geschichte des Altertums*, II, 2 (2nd edition). (Stuttgart).
——, 1953. *Heinrich Schliemann Briefwechsel*, I. Aus dem Nachlass in Auswahl herausgegeben. (Berlin).
Mingazzini, P., 1968. Il Porto di Carthagine ed il Kothon. *Atti, Academia Nazionale dei Lincei*, Anno CCCLXV, 1968, Serie ottava, Rendiconti, Classe di Scienze morali, storiche e filologiche XXIII, 3-4, 137-152. (Rome).
Moscati, S., 1968., *The World of the Phoenicians* (London).
Movers, F. C., 1850. *Die Phönizier*, Pt. II (Bonn).
Münter, F. C. C. H., 1790. *Nachrichten von Neapel und Sizilien auf einer Reise in den Jahren 1785 und 1786* (Kopenhagen).
Neiman, D., 1965. Phoenician Place Names. *Journal of Near Eastern Studies*, XXIV, 113-115.
Nicholls, R. V., 1958-9. Old Smyrna: The Iron Age Fortifications and Associated Remains on the City Perimeter. *Annual of the British School at Athens*, LIII-LIV, 35-137.
Niemeyer, H. G. and Schubart, H., 1969. Toscanos. Die altpunische Faktorei an der Mündung des Rio de Velez. Lieferung 1: Grabungskampagne 1964. *Deutsches Archäologisches Institut, Abteilung Madrid. Madrider Forschungen*, Band 6. (Berlin).
Nissen, H., 1892. chapter "Griechische und römische Metrologie" *Handbuch der Klassischen Altertums-Wissenschaft in systematischer Darstellung* (ed. I. v. Müller) vol. I, 833-890. (München).
Orlandini, P., 1966. Lo scavo del thesmorphorion di Bitalemi e il culto delle divinità ctonie a Gela. *Kokalos* XII, 8-35.
Pace, B., 1915. Prime note sugli scavi di Mozia (1906-1914). *R. Academia dei Lincei, Notizie degli Scavi di Antichità.* 431-446.
1935. Arte e civilta della Sicilia Antica, Vol. I. (Milano-Genova-Roma-Napoli).
1938. *Ibid.*, Vol. II.
1945. *Ibid.*, Vol. III.
1949. *Ibid.*, Vol. IV.
Parsons, A. W., 1936. The Long Walls to the Gulf, in R. Carpenter and A. Bon, op. cit, 84-125.
Partsch, J., 1891. P. Clüver der Begründer der historischen Länderkunde. Ein Beitrag zur Geschichte der geographischen Wissenschaft. *Geographische Abhandlungen herausgegeben von Prof. Dr. A. Penck*, Bd. V., Heft 2, 1-47 (Wien).
Paterno, Castello Biscari, I., 1718. *Viaggio per tutte le antichità della Sicilia* (Napoli).
Perkins, J. B. Ward-, 1953. Sabratha, Tripolitania. *Fasti Archaeologici* VI, 1953, 379 no. 4877.
1959 Excavations beside the North-West Gate at Veii, 1957-8. *Papers of the British School at Rome*, XXVII (N.S. XIV), 38-79.
Pesce, G., 1960. *Sardegna Punica* (Cagliari).
1964. Scavi e scoperte puniche a Tharros. *Oriens Antiquus*, III, 137-8.
Poidebard, A. and Lauffray, J., 1951. *Sidon: aménagements antiques du port de Saida (Beyrouth).*
Pritchard, J. B., 1970. The Megiddo stables: a reassessment, in J. A. Sanders (ed.), *Near Eastern archaeology in the twentieth century* (Essays in Honour of Nelson Glüeck) (Garden City, New York), 268-76.
Riedesel, J. H. von, 1771. *Reise durch Sicilien und Grossgriechenland* (Zürich).
Rocco, B., 1970. Morto sotto le mura di Mozia. *Sicilia Archeologica* III, 9: 27-33.
Säflund, G., 1935. The dating of ancient fortifications in Southern Italy and Greece, with special reference to Hipponium. *Opuscula Archaeologica* I, 87-119.
Saint Non, J. C. Richard de, 1788. *Voyage pittoresque ou description des royaumes de Naples et de Sicile.* Paris.
Sayve, A. de, 1822. *Voyage en Sicile fait en 1820 et 1821.* (Paris).
Schmiedt, G., 1963. Contributo della fotografia aerea alla ricostruzione della topografia antica di Lilibeo. *Kokalos* IX, 49-72.
——, 1965. Porti antichi di Italia. *L'Universo* XLV, 225-274.
Schröder, P., 1869. *Die Phönizische Sprache* (Halle).
Schubring, J., 1866. Motye-Lilybaeum. *Philologus* XXIV, 1866, 48-82.
Sellers, O. R., 1962, Article " Weights and Measures", *The Interpreters' Dictionary of the Bible* (ed. G. A. Butrick and others), vol. IV, 828-39 (New York and Nashville).
Shilo, Y., 1970. The Four-Room House- Its Situation and Function in the Israelite City. *Israel Exploration Journal*, 20, 3-4, 180-190.
Smyth, W. H., 1824, *Memoirs descriptive of the resources, inhabitants and hydrography of Sicily and its islands.* (London).
Stern, E., 1968. The dating of stratum II at Tell Abu Hawam. *Israel Exploration Journal*, 18, 213-219.
Stolberg, F. L. Graf zu, 1794. *Reise in Deutschland, der Schweiz, Italien, und Sizilien.* (Königsberg and Leipzig).

Tagg, G. F., 1964. Resistivity Surveys at Motya, Sicily. *The Evershed News*, 8, 2: 2-9.
Tarradell, M., 1960, *Marruecos Punico* (Tetuan).
Taylor, J. du Plat, 1964. Motya, a Phoenician trading Settlement. *Archaeology*, 17, 2: 91-100.
Titone, E., 1964. *Civiltà di Motya* (Trapani).
Trinquet, J., 1957. article "métrologie" in *Supplements au dictionnaire de la Bible* (ed. H. Cazelles) vol. V, cols. 1212-1250 (Paris).
Tusa, V., 1964. Scavi a Solunto. *Oriens Antiquus*, 3, 138-9.
1967. La questione Fenicie- Punica in Sicilia. *Eretz-Israel*, VIII, 50*-57*.
Van Buren see BUREN, L. D. Van.
Whitaker, J. I. S., 1921. *Motya, a Phoenician Colony in Sicily* (London).
Winter, F. E., 1971. *Greek Fortifications* (London).
Wright, G. R. H., 1968. Temples at Shechem. *Zeitschrift für die Alttestamentliche Wissenschaft*, 80, 2-35.
Ziegler, 1933. "Motya" in A. F. Pauli, *Real-Encyclopaedie der Classischen Altertumswissenschaft*, neue Bearbeitung begonnen von G. Wissowa (ed. N. Kraft) XVI, 3, col. 387-407. (Stuttgart).

GENERAL INDEX

PLATES 1-26

1. Father and daughter: Joseph I. S. and Delia Whitaker.

2. The stagnone with Motya, seen from the Spagnola Road.

1. Air photo of Motya and the lagoon, showing reef across the entrance near Marsala.

2. Air photo of the northern end of the lagoon, showing present entrance near S. Teodoro.

3. Air photo of Motya and the causeway with surrounding waters.
Photographs 2 and 3 by courtesy of the Aerofototeca, Ministero di Pubblica Istruzione, Rome; photograph no. 1 by courtesy of the Deutsches Archäologisches Institut, Rome.

Motya, vertical air view of the island. Photograph reproduced by permission of Messrs. Hunting Surveys Ltd.

1. Motya, view of the Island across the water from the east. The South Gate is near the left extremity of the picture, Villa Whitaker in the middle and the North Gate beyond the right edge of the island.

2. Motya: Oblique air view. Ministry of Defence (Air Force Division) photograph, Crown Copyright reserved.

1. Motya, geological section showing tufa cliff.

2. Western geological section showing rock and natural soil.

3. Eastern geological section.

1. View in the interior of the island. Villa Whitaker in the background.

2. Motya, north coast with reef.

Air view of Motya. Significant features discussed in Part II, Chapter 5 are drawn in. (Ministry of Defence (Air Force Division) photograph. Crown Copyright reserved).

1. South-West corner of the Island, with Cothon Channel and South Gate. The entrance of the Cothon Channel is near the centre of the picture.

2. The South Gate seen from the sea.

3. The South Gate entrance, looking inland from the sea.
Note Wall XIX and the section of Pit A, behind the Gate.

1. View of the Town Wall and bastion West of the South Gate.

2. Rooms 25-6 during excavation: foundations of the Period IIA building. Note the Well.

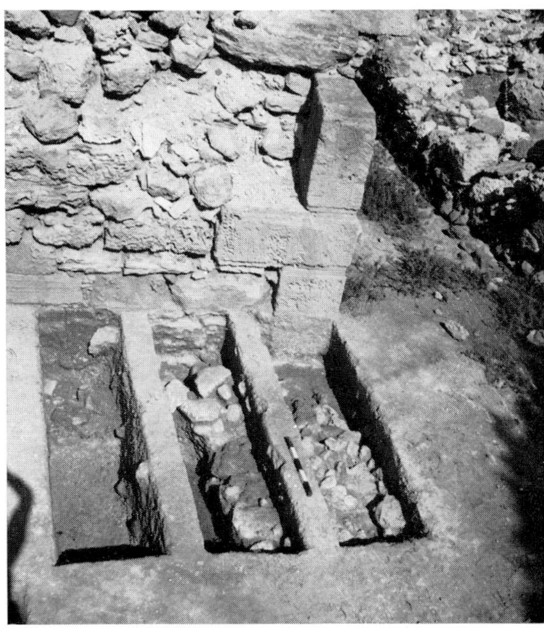

3. South Gate, detail of excavations near northwestern corner, with Trenches 5, 5a, 5b.

1. Room 29 seen from the South Gate. The corner of Room 28 is on the right, Wall XIX on the left. (Working shot).

2. View of Wall XIX and of the South Gate from the north.

1. Panorama of excavated ruins inside the South Gate (composite photo).

2. Trench 4a, inner face of Town Wall.

3. Trench 4b, outer face of Town Wall.

1. Pit A, detail: Inner pit A2, outer pit A1 and Wall III below a streak of slipped stones in top.

2. Trench 5a from the east. Note end of column in Town Wall. Footings of Wall XIXa on the right.

3. South-East corner of Room 1, looking westwards. Wall XIII above debris of IB in rear. Wall XIX on left.

1. South Gate excavations at the end of 1962 season, looking west.

2. Room 5 under excavation. seen from the south. Note pebble pavement.

1. Well W2 before excavation. Note clay pipes on left.

2. Well W2 after excavation.

3. Room 17a from the east. Composite picture of section.

4. Well W1 partly excavated. Fill (13) and (14) shown in rear.

5. Window-like opening in the Casemate, from the south. Note mud brick fill in the rear.

1. Casemate entrance at the beginning of the excavation.

2. The inside of the Casemate (Room 22a) after excavation.

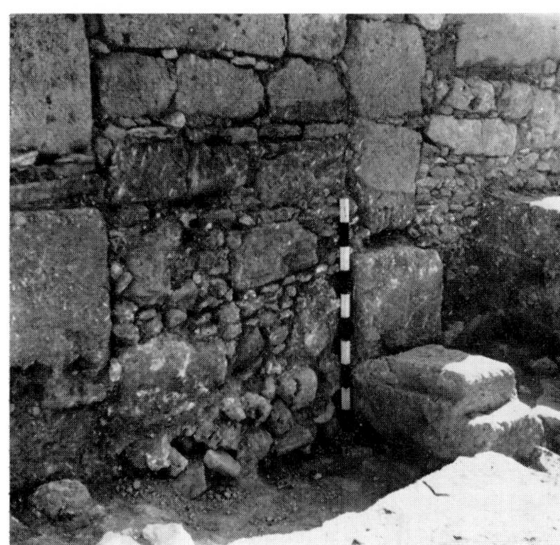

3. Blocked doorway to the casemate: lower part, from the outside.

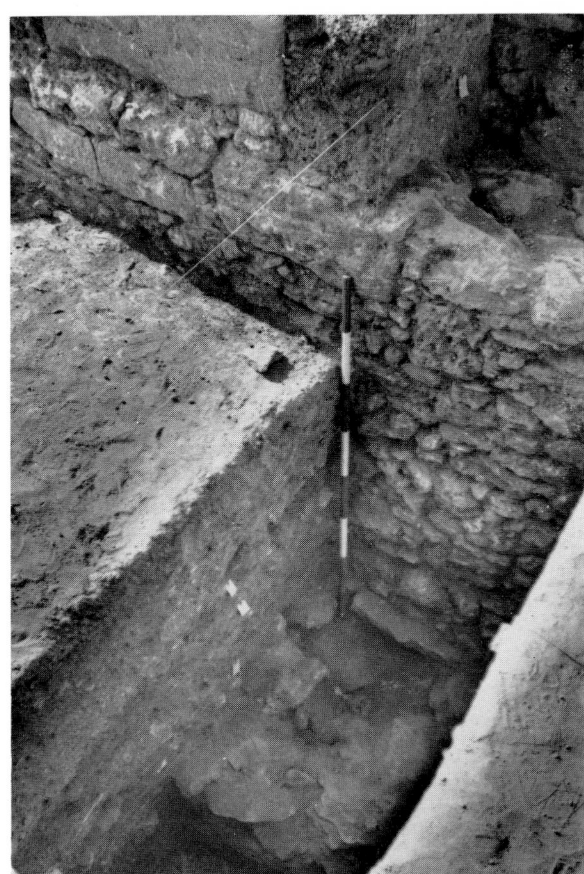

4. Trench 21d, looking south-east. Note the footings.

1. The Tower, from the west. Block A is seen above pavement in center.

2. The Tower, east wall.

1. The Cothon Channel before excavation, looking west.

2. The Cothon Channel, eastern quay, soutern part, showing wing wall.

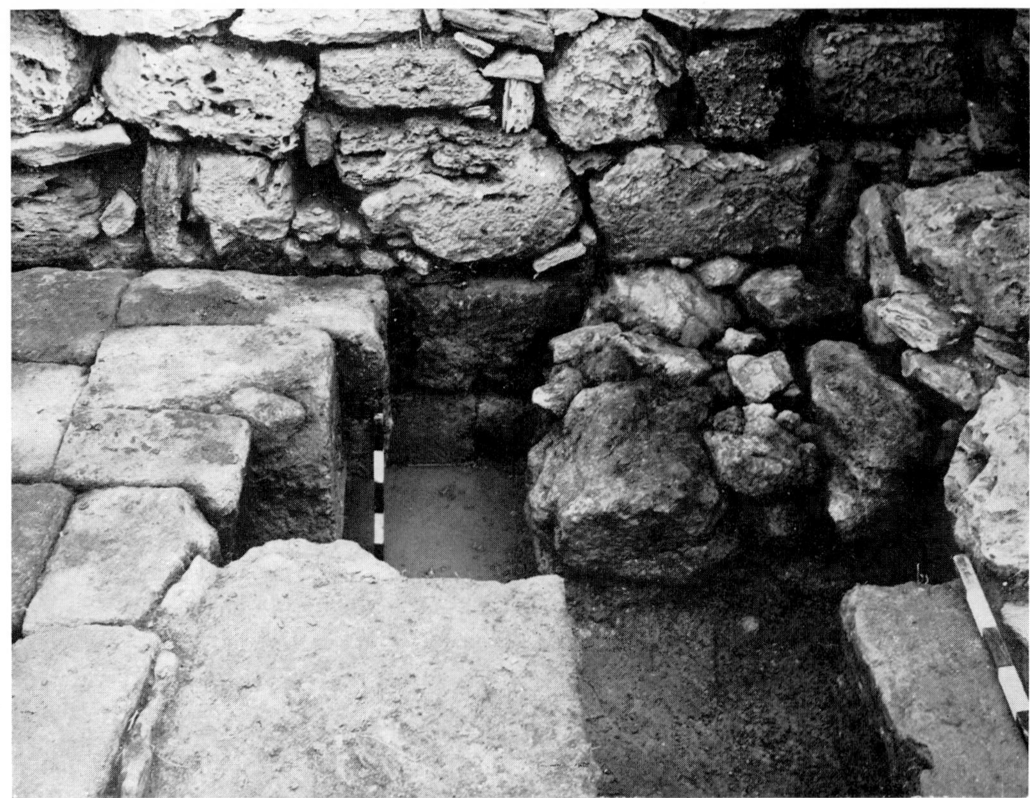

1. Trench 15a from the south. Note the wing wall above the quay. Wall XLII partly removed.

2. Trench 14a from the south. Note the cobble layer.

1. The North Gate from the sea, looking south.

2. The Eastern Sanctuary showing urns between masonry kerbs IV and III.

3. Trench ZA showing section across road outside North Gate (looking east)

1. Cobbles on North Gate Roadway with arrowheads *in situ*.

2. North Gateway, showing cart ruts and dividing wall.

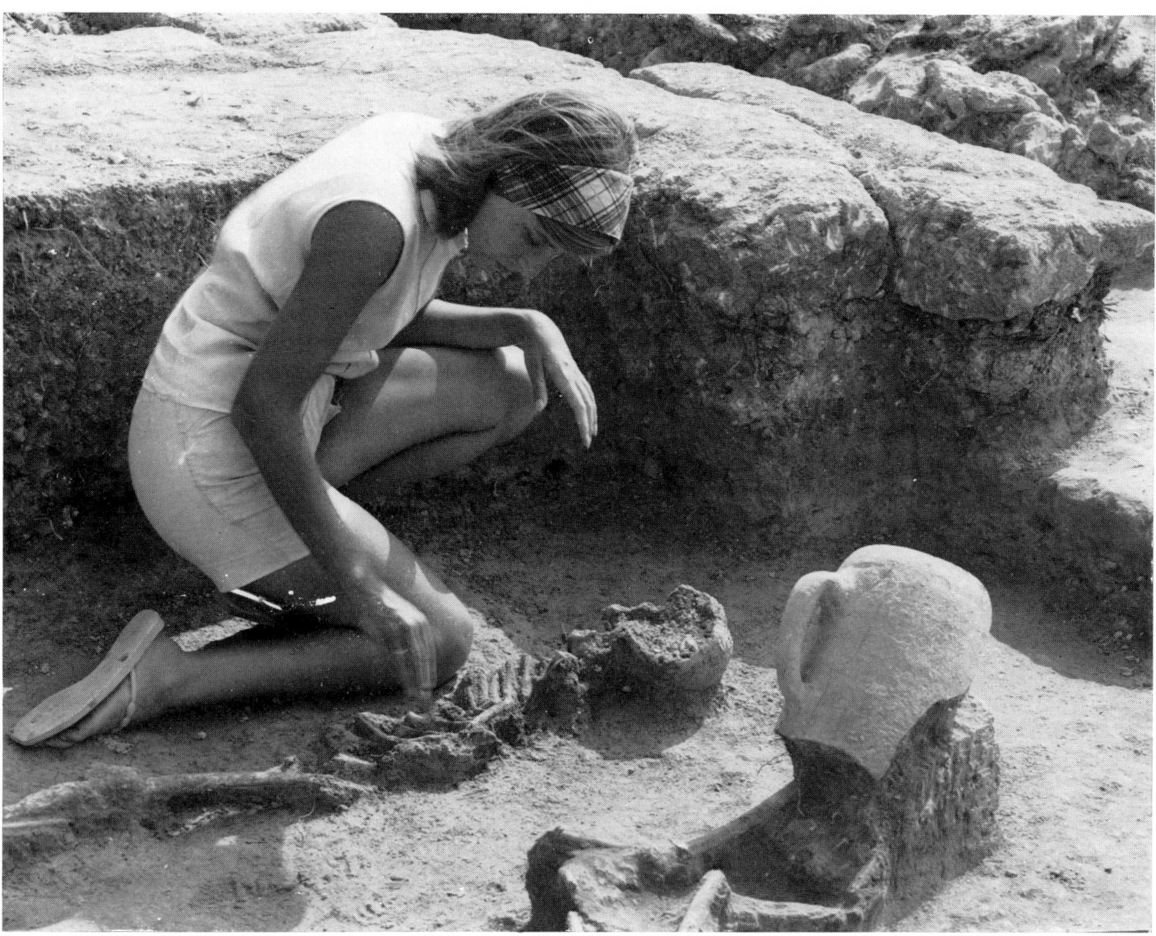

1. Skeletons outside North Gate. Kerb IV in background.

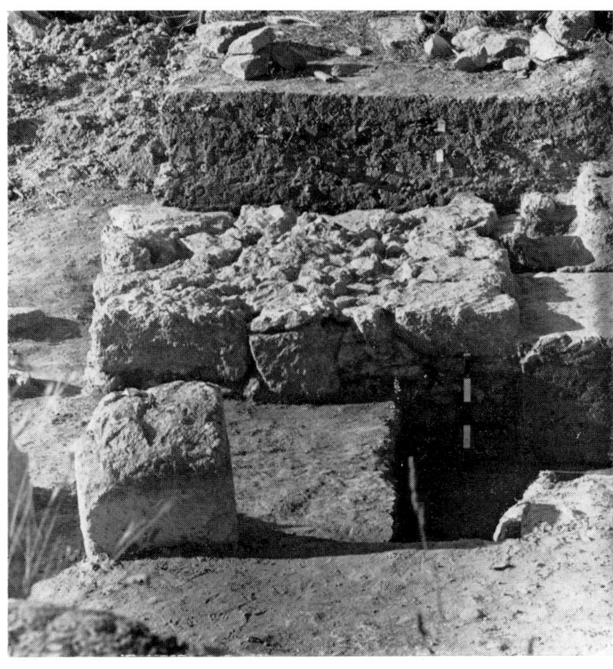

2. Altar belonging to Western Sanctuary.

3. The causeway to Birgi viewed from the North Gate.

1. Western Sanctuary, ashlar masonry at southwest corner.

2. Western Sanctuary, wooden stakes to north of shrine (near metre rod).

1. Western Sanctuary, Wall I and fortifications, looking south.

2. Western Sanctuary, looking north.

1. Western Sanctuary, Doric Capital (A).

2. Oriental engaged capital (B).

3. Oriental engaged capital (C) as found.

1. Wall I and West Bastion, looking west.

2. Junction of West Bastion with ashlar wall.

3. Limestone relief from Western Sanctuary.

1. Exploratory Trench A in interior of island

2. Exploratory Trench B

3. Detail of masonry in Trench A

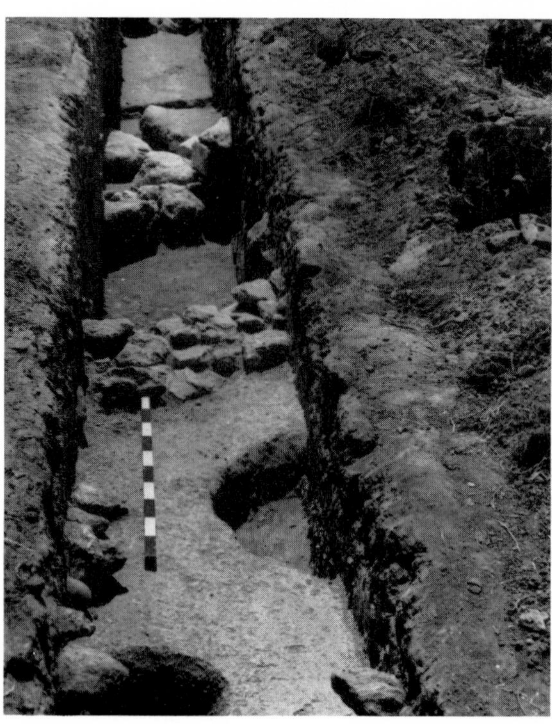

4. Detail of domestic structure traversed by Trench B